T0041052

Out of the Park

Out of the Park

Memoir of a Minor League Baseball All-Star

ED MICKELSON

with a foreword by
Lowell Reidenbaugh

McFarland & Company, Inc., Publishers
Jefferson, North Carolina, and London

LIBRARY OF CONGRESS CATALOGUING-IN-PUBLICATION DATA

Mickelson, Ed, 1926–
    Out of the park : memoir of a minor league baseball all-star
/ Ed Mickelson ; with a foreword by Lowell Reidenbaugh.
        p.   cm.
    Includes index.

    ISBN-13: 978-0-7864-2889-2
    (softcover : 50# alkaline paper) ∞

    1. Mickelson, Ed, 1926–   2. Baseball players—United
States—Biography.   3. Minor
    league baseball—United States.   I. Title.
    GV865.M513A3   2007
    796.357092—dc22   2007007786

British Library cataloguing data are available

©2007 Ed Mickelson. All rights reserved

*No part of this book may be reproduced or transmitted in any form
or by any means, electronic or mechanical, including photocopying
or recording, or by any information storage and retrieval system,
without permission in writing from the publisher.*

Cover photograph: Ed Mickelson, Cover of *Sunday Oregonian Northwest Roto Magazine,* April 17, 1955

Manufactured in the United States of America

*McFarland & Company, Inc., Publishers
    Box 611, Jefferson, North Carolina 28640
    www.mcfarlandpub.com*

To the memory of my late wife, Jo Ann Menzel Mickelson, who attended every home game and was my constant support during my playing career and in writing this book.

To my present wife, Mary Steffen Mickelson, without whose newly-learned computer savvy I would not have completed this book.

To my son Eric and my daughter Julie, and her three children, Eileen, Michael and Matthew.

My mother and father

And to my fellow 8500 minor leaguers who also loved the game.

Acknowledgments

My special thanks to friends who read the manuscript and gave me encouragement and suggestions. They were Donna Keebey, Dennis Hugo, Bob Broeg, Erv Fischer, Roger Richardson, Jim Riley, Bob Case, Lloyd and Alice Brewen, Dave Stauffer, Gary Chesley, Bill Hensley, Carl Beck, Jane and Paul Dohrman, Tim Gannon, Bill Borst, Erv Fischer, and my wonderful parents Mary and Ed Mickelson.

Special thanks to the late Lowell Reidenbaugh and the late Oscar Kahan of the *Sporting News* for letting me use the *Sporting News* facilities in my research. Special thanks to Mr. Reidenbaugh for his encouragement and suggestions and his splendid foreword.

Special thanks to baseball authors Rich Marazzi and Len Fiorito, authors of *Aaron to Zuverink*, for their help and encouragement. Inspiring words also came from Milt Richman, who read the manuscript and said, "I enjoyed [it] immensely." This kind of praise coming from the sports editor of United Press International enabled me to increase my efforts to seek a publisher.

Thanks to Rhonda Meyers, who typed the first rough draft in 1978, and Annette Stranz, who re-typed it in its entirety. Carol Engle helped with the typing in the late stages of the book.

Special thanks goes to my late wife, Jo Ann, who sat with me many late summer nights in 1976, '77, and '78, when we first got my memoir going and who had much to do with the contents by keeping scrapbooks over the eleven years I played baseball. Most of my ideas were bounced off her, and some we went with and some we discarded. She also typed one of the first drafts. Jo Ann was my support and soul mate during the baseball years and during life.

I also give thanks to my children, Julie and Eric, who were patient throughout all of this. Lately my wife Mary helped with the final editing of the book. Thanks to Chase Groomes, the book got a new life using modern technology and updated ideas. It has been fun and a labor of love. Thanks to Tom Wheatley of the *Post-Dispatch* for taking time to edit the book with his penchant for tightening things up and pulling out things that were redundant.

Contents

Foreword

by Lowell Reidenbaugh

In the Golden Age of baseball, when as many as fifty-nine minor leagues operated in a single season, dreams of diamond glory proliferated across North America.

Hundreds of returning G.I.s from World War II competed with youthful aspirants for a chance to demonstrate their athletic skills that, hopefully, would lead them to the major leagues. The siren song of fame and fortune was never more seductive than in the late 1940s. Long-forgotten leagues like the Tobacco State, Coastal Plain, Kitty and Lone Star were staging areas for legions of young men who were willing to ride antiquated buses, play on dimly lighted fields, and endure gastronomic hardships for serf-like emolument, all in pursuit of a goal represented by four hundred jobs on sixteen major league teams.

Ed Mickelson was one of those who cast his lot with professional baseball in this era. Unlike many others, however, he did not start at the absolute bottom. From the day he earned a token bonus to sign a minor league contract with the St. Louis Cardinals, he was considered a prospect with remarkable potential, a potential that existed almost to the day when he found his aspirations no longer tenable and he bade farewell to the diamond and dreams.

Before the final curtain there were many peaks and valleys to cross, many moments of high exultation and gut-wrenching dejection. So often the highway of hope was studded with roadblocks or seemed to lead nowhere. Advancement was spelled m-i-r-a-g-e.

With extraordinary recall and vivid clarity, Ed Mickelson relates his eleven-year struggle against the odds of success. Oh, yes, he did enjoy the proverbial cup of coffee in the major leagues, three cups, in fact. But, for reasons not always clear, he was denied the euphoric pleasures of caviar and champagne.

There were, to be sure, a few moments to be remembered, mainly by members of his family and profound scholars of the game. Like the day, when substituting for an ailing Stan Musial, Ed collected one of two hits against Hall of Famer Warren Spahn. And nobody will deny him the distinction of driving in the last run in the history of the St. Louis Browns.

On the other side of the ledger was his brief and baffling stint with the Chicago Cubs. While a member of the Portland club, Mickelson was informed that the Cubs wished to purchase him. At the time he could have refused such a move as a player in the "Open Classification" Pacific Coast League. He acquiesced only after Cubs officials promised him that he would play regularly against left-handed pitchers.

Disillusion was almost instantaneous. He sat on the bench against all types of pitching. "Why," he asked the team's authorities, "did you buy me if you didn't plan to play me?" There was only silence.

There was also a sticky puzzlement while Ed was with Lynchburg in the Class B Piedmont League. In early May he rapped out four hits in five trips to the plate, driving in five runs for the enjoyment of his favorite good luck charm in the stands, his mother-in-law. Prospects for a premier season—and promotion—were never brighter. Yet shortly thereafter he was summoned to the manager's office for a post-game conference. The purpose, Ed surmised, pertained to his league-leading .393 batting average.

He was ill prepared for the news: He was being assigned to Montgomery, Alabama, in the Southeastern League, another Class B circuit. There was apparently no reason for such a lateral move, and the player questioned the rationale. He was informed that another first baseman in whom the Cardinals had a substantial investment was being demoted from a higher league and would play only in Lynchburg. "Be a good soldier and go," he was told.

Bitterly, Mickelson packed his bags and headed south, wondering why the transfer had to be made immediately after a shopping expedition in which he had laid in a week's supply of groceries.

At Montgomery, Ed scaled his statistical Matterhorn with a .417 batting average. Still, with two lofty averages for two clubs, he failed to qualify for the batting title in either league because of an insufficient number of plate appearances.

Such were the circumstances in a career that alternately mixed sunbursts of optimism with cloudbanks of pessimism.

But anyone who accompanies Ed Mickelson on his baseball odyssey will find delight in tales of friendships formed along the way in his eleven-year career, of witty repartee, and the search for entertainment when cash was low and hopes still high.

Like the inexpensive pleasure of peering through the open transom of a hotel room and gazing on the X-rated exhibition within. These were unsophisticated times when athletes played for the love of the game, motivated by goals that always seemed just beyond their fingertips.

And who can suppress a chuckle when reading about Mickelson's winter-time experiences in Venezuela? How an assigned chauffeur, Felix Garcia, disdained the use of an automobile horn and instead beat vigorously on the side of his car to notify other drivers that he was about to pass the vehicle ahead. In case his system sprung a flaw, Felix never failed to cross himself before venturing into another lane of traffic.

Raw humor was a constant companion of those who labored in the "bushes" of baseball half a century ago. There was, for example, an all-night bus ride through the mountains of the Northwest. It was a junket beyond compare. Pocatello players, fortified by beer and hard-boiled eggs, polluted their vehicle with sulphurous odors as they competed for the championship of the "Rectal Gas League." At the completion of the trip, the scorekeeper awarded the title to he who had recorded 31 anal explosions.

Throughout the following pages one personality stands rock-solid, unflappable no matter what the winds of baseball brought her way. She is Jo Ann Menzel Mickelson, the leading lady in her husband's quest for the brass ring of baseball. She learned to read road maps that guided her along unfamiliar highways to unfamiliar cities. She supplied the domestic touch that gave fulfillment to her husband's career. She picked him up during emotional lows and leveled him off during emotional highs.

And Jo Ann was there in Portland on that late July day in 1957 when the final curtain fell. Despite impressive statistics—the second highest batting average in the Coast League and the best fielding percentage among first basemen—Ed Mickelson decided that professional baseball had become an ogre. Gone was the thrill of competition, the clubhouse humor, the cities and the fans he had come to love and appreciate.

At thirty-one years of age, he decided to pack it in. Physically, he was unchanged from the productive season of 1956. He was simply drained, no longer the gregarious individual of other years. Then he had been sociable. Now he was reclusive.

The 1,500-mile automobile trip back to St. Louis marked the climax to a career battered by the freakish winds of baseball. One can only ponder the career that might have been if the Cardinal system had not been overloaded with first basemen at the height of Ed's productivity. Or if the Browns had remained in St. Louis one more season to afford the player a full-length trial. Or if the Cubs had given him the thorough chance that had been promised.

Who can tell?

The late Lowell Reidenbaugh was the corporate editor of The Sporting News.

1

The Beginning

I don't know when it started—that feeling that I had about baseball. My earliest recollections are those of throwing a ball in the air against the second floor of our home in Marseilles, Illinois, in the summer of 1933. I remember listening to the radio as the play-by-play announcer from Chicago related that KiKi Cuyler was going after a fly ball. I suddenly became Cuyler and I was running under that same fly ball—only mine had rebounded off the side of our wooden house. A ground ball, as reported by Bob Elson, the Cub radio announcer, hit to Billy Herman, the Cubs' second baseman, meant I had to lower my sights from between the upstairs bedroom windows to an area on the first floor below the dining room windows. A crashing grounder would rebound off the house and skim along the grass. I would neatly backhand the ball a la Herman and make a level throw. Then the ball would rebound to me again and I had become the Cubs' first baseman, Charlie Grimm, finishing the out.

I was seven then, and the radio reports came in daily when the Cubs or the White Sox were playing at home. My games against the side of the house were also daily, for I followed each game, pitch by pitch, play by play. There must have been a thousand-a-day tennis ball thumps against that house. Dr. Clark, our family physician, and my mother were trying to discover why she was having headaches at this period in her life. I doubt they questioned the thumping noise constantly vibrating throughout the house during those summer days.

My parents lived on Clark Street in Marseilles during that summer of '33. Marseilles was a sleepy, peaceful little town of about 4,000 settled a hundred years earlier in the Illinois River Valley, some 70 miles southwest of Chicago.

In 1934 we moved to a two-story brick structure west of town in what was called the "new addition." It was there that Vernon Twait, the Schumanski boys and I built a baseball field. We cut the weeds, mowed the grass, laid out the bases and built a backstop. My dad loved sports, so there was always excitement for me when he could take the time to play with us in the evenings or on Sunday. Baseball was just part of our summer days in

Illustration by Ronnie Joyner.

Marseilles. We fished, swam on the Richmonds' farm in a dammed-up creek and roamed the woods the year around. Winter meant sleigh riding down the steep hills and ice-skating on the frozen river.

We moved to Chicago in September of 1935 and into apartment living. We played baseball on the corner lot on Parnell Street, with enough kids for 7 or 8 on a side. Down the left field line was a three-story apartment building, with what looked to be a hundred windows. Down the right field line was open space. I became adept at hitting the ball to right field, which isn't easy for a nine-year-old, right-handed hitter.

The street kids of Chicago had a game called step ball. We played it for hours on end. Two or more guys would throw a rubber ball against concrete steps. We used to play underneath the elevated train on the steps used by passengers coming down from the tracks overhead. Hitting the edge of the step with a throw counted 100 points. The throws that hit the back or top of the step and rebounded were worth 10 points if caught on the fly. We would play to 5,000 or 10,000 points. It might take all morning for someone to get 10,000 points.

My biggest thrill in Chicago came when my dad took me to see the White Sox play the Yankees in a Sunday double-header in 1936. It seemed hard to believe that I was actually seeing Lou Gehrig, Bill Dickey and Red Rolfe for the Yankees, and Luke Appling, Al Simmons, Ted Lyons and Zeke Bonura for the White Sox. I don't recall who won the games, but I can still remember the action and recall the excitement of my first big-league game.

We came to the St. Louis area in 1937. I was 11 years old when I entered Delmar Harvard Elementary School in University City for the last few weeks of fifth grade. These were fun years and I remember vividly my playmates Bob O'Connor, Harold Fridkin, Mark Saphian, Norm Zwibelman, Gene Alper, Sonny Julius and a host of other boys. We had a great time playing cork ball, which is native to St. Louis.

A cork ball is about half the size of a baseball. We played with a tennis ball, though, because cork balls cost 25 cents, which was a lot of money for a kid in the '30s. An old tennis ball, on the other hand, was easy to acquire and cost nothing. Sawed-off broomsticks were bats. Each team had a pitcher, catcher and outfielder and got three outs an inning for a nine-inning game. Any pitch that was caught cleanly by the catcher after a swing and a miss was an out. A foul tip of any kind behind home plate was also an out, as was any ball caught on the fly. A ball that was hit in front of the plate and not caught on the fly was a hit, and four hits scored a run. If the game went extra innings, hits would count as runs. A good pitcher could throw curves with the tennis ball and make fastballs hop.

When we weren't playing cork ball, we were playing Indian ball, which I believe is also unique to St. Louis. The game can be played with two on a side, but is better played with two infielders and two outfielders. The bases are placed 30 to 40 feet apart with two infielders guarding this area from ground balls. Home plate is stationed 100 feet or so from the opposing infielders. The outfielders are placed about 150 feet behind the infielders to catch the line drives or fly balls before they drop in the outfield for a hit. The team at bat has one of their members toss the softball (12 inches) underhand to the batter. No balls or strikes are called and the batter swings only at desired pitches thrown by his teammate. A ball hit on the ground and caught cleanly by the infielder is an out, but if the ball goes past the infielder or is juggled it's a hit. Any caught fly ball is an out.

After three outs, the fielders take their turn at bat. Three hits in a half inning will load the bases and each succeeding hit scores a run. A home run is a ball landing behind the outfielders, over their heads. As in cork ball, extra-inning hits count as runs. We kept league standings in Indian ball. But unlike cork ball where we could play 15 to 20 games a day, only seven or eight games of Indian ball could be played in a day. We played from morning until twilight.

We also had our summer playground activities such as horseshoes and arts-and-crafts projects, but the main activity for me was the Eastgate Softball team. I generally played shortstop. We had a good team and won most of our games, except when we played the Bartmer playground team in the University City Softball Playground League. The Bartmer teams were composed of some pretty tough kids. The teams were made up of kids aged 13 and 14. But the Bartmer kids (all of whom were 14) always seemed to have beards and mustaches, and it was rumored that two or three had more than brief encounters with the law. When you played Bartmer, you played their fans, too. It sure was difficult to bat with peas, B.B.s and rocks bouncing off your head. Beating Bartmer on their home field could mean trouble. Thankfully, in our first two games played on the Bartmer playground in '37 and '38, we never found out if the rumors were fact. But in '39 we were brash enough to beat Bartmer on their field, and we were all thrown in their wading pool. It did help to cool us off from the hot St. Louis summer day, and we were relieved that nothing more happened.

In junior and senior high school, it was basketball for me. We did not have a baseball team. So I went out for track also but I was, at best, mediocre and uninterested. Speed was certainly not one of my strong points. In my senior year, I went out for the football team at University City High School. Forest "Frosty" England, the coach, had enticed me to play. Our team went on to have a very successful season, and I found myself wishing I had played football earlier under the excellent football mentor, Clarence "Stub" Muhl, who had played for Illinois during the Red Grange era and was a legend at U. City. During my senior year, he was away in the service, and Frosty England was his replacement. The first City-County Playoff game was played at Walsh Stadium on Thanksgiving Day in 1944, and was witnessed by 13,000 fans.

Ed Mickelson, Ward Junior High basketball player, a student in the University City, Missouri, school system, in 1939. My coach, Howard Mundt, was an early mentor. He encouraged me to concentrate on basketball through high school and took me to basketball games around town. I have great respect for him.

My senior year in high school, then, I went from football to basketball to baseball. As our high school did not have baseball in the athletic program until my senior year, I played my first baseball game in uniform at the age of 17. One game that I especially remember during the spring of '44 was at the Webster Groves High School field. I was having a good

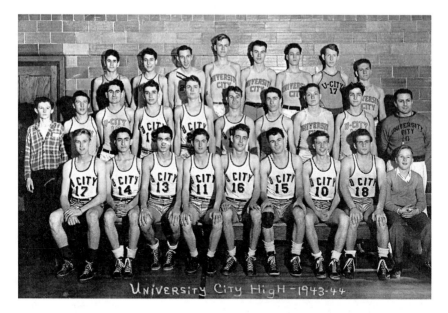

University City High School Basketball Team, 1943–44. Left to right, top to bottom: Hirsch, Slonim, Taylor, Metz, Barks, Friedman, Chandler, Parnas; Hamilton, Orr, Robinson, Benson, Ballard, Taylor, Adzick, Spielburg, Polinsky, Coach England; Pugh, Molasky, Stone, Greenblatt, Barringer, Mickelson (15 in front), Haley, Lasky, Hetzler. Forest England went on to be a successful college football coach at the University of Toledo. (University City High School Yearbook, 1944.)

game, going 3 for 3 with a home run over the left fielder's head. An elderly man came up to me, smiled and said, "I'm Jack Ryan, a scout with the St. Louis Cardinals. I like the way you swing the bat. Let's see you really hit one next time, kid!"

Fortunately, luck was with me, and the next time at bat I hit a line drive off the chest of the umpire who was positioned behind the pitcher's mound. I decked him and reached first base on the hardest ball I had hit all day. Contrast this scene: The umpire on his back writhing in pain while signaling a base hit for me, and Jack Ryan in the stands doubled-up in laughter. I knew I had made an impression on both men.

I went on to attend the University of Missouri in the fall of '44 and went out for the football team. Because of World War II, the University of Missouri's crop of football players that year was very lean, and I became a starting end. The second game of our season, we played Ohio State with Heisman Trophy winner Les Horvath in the backfield. Seven of their starting eleven would make first or second team All-America. They had the Navy V-12 training program at their school as a recruiting tool, along with a host of other outstanding football players. And they annihilated us 54–0.

Before the game, during halftime and after each of the eight touchdowns, they played the Ohio State fight song. I learned that song word-for-word that day. My personal battle was waged with Bill Willis at tackle and Jack Dugger at end. Willis later went on to make All-America, became an All-Pro lineman with the Cleveland Browns and was enshrined in the Pro Football Hall of Fame in July 1977. Dugger also made All-America at the end of that '44 season. Those two guys turned me every way but loose on that fall day in Columbus, Ohio. I also started at right halfback against Oklahoma University in Norman and against the University of Nebraska in Lincoln. What Chauncey Simpson, our head coach, saw in me as a halfback I'll never know. I did score a touchdown against Nebraska—with a magnificent carry from the one-foot line. The University of Missouri's lack of talent during the war years in basketball also enabled me to start as a freshman for the varsity team. It was sure a lot of fun, but before the end of the season, Uncle Sam beckoned. Life as a foot soldier didn't sound too thrilling, so I enlisted in the Army Air Corps in September of 1944. I left Mizzou in February 1945 for Biloxi, Mississippi and basic training.

After basic training at Keesler Field in Mississippi, I was sent to Scott Field in Illinois and was placed in Special Services, playing basketball and baseball for the base teams. That was really a rough life, stationed about 30 miles from home and my high school sweetheart, Jo Ann Menzel, who was later to become my bride. Our Scott Field basketball team flew all over the country. My teammates were All-Americans such as Pete McCloud of Colorado University, Ray Lumpp of New York University and later the New York Knicks, Norm Kohler of Long Island University, Vic Kraft of the Harlem Globetrotters and Bill Weimar, who went on to star at Denver University.

This was a tremendous experience for me. I started most of our games at center despite being only 6'4" and 215 pounds. We played 30 games and won all but a few in the 1945–46 season.

I also had some excellent experiences playing baseball at Scott Field. The competition wasn't that keen, but we practiced every day and played 30 or 40 games a season. We flew to Michigan, Indiana and several other Midwest states to play service teams. I played first base in every one of our games in that summer of '46. We had no former major leaguers playing with us. In fact, we had only a few who had any professional experience at all. But we had a lot of fun and did entertain a lot of soldiers who came to cheer us on.

One of the rewards of playing for Scott Field was knowing Mike Cudemo, our catcher. Mike was a cook, and every night after practice he presented me with the same cheerful option, "Hey Ed, how do you want your steaks?"

University of Missouri Basketball Squad, 1944–45. Back row, left to right: Harold Schrader, forward, William Whitaker, forward; Dale Freeman, guard; James White, center; Robert Heinsohn, center; Edward Mickelson, center (22, standing); John Heimburger, forward; Thomas Walsh, guard; Lane Bauer, forward. Front row left to right: Eugene Kurash, guard; Harold Weir, forward; Earl Stiegemeier, forward; Paul Collins, Capt., guard; William Dellastatious, guard; Leonard Brown, forward; Gerald Patterson, forward; Ozzie Sherman, guard. These guys were a mediocre basketball team, but incredibly lucky in collegiate life. Enrollment at that time was 50 women to 1 man. (Used by permission of Chad Moller, Director of Media, University of Missouri.)

When my son, Eric, was 12 years old, he was an avid fan of Westerns and old war movies. On several occasions, after viewing some John Wayne movie about World War II, he would turn to me and ask, "Hey Dad, what did you do in the war?" I would tell him I played baseball and basketball for Scott Field to entertain the troops. His response was generally a look of disappointment as if to say, "You mean that is all you did during the war!"

All of my coaches made a tremendous impression on my life—Stub Muhl, Frosty England, and Henry Schemmer, to name a few. But Howard Mundt, my junior high school coach, took me under his wing when I was in need of someone who cared. I made two quick moves in three years in the mid-'30s and was in the midst of the terrible teens. I was close to both my dad and mom, but Howard Mundt took a special interest in me and took me with him to college basketball games at Washington University in St. Louis. He would take the time to explain the game while it was in progress, encouraged me and taught me the fundamentals. In the early '40s,

Mr. Mundt took me to the Washington University Field house to see the Aggies of Oklahoma A&M University coached by Mr. Henry Iba. They played basketball with great intensity and teamwork. And I secretly hoped that someday I would play for Mr. Iba and the Aggies.

The Aggies won the NCAA basketball championship in '44 and '45 led by seven-footer Bob Kurland. I went to Oklahoma A&M on a baseball scholarship after being discharged from the service in September 1946. There were numerous returnees from the NCAA championship basketball teams. I tried out, and I felt good when they let me continue to work out with the select group of 20 varsity members. I had to learn Mr. Iba's intricate offense and especially learn to play defense. The first part of the season I sat and watched. Then, though I didn't start, I played in each of the last 16 games of the season. I learned that if I didn't shoot, moved the ball more and played good defense, I would get to play. With Mr. Iba, a "maybe" shot was never taken. It had better be a sure shot.

Mr. Iba was the greatest coach I have ever played for in any sport. I respected the man as a coach, a human being and a disciplinarian. In my mind he was the greatest college basketball coach of his era, and he went on to coach several U.S. Olympic basketball teams.

In the 1946–47 season in Stillwater, we played St. Louis University with "Easy" Ed McCauley, the future pro basketball Hall of Famer, and we were beaten, 39–20. Mr. Iba always had meetings after the game, and when he entered the room after that St. Louis U. loss, a hush immediately fell over the team. I've never known a man who commanded such respect from his players. Mr. Iba simply said, "Boys, I've been coaching basketball close to 20 years and this is the first time I've ever been beaten that badly—by 19 points."

I thought to myself: Imagine coaching two decades, hundreds of games, and never really being blown out of any one of them—that is remarkable.

He turned and left the room. Fifteen basketball players sat in silence, inwardly vowing that it would never happen again. That team, which really was not strong on talent, went on to beat one of the greatest assemblages of college basketball players, the 1946–47 University of Kentucky team, in the Sugar Bowl Tournament in New Orleans. Mr. Iba was really responsible for that win.

Also that season, a young radio announcer was just getting his start doing play-by-play for our home basketball games. His name was Curt Gowdy, who became a television broadcasting legend.

Henry P. Iba went on to win 767 college basketball games. He was called the "Iron Duke" of defense of college basketball for over 40 years. He built Oklahoma A&M into a national powerhouse. With Bob Kurland leading the way, the Aggies won the NCAA title in both 1945 and 1946. Mr. Iba was elected to the Oklahoma Sports Hall of Fame, Missouri Hall of Fame, the Helms Foundation Hall of Fame, the Hall of Fame for College Basketball Coaches, and Basketball's Hall of Fame at Springfield, Massachusetts.

In the spring of '47 at A&M, I played first base for Toby Greene's Aggies. I was the greatest pre-game hitter in college baseball. I would hit about every third pitch over the fence in batting practice, but during the games it was a different story. I went 1 for 23 that season, my only hit being a dribbler between short and third against the University of Oklahoma at Norman. My confidence was crushed. It was my first real experience with athletic humiliation and frustration. That experience would help me years later.

I came back home that summer very morose, but not for long. Mr. Collins, our druggist, told Leo Ward, the St. Louis Cardinals' traveling secretary, of the prodigious hitter in their midst. Mr. Ward got a try-out for me at Sportsman's Park.

Butch Yatkeman, the clubhouse manager, put me in the scrubbini area of the Cards' locker room, where the scrubs dress. He gave me a shirt with a so-called donkey number—56—on the back and the pants of Hall of Fame slugger John Mize, which were too big for me, and away I went to take batting practice.

Del Wilber had a great batting practice pitch. Good velocity, but not too quick, and each pitch was in the same area. Sure enough, I hadn't lost my batting-practice eye. Of his first eight or ten pitches to me, I hit four into the left field bleacher seats. One ball knocked over two cases of beer neatly stacked, one upon the other. I can still hear Harry "The Cat" Brecheen, the veteran pitcher, yelling, "That's the way to hit, Okie!" Harry was from Ada, Oklahoma, and must have been told that the big kid at bat was from Oklahoma A&M. I can also remember Dick Sisler, the Cards' first baseman, advising me to be sure and try out with other clubs. He wouldn't have been worried if he had known my A&M batting average.

In a few days I was offered a contract with the Cardinals for what seemed like a sizable sum of money—$2,000. But before I signed I called Oklahoma A&M because I wanted to talk to Mr. Iba. His secretary said that he was on a fishing trip. I believe that had he answered and told me not to sign the contract, I would not have signed. Now I had to make up my own mind. When I asked my father, he said, "You should do what you want to do most." I was torn between basketball with Mr. Iba and baseball. The money was not that important. In the end, that feeling for baseball which started way back in 1933 in Marseilles, Illinois, won out. I signed and was sent a few days later to Decatur, Illinois, a Class B Cardinal team in the Three I League.

All my years of play—on steps and in alleys, on sandlots and playgrounds, for high school and college and service teams—put me in good stead for the years ahead of me. As I had moved up the competitive ladder, lessons were learned and experiences were gained that would better enable me to compete in professional baseball.

2

The Rook

It was said of Sam Breaden, the owner of the St. Louis Cardinals when I signed in 1947, that he was lucky. For Sam Breaden, it never rained on Sundays, holidays, doubleheaders or any other time that the Cardinals might have a big home crowd at Sportsman's Park. I say Sam Breaden was not only lucky, but he was a shrewd businessman. I got a $2,000 bonus to sign and supposedly another $250 a month to play the last two months for Decatur of the Three I League. I thought that meant I would have earned $2,500 when the season closed on September 1st.... Not so! Mr. Breaden had arranged it so my playing time at Decatur came out of my bonus money. So in essence, I was paid a $1,500 bonus to sign, and played the last two months of the season at Decatur for $500. I do not have a confrontational demeanor, so I stuffed my feelings and rationalized—how could he give $2,500 to a guy who got only one hit in 23 times at bat in college?

My dad and my uncle Jim Kilgore drove me from St. Louis to Springfield, Illinois that Saturday afternoon, July 5, 1947. I kept thinking, God, if I could only get one hit this spring in college ball, what will happen to me in professional competition? Gene Corbett, the Decatur manager, met me at the clubhouse steps. We shook hands as he said, "You're in the lineup tonight." I was given my uniform—they were just like the parent Cardinals' uniforms, only from three seasons past. Corbett went over the signs with me, and I met the guys on the team, and before I knew it, it was time for batting and infield practice. I was very nervous, but playing immediately was a blessing. It didn't give me time to think.

All the games in the Three I League were played at night and game time was usually at 8 p.m. Decatur was playing Springfield, a St. Louis Browns farm club, and I was impressed with the well-kept ballpark. The field was better than anything I had ever played on in the service or in college baseball. The outfield grass was freshly cut and the infield grass and dirt were smooth, and much better than I had anticipated. The lights left something to be desired, something I was to find true of most of the lower minor-league ballparks. The clubhouse was small, but it had been freshly painted and it was clean.

16

Illustration by Ronnie Joyner.

My anxiety about how I would perform eased when in the fourth inning I hit a single and drove in a run. We won the game 5 to 3, and that was no mean feat for the Decatur ball club. After the game, the skipper congratulated me on my play and I quickly started to feel like a member of the team. I remember a statement of his about hitting that was simple but helpful. "Always be ready for the fast ball, and if it is a curve or off-speed pitch, you will be able to adjust." It was very basic and it helped. Little did I know that I was joining a team that would establish itself as one of the worst clubs in all of organized baseball that year.

I found the newspaper reporting in the minors to be much better than given credit for. However, the first paragraph of Sports Editor Howard V. Millard's in the *Decatur Herald & Review* that next day read, "With manager Gene Corbett taking a rest from active duty to direct traffic at the third base coaching line while new Joe Mickelson worked at first base, the Commies came through with another good game here tonight to take the first set with the Brownies, 5–3." The game was played in 1 hour and 50 minutes. An old adage in baseball is "You can't beat the hours," but that night we did.

Hank Arft played first base that night for Springfield and he led the Three I League in batting average that season. He went from there to the big leagues. Hank was a gentleman and a good hitter.

I learned one thing quickly that night: There are generally only two or three showerheads that work in a minor-league clubhouse. So you do either one of two things: Rush in after the game, rip off your uniform and run to the shower, or slowly stroll in off the field, take your time getting to your hook (individual lockers were rare below Class A ball), and leisurely undress. There was a prolonged wait while 17 or 18 guys showered two at a time. That night I waited until just a few were left. I showered, dressed slowly and was one of the last to leave the clubhouse—a pattern I was to follow for over 1,400 regular season games.

My wife would attest to this later and it became one of her pet peeves. "Honey, why are you always one of the last out of the clubhouse?" she would ask repeatedly throughout the years. I would shrug my shoulders, not responding.

How could I explain to her that on July 5, 1947, in Springfield, Illinois, I decided, "To hell with it, why fight for only two showerheads?" In the Three I League that year, some clubhouses had only one showerhead that worked.

The next night we got beat 5–1, but I got a triple and I was feeling great. I already had one more hit than during my entire college season. I bounced into the locker room elated, but I sensed an atmosphere of dejection. In professional baseball, silence reigns as gloom stalks the clubhouse after defeat. You could go 5 for 5 with 3 home runs, but if your team loses you had better not show any outward signs of glee. Before the '47 season was over I would have plenty of practice looking dejected, but after several weeks of losing the feeling had become genuine.

We played the Evansville Braves in mid-July and Tom Zikmund, a likable first baseman, was honored by the Evansville fans. He was given a brand new 1947 Plymouth sedan. Sometimes in some places to some people, minor league fans can be very generous. Most of the minor leaguers used to joke to one another about having a "day" by saying, "The only day they'll ever give me is a day to get out of town."

On July 23 we had a double-header, and in the second game I got a double and a single off of a hard-throwing right-hander named Carl Erskine. A few nights later in Waterloo, Illinois, another hard-throwing right-hander named Howie Judson was on the mound. I lucked out and went 3 for 5 with two doubles. Both Erskine and Judson went on to major-league stardom, but Johnny Perkovich was the hardest thrower in the league, with good control and an excellent curve ball. I faced him on several occasions, and "got the collar" on August 13 and 22. On the 22nd Perkovich pitched a two-hitter and struck out 12, beating us 1–0 before 4,500 fans.

August 8 was Decatur Night, a double-header. Attendance gifts worth more than $700 would be presented after the second game. These included a Bendix washer worth $249.50, a Philco refrigerator priced at $199.75, a

Philco freezer valued at $169.50, an FM radio worth $79.95, plus other gifts. As usual, the Commies lost both games before 4,202 fans, but Forrest P. Kyle reported in the *Decatur Herald & Review*, "The handsome crowd at Fans Field were kept in a more or less happy mood by (1) frequent announcements that the St. Louis Cardinals were winning, (2) two or three dramatic protests by Morrie Arnovich, the Cubs' manager, (3) the spectacle of umpire Gene Allinger calling balls and strikes on the first two batters before discovering that he had neglected to don his mask."

The crowds at most ball games in the Three I League were around 1,500. Some special nights might draw over 4,000 but a crowd of 3,000 was considered good. At Decatur, because of a poor ball club, we drew much smaller crowds. My joining the Decatur Commies (short for Commodore Stephen Vincent Decatur, not the Russian Reds) did little to change their fortune. True, we won the first night I played, but then we lost four in a row before beating the Cub affiliate in Davenport, Iowa, 12–1. Then we lost four more in a row.

That season, Decatur had numerous one-game winning streaks and several times we actually won two in a row. We went on a couple of 10-game losing streaks and in the latter part of August we lost 14 straight. We wound up last in the league in team batting average at .242 and next to last in team fielding with a .939 percentage. I contributed to that fielding mark by making eleven errors in 53 games for a poor .975 fielding percentage. A first baseman with a good fielding percentage will finish in the .990's and make no more than 10 errors for a season of 150 or more games. Walt Soderlind did an amazing job of pitching for us, winning 10 games while losing 9. Our other pitchers' records were as follows: John Remke (5–5), Bill Buck (2–6), Tiny Osborne (4–8), Ed Beane (4–14), Joe Stacy (0–9), Ray Wollgast (0–5), George Kemp (0–6), Bob Zachritz (0–9), and Ray Gamache (1–5).

There were 51 minor leagues in existence at that time with over 400 teams playing in organized baseball. Only Grand Forks, South Dakota, had a record worse than the Decatur Commies in 1947. Grand Forks won 28 games while losing 93 for a .233 winning percentage. We ran a close second from the bottom, winning 31 games and losing 93 for a .250 percentage, and we drew only 33,069 fans for the entire season. Eat your heart out, Joe Garagiola! Your Pittsburgh Pirates of the early '50s look like the '27 Yankees by comparison. More than 70 different ball players wore a Decatur uniform that season, for we had become the proving grounds for all of the St. Louis Cardinals' scouting mistakes. I would arrive at the ballpark very early in those days to make sure no one else got my uniform.

I learned a number of lessons during my first season in pro ball. Baseball executives are much more adept at negotiating contracts than players are. Two dollars a day is not enough for meal money on the road. Movies are an everyday occurrence for ball players to prevent the onset of boredom and loneliness. Minor league managers are helpful to rookie ball players, as they constantly shout, "You had better wear a cup, son, or they'll ring your bell!" Most of the fields were in fairly good playing condition. In some parks players would be asking, "I wonder when they are going to turn the lights on?" after they were already on. Some minor-league parks could substitute for airports during inclement weather. Most baseball players of that era did not chew tobacco. Managers are called "skipper." The curve ball is not an "optical illusion." When in doubt, order a Salisbury steak (glorified hamburger).

Also, I found out there were some very good ball players in Class B baseball in the Three I League in 1947. How about these outstanding future big-league players: John Logan (Milwaukee), Hank Arft (Browns), Willie "Puddinhead" Jones (Phillies), Howie Judson (White Sox), Carl Erskine (Dodgers).

Johnny Perkovich did not achieve major league stardom, but in my opinion, nobody in the Three I League had more stuff and location. Perkovich won 17 games while losing 9 for a Waterloo, Iowa, team that finished in fourth place. He struck out 207 batters, walked 93 and gave up only 157 hits in 211 innings pitched. His earned run average of 2.50 was the best in the league. But John hurt his arm after that season and never reached his full potential.

It is extremely important to have good timing in baseball. I'm thinking back to the night of July 17, 1947, when I hit a lazy fly ball to Ray Fletcher, the Evansville right fielder, in the second game of a doubleheader in Decatur. A smoke pall had just been laid down by a freight train passing on the Wabash tracks behind the right field fence. Fletcher lost the ball in the smoke as I circled the bases, driving in two runners before me for an inside-the-park home run. Now that is good timing!

A big thrill for me was playing alongside and rooming on the road with Andy Phillip. He played on the great Illinois "Whiz Kids" basketball team of the early '40s, one of the finest college teams of all time. Andy was the leader of that team, as well as their leading scorer and everybody's All-American. At the time, though, he was interested in professional sports primarily as a means for helping out his parents in Granite City, Illinois. Andy could have become a good baseball player. But he hurt his knee playing the outfield for Decatur, and the '47 season was the last for Andy Phillip in baseball. That injury started Andy into thinking that basketball was his future and that he had better travel that route. He went on to fame and fortune in professional basketball, playing in five All-Star Games. As an unselfish team player, he had 3,759 assists in his career and averaged

5.4 assists per game and is enshrined in the Pro Basketball Hall of Fame. Andy was a gentleman and it was my privilege to have known him.

As I look back on that rookie season, two things stand out: Baseball played professionally is a tough, competitive game in which I felt I could survive. And some of the toughest and most competitive men are quiet and thoughtful people like Andy Phillip.

I had many adjustments to make that first season and the biggest ones were not on the field. The day-to-day living away from home and the loneliness brought on by the long boring days before night games were certainly difficult. The constant travel and the irregular sleeping and eating patterns created problems as well. But the biggest problem, for me at least, was dealing with the emotional strain caused by the highs and lows of good games versus bad ones. It was hard for me to keep from getting too high or too low. Baseball can drive you crazy if you think about it too much. I was learning to cope with my feelings and I had gained a great deal of confidence. It is my observation that every ball player carries with him from day to day a feeling of nervous apprehension that builds before each game—not unlike the salesman wondering, "How am I going to do today?"

3

Pokie

The biggest event in my life took place at the end of the 1947 season. On November 8, 1947, I married my high school sweetheart, Jo Ann Menzel. She was by my side day in and day out. She never missed a regular season game at home and she listened to most every road game by following the radio play-by-play. In those days the announcer for the minor league away games sat in the studio of the radio station and created the play-by-play from information given him from a ticker tape. The information was usually an inning or two ahead of the announcer. Information was sparse, though, and he had to create the excitement and a full description of what each batter, pitcher, catcher and fielder did, even the umpire dusting off the plate. Jo Ann kept score and always had a box of popcorn during the game. We didn't keep track of the number of boxes of popcorn she ate, but I'm sure it would be in the thousands. Baseball wives in the minor leagues have one common trait. With few exceptions, they are beautiful. My wife was not only beautiful, but she was a source of strength and support throughout all my baseball years and those years that followed.

Baseball people don't always follow through with what they say. Typical example: Eddie Dyer, the Cardinal manager, told me as I was about to leave to play for Decatur after signing in the Cardinal organization, "Son, if you can hit .250 at Decatur with no spring training in your first year of organized baseball, I'll take you to St. Petersburg for spring training next year." I should have replied, "Put that in writing and sign it, Mr. Dyer." I hit .251 at Decatur but never heard a word from him about spring training.

In February of '48 I received by registered mail (every contract I ever got came by registered mail) my contract for $300 per month to play with the Columbus, Ohio, team in Triple A. My chance of making that veteran team ball club with only a half year of minor league experience was between slim and none.

I signed the contract and sent it back to Al Bannister's office. Mr. Bannister had a long successful career in baseball and ran the Cardinal Triple A entry in the American Association at that time. Shortly thereafter, I

WE'VE PLAYED IN SOME BIG PARKS, ED, BUT THIS IS RIDICULOUS!

Illustration by Ronnie Joyner.

received $26.61 for train fare from St. Louis to Daytona Beach, Florida, where the Columbus club trained. I also received $5.00 for meal money while on the train. I did not attend college the second semester, which was to become a common pattern throughout my baseball life.

I got the train out of St. Louis in early March, 1948, and I was heading toward my first spring training and my first full season of professional baseball. I rode coach all the way to save money, and the sandwiches and fruit from home enabled me to stay out of the expensive dining car.

I arrived at Daytona Beach in time for the opening of spring training on March 5, 1948. I was moving into fast company and minor leaguers were moving into a golden age. Servicemen had returned to baseball by the hundreds, and blacks and Latin Americans would soon be entering baseball in large numbers. Major league teams were holding tryout camps everywhere. In 1948 the St. Louis Cardinals had over 20 minor league teams. Some they owned outright and others they had working agreements with. By the '50s, they would increase this number to about 25 farm teams. Brooklyn and the Yankees got the message from Branch Rickey's farm club creation for the Cardinals in the '30s. In 1948, Brooklyn had 25 farm clubs and the Yankees had 21. In that year, there were 50 professional minor leagues, with each league consisting of approximately eight teams. In 1978, there were only 17 minor leagues and in 1994 there were 10.

Operating in the tough American Association, the Columbus, Ohio, club manned its team about the way most Triple A teams did at that time. Two or three regulars were older men in their late 30s and early 40s—men with a number of years of major and minor league experience. Another two or three regulars were near 25 years of age, but had anywhere from two to six years of experience in pro ball. A smaller segment of the team, possibly only one regular and one or two pitchers, was composed of youngsters around 20 years of age with little or no experience but tremendous raw talent. It was not uncommon to see players in their late 30s and early 40s hanging on in the minor leagues in the 1940s and 1950s. If one looks in the records concerning the three Triple A and two Double A associations, the official Baseball Guide published by *Sporting News* in 1949 reads like a Who's Who of ex-major league ball players.

The Columbus, Ohio, Redbirds were no different than any other Triple A team at that time. They had the ex-major leaguers, the experienced Triple A performers and a few youngsters who showed potential.

The man at first base for Columbus was a veteran, Mike Natisin. Mike was typical of any outstanding Triple A ball player at that time. All he needed to play in the majors was a chance. He went on year after year knocking down the fences in the American Association only to be sent back the next season to do it again. Mike's only problem was a fellow named Stan Musial—also a pretty good hitter—who was at first base for the Cardinals. So he went about his business of getting in shape to have another good year in Triple A ball. The record shows that he did, for during the 1948 season at Columbus, Natisin hit .305 with 33 doubles, 5 triples, 30 home runs and drove in 132 runs in one of the best leagues in baseball next to the majors. Mike is still wondering, if he's living today, what you have to do to get a chance to play in the major leagues.

My roommate in spring training was Charlie Stanceau. Charlie had pitched briefly for the New York Yankees and had lost some time in service during World War II. Charlie was a mild-mannered fellow from Canton, Ohio. My most vivid recollection of Stanceau was his arising from his cot in our small room, reaching over to the nightstand, pulling out a cigarette, lighting it and inhaling deeply. I always thought, "My God, how can a guy do that first thing out of bed?"

The spring of '48 went by quickly. It was exciting learning the routine of spring training, which didn't seem to vary from camp to camp and spring to spring. Our schedule was: Up at 8 a.m., on the field by 9:30 and practice until 12:30 or 1:00 p.m. The practice routine always followed this order: Stretching, throwing, batting practice, infield practice, specialty practice (pick-off plays, base-running, etc.), and wind sprints.

Pepper was a fun game that we played before stretching. After the exhibition games started, we played it outside the foul lines in the outfield. Pepper is played with one batter and several fielders about 15 to 20 feet away. One fielder pitches the ball to the batter, who hits it back on the ground. The batter generally hits the ball in a sequential pattern from one fielder to the next until each has had a turn, and then the pattern is repeated. It promotes good bat control for the batter, while the fielders sharpen their reflexes and stretch the backs of their legs. Usually the fielders are in a position where the body is bent at the waist with the knees flexed, feet planted and arms dangling toward the ground. It exerts a constant stretch on the calf muscles of the lower legs and the hamstrings, as well as the muscles of the lower back.

Some of the damnedest fights and arguments have been the result of disagreements from pepper games played for Cokes. Every grounder or fly ball juggled counts for a Coke against the errant fielder. There were always disagreements as to whether the ball was caught cleanly or not. Some guys would purposefully lose count of how many Cokes they owed. Also the batter might hit the ball harder to one fielder than another, provoking cries of indignation from the one who felt picked upon. Mo Mozzali, Billy Costa, Bill Howerton, and Roy Broom were always in the same pepper game, and the noisy arguments they had were of a kind rarely heard in baseball.

Ball players are notorious for finding good eating places. One of the local hotels in Daytona Beach had been turned into an apartment-type complex for retirees. Each Sunday the management would put on an out-of-sight smorgasbord for $1.50. That was a lot of money in 1948 for a meal, but when you could go back for unlimited helpings, well.... The word got around, and before long the 60 or more players, coaches, trainers and everyone connected with the Rochester Red Wings and the Columbus Red Birds—both Triple A Cardinal teams trained in Daytona Beach—arrived promptly at noon for the feast. The management had been used to catering to elderly people picking at their food, not the hungry animals young ball players can be. Needless to say, we cleaned them out. The next Sunday was a repeat performance, and by the third Sunday the doors to the dining room were closed, and remained so each Sunday until the ball clubs left town.

I met a fine young man in spring training. He was about 5'11" or 6' in height, weighing about 170 pounds. He had a broad and perpetual grin on his narrow face. His body was lithe, trim with muscular shoulders and arms and a narrow waist. His only drawbacks were his legs. They were very thin below the knees, almost birdlike. But this youngster could run like a deer, and for a pitcher he had hit one of the longest balls I had seen hit that spring. It was a tremendous wallop to right center, a good 420 feet. Watching that ball travel over the outfielder's head I thought, "My God, if pitchers can hit a ball that far in professional baseball, how far will a first baseman have to hit them?"

This young pitcher from South Vienna, Ohio, became my close spring training buddy. We were green as grass and shared the experience of smoking our first few cigars together, the wooden-tipped Hav-a-Tampas. We didn't want to be different from the rest of the guys, so Miller High Life was a part of our post-training daily routine. We always found time to have a couple of beers before bedtime. It struck me that I was running the beaches and going to the movies with a highly talented young baseball player. But what really threw me was that he told me he had been a left-handed shortstop in high school. The more he pitched, the more I knew he would make the club that spring and go on to greater things.

This proved to be true because my buddy that spring was none other than Harvey Haddix, who became one of the finest left-handed pitchers in baseball. His 12.2 innings of perfect, no-hit baseball for the Pittsburgh Pirates against the Milwaukee Braves stands as one of the all-time great pitching feats. Harvey was an outstanding fielder at his position, so the Cardinals nicknamed him The Kitten. His predecessor with the Cards, Harry Brecheen, had been called The Cat.

I didn't play much that spring, but I learned a lot of baseball from our manager, Hal Anderson. Hal had spent many years as a fleet defensive outfield wizard in the minors. He was a good base runner and taught quite well the arts of running and stealing bases. He was also good at teaching team fundamentals such as hitting the cut-off man, backing-up bases, bunting techniques, etc. I liked the man and he liked me, but at the end of spring training he said what I was to hear from several other managers: "The hardest thing for me to do in all of baseball is to tell a youngster like you that I am going to have to send you down."

Harvey stayed and I went. It was right because I didn't belong in Triple A baseball. I knew it and I wanted to play regularly. But it was from Daytona Beach to Columbus, Georgia, for me. I trained there for a few more days and then headed to Pocatello, Idaho.

I was waiting in the air terminal at Columbus, Georgia, to catch my flight to Chicago, which left there and went out West. It was there that I met Ray Sowins, who was joining me for the trip to "Pokie." Ray was a small fellow, no more than 5'7", but he had arms and legs that were something to behold. He weighed over 185 pounds and was all muscle. We introduced ourselves and headed toward the plane. That was the start of an unforgettable friendship—and season.

We weren't aloft five minutes before I could see we were in trouble. I kept telling Ray to look out the window next to me and see the landscape below. The third time Ray looked out of the window, he turned the most awful-looking grayish-green color. Ray was a man of few words but, I was to find out later, what he said he always meant. Ray started in a low monotone, "The next time this plane lands I'm getting off." We landed in Jackson, Mississippi, and from there cashed in our plane tickets and took the train to Pocatello, Idaho. I was elated when I found out it went through St. Louis. I stopped off there for a day and got to see my wife.

Ray and I proceeded by train to Denver, where we got off the train to get something to eat and look around. When we came back to board the train, it had already pulled out of the station and all we could see was the observation car in the distance. We grabbed a cab, just like in the movies, and beat the train to the next town where we boarded it. Life was to be like that with Ray Sowins as my roommate. We pulled into Pocatello before sunrise with snow on the ground. It was 26° F.

The '48 season opener in Pocatello was a big night. The stands, which held close to 4,000 people, were filled. The temperature on this mid-April night was about 28° and a few snowflakes were falling. My roomie, Ray, played center field in a warm-up jacket. He was a pretty good "moaner," and that night was no exception. During an at-bat, Ray caught a fastball on his fists and the "bees were stinging his hands." Dom Barczewski, our second baseman, and I heard Ray come in complaining again and again about the cold weather. Finally, about the 7th inning, Ray leaned over to Dom and me and said, "I've just got to take a leak! I can't hold it any longer." But in the lower minors there are no restroom facilities in the dugout. If a ball player has to relieve himself, he must go back to the clubhouse, and ours was located underneath the stands. After our chat, Ray proceeded to move to the on-deck circle and from there to the batter's box. At bat, he singled to right after taking a couple of pitches. Ray was on first base shifting from one leg to the other in agony. Dom and I were watching him as he got an unbelievable lead off first base. Our look to each other conveyed, "He must be trying to steal!" But the lead got even bigger—he was almost half-way to second base. The pitcher stretched, whirled and threw to first. Ray casually tiptoed back to first, leaving the umpire to make the easiest decision of his whole year in the Pioneer League. "You're out!" the umpire cried as Ray, not breaking stride, went through an open gate, picked up his pace and was last seen sprinting behind the stands to the clubhouse.

We won that night handily, as we did all season. We had a great hitting club, average defense and good pitching, a combination that would prove hard to beat.

Harvey Haddix, ca. 1954. Harvey pitched what some would say was the best game ever pitched in baseball. On May 26, 1959, at Milwaukee, pitching for the Pittsburgh Pirates against the Milwaukee Braves, he retired the first 36 batters he faced. No one reached base. Perfect game. He lost the game in the thirteenth inning, when Felix Mantilla reached base on an error, and moved to second on an Eddie Mathews sacrifice. Hank Aaron was walked intentionally. Joe Adcock, the next batter, hit a homer, ending the game. The score was listed officially as 1 to 0 because Adcock inadvertently passed Aaron on the base paths. (National Baseball Hall of Fame Library, Cooperstown, New York.)

The Pioneer League, Class C, had beautiful scenery. The states of Idaho, Montana, and Utah housed the eight teams in our league. We had to travel 420 miles to Great Falls, Montana, and 280 miles to Billings. Those trips were made over mountainous terrain in an old Ford school bus with no radio, no reclining seats and a heater that did not work. Every time we made one of those long trips on the old school bus, my knees would be sore from banging against the seatback in front of me.

Our first trip, to Great Falls in early May, was scenic and eventful. We went through Yellowstone National Park and heavy snow lay on the side of the road. It was still cold in that northern part of the country in late spring. Someone had to get out to open the gate to the entrance, as visitors were not allowed in the park so early in the year. What a sight it was for a city boy from the Midwest to see mountains, pine trees, and hundred of mallards in the stream by the roadside. Fish were abundant and could easily be seen swimming in the swift-running, crystal-clear streams. We saw all kinds of wild animals—deer, antelope, elk, moose—and beautiful foliage and trees. It was something to behold.

Ray Sowins, the Chicago boy, just had to see a bear. His strict orders to all concerned were that he must see a bear, even if it meant being awak-

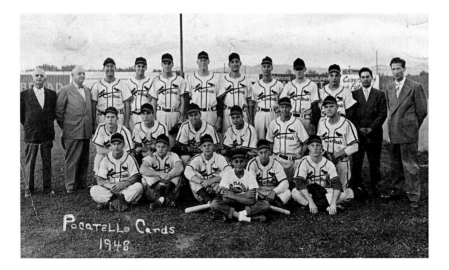

The Pocatello Cardinals, 1948. Top row, left to right: "Pop" Bailey, Mr. Hinckley, Roland LeBlanc, E. Toolson, George Koby, Ralph Beard, E. Glass, Bean Torres, Bob Maloney, B. Powers, Mr. Marvin Milkes, "Bus." Middle row, left to right: Ken Dudrey, Dom Barczewski, Ed Mickelson, Larry Swederske, Ned Sheehan, Al Neil. Bottom row: Ray Sowins, Erv Schuerman, Kent Hadley (bat boy), Bill Weatherwax, Bob Curley. Some of these guys moved up to the big leagues: Ralph Beard, Bob Maloney, bat boy Kent Hadley, and me. Kent grew up to play baseball at Southern California then in the big Leagues for Kansas City and the Yankees. I played against him during a spring training game between Southern Cal and the Portland Beavers.

ened from sleep. As dusk came, a disappointed Sowins rested in his seat. As it grew dark, Gene Sack, a catcher-utility man on the team, shouted, "Hey, Ray, there goes a bear!" Ray bolted upright exclaiming, "Where, where?" Gene replied, "Aw, shucks, Ray. He just went behind a boulder over there." This was to be repeated every hour on the hour until 5 o'clock in the morning. Then everyone became too exhausted from the ride and laughing at Ray, who kept being awakened to the sight of a bear that never existed. The last time Ray was awakened, he took off directly toward the guy who woke him, ready to do battle. Ray had realized by this point that it was a hoax. Believe it or not, just as the sun rose, there was Ray's bear. Everyone yelled for Ray to look. Because he was too tired from constantly being awakened, or because he just sensed another trick, he just grunted and slept on. Ray was the only man on the team to miss seeing a bear on that trip.

One night early in the season, the Pocatello radio announcer interviewed me before the game. Among other questions, he asked, "What is it like to room with Ray Sowins?" I quipped, "Ray is no trouble at all to

Self. Illustration by Ronnie Joyner.

room with. He's never home." Ray heard about that and the next day said, "Hey Mick, what are you doing telling everybody I am out all the time and you never see me?" I laughed and said, "I don't know why I said that. I just thought it would lend an air of mystery to you." Ray walked off, still not too happy with my reasoning.

Four of us lived at Mr. and Mrs. Buffalo's home in Pokie. Sowins and I were in a back room on the first floor, with Barczewski and Ralph Beard on the second floor. The Buffalos were a nice family. They had to be to quarter a quartet of ball players. The living room was just off our bedroom, and Ray had a penchant for phoning his girlfriend in Moultrie, Georgia. It would be 3 in the morning, after we would have been in bed an hour or so, and Ray would tiptoe to the phone and call Lottie. This happened quite frequently, always about the same time at night. Ball players get lonely. Ray married Lottie the next year.

My wife came out to Pocatello by train on her two-week vacation. We couldn't afford for her to give up her job in St. Louis. We needed the money to get us through the winter months. She met me in Ogden, Utah, and stayed for the series. Then we returned to Pocatello for 10 days of

Ray Sowins, 1948. Ray never swung at the first pitch. He appeared in "Ripley's Believe It Or Not" for walking 7 times in a 9-inning game.

home games. In those days there were slot machines everywhere. Drug stores, grocery stores, restrooms, hotel lobbies. Jo Ann enjoyed playing the slot machines and quite often I would see her slip a quarter, dime or nickel into those one-armed bandits. There were even silver dollar machines. I wish I had known then to save a few coins.

I really enjoyed having her there, and I wished she could have stayed the whole season. I had promised her a home run and fortunately I came

More Pocatello teammates, 1948, left to right: Dom Barczewski, 2B, and my running mate, along with Sowins; Al Neil, OF, and leading hitter, who always checked
his batting average on his sleeve; unknown pitcher.

through by hitting one off Ken Lehman, one of the better pitchers in our
league, who later spent 10 years in the majors.

    A few days after my wife's arrival, one by one my teammates would
comment how my eyes were starting to clear up. Toward the end of Jo Ann's
stay, Gene Sack jumped on a trunk in the clubhouse and screamed, "Hey,

Pocatello teammates, 1948, left to right: Erv Schuerman, SS, who lived in Pocatello; Gene Sack, utility, who was always short of money, and Larry Swederske, third base, who was our flatulency ace.

guys, don't worry about Mick losing so much weight these past few days. His wife is leaving soon. One thing about it that has been good is that the red streaks in his eyes have all been drained out." Ball players are often crude, but they are quick to cut through the bull and keep their own kind humble.

We always had pretty good luck in Great Falls. We had hit well and were winning most of our games. Sowins, Barczewski and I were in our room on the second floor of the Park Hotel talking baseball. Back then in the lower minor leagues, when a player needed instruction he rarely got it. LeBlanc was a good manager, an excellent catcher and a knowledgeable player, but he had to play every day and still worry about winning ball games and keeping a team of youngsters out of trouble. He did go out to the park with us for extra workout sessions at times, but nothing too organized and not with any regularity.

The paradox in professional baseball then was that a major leaguer, who was already supposed to know everything, had coaches for pitching, hitting, etc. In the lower minor leagues, where players were supposed to be learning the game, there was one manager and no coaches, and some managers like LeBlanc played every day, too. What a player learned in the minors, he generally learned on his own.

So the subject we were discussing in the hotel was sliding. Dom and I admitted that we didn't know how to slide, at least not very well. We decided to take the blankets off our beds and put them in the hallway to slide on, in order to pick up a few ideas from each other. It was 12:30 a.m. and most of the team was asleep. Dom, Ray and I started our run down the hall as if we were stealing second base, dressed only in our Jockey shorts. We made slide after slide on those blankets, and for some unknown reason, we didn't wake anyone. After a half-hour of sliding practice, we grabbed our blankets and headed to bed, vowing that practice would be resumed again the next night.

We kept on hitting and winning, and the temperature finally warmed up, too. We were playing one evening in Pocatello, and Barczewski and I were looking in from our infield positions at the catcher giving his signs. The 1,500 people in the stands had slowly started snickering and before long, a raucous laughter broke out in the stands. The pitcher, Ralph Beard, stepped off the mound in the middle of his wind-up and looked to right field. Dom and I did an about-face and as I gazed to that spot, Ned Sheehan, our right fielder, was nowhere to be found.

Suddenly my eyes caught something moving atop the light standard behind the right-field fence. It was Sheehan! He had climbed the light tower to its top and was waving, yelling and smiling at the crowd. I guess it takes all kinds to make a minor-league ball club.

One night, the door to Ned Sheehan's hotel room in Billings, Montana, was ajar and I could see Ned at work, massaging his scalp. Ned was rapidly losing his hair but was still far from bald. He had read somewhere that if you spread your legs, bent over at the waist and placed your head between your knees while massaging vigorously, the blood would rush swiftly to the hair root endings and bring fresh nutrients to your hair—

thus preventing baldness. I don't know how long or how often Ned did this, but some of the guys said it was six or seven times a day for ten minutes a stretch.

A few nights after the light pole incident, we were playing in Ogden, Utah, a Cincinnati farm club. Sowins was on second base, edging off the bag toward third. He had his back to the pitcher and was looking to see where the outfielders were positioned. The pitcher had gone behind the mound to pick up the rosin bag and saw Sowins with his back turned. The pitcher put the bag down and took a few steps toward Sowins, who still had not turned around. The pitcher then started sprinting toward the sleeping Sowins, and before the third base coach could get Ray's attention, the pitcher was upon him and tagged him out.

The embarrassed Sowins came into the dugout just as LeBlanc charged toward him, questioning not only his mentality but his ancestry as well. Ray won the team's unofficial award for "The Longest Look to the Outfield While Leading off a Base."

Big Al Neil, our chief RBI man, was the best hitter in the league. He was a tough out and hit the ball with authority. He often stepped out of the box and tugged at the sleeves of his sweatshirt. Barczewski and I always contended that the reason Big Al did that was because he was super conscious of his batting average, and had it written down on his sleeve. The up-to-the-minute average, that is. He would pull up his sleeve, glance at it and then step back into the batter's box to rip another line drive. All the while, Dom and I would be saying to each other, "There he goes again. The Big Moose is always checking his average and cracking out another hit." Could it be that we were envious?

Ken Dudrey was a relief pitcher on our Pokie team. He didn't throw hard but had a fairly good sinker ball, some would say from lack of speed. Ken was from Sundance, Wyoming, one of those catchy names that you just don't forget. Ken could throw strikes, which is what a relief pitcher has to do. But sometimes his strikes turned into line drives that could get an infielder killed. Kenny's claim to fame was his play at the slot machines at the local Elks Club. What an eye Ken had for the slots. They paid 60–40 odds to the house, which is about as high a ratio in favor of the player that you could find. After somebody had primed the pump for a half-hour without a jackpot and walked off in disgust, in would move Eagle-Eye Dudrey. He would make a few more pulls of the one-armed bandit, hit a jackpot and then send money home. Ken sent home $300 a month, which was probably more than he was making from baseball.

We had a payday ritual in Pokie that went something like this. The guys got paid on the 1st and 15th of each month. Gene Sack, our utility catcher and chief hustler, was a super con man out of Damon Runyon's

Guys and Dolls. Gene dressed flamboyantly, and this was in the austere '40s. Gene would come into the locker room after cashing his paycheck, and he'd have on a yellow shirt, green pants, red socks, white shoes and a purple straw hat. All the while he'd be constantly chewing a cigar that dangled out of the corner of his mouth. He would then make the rounds of the clubhouse saying, "Here's your $5, George, here's your $3, Larry, here's your $2, Dom," and so on.

A few days later Gene would make the same rounds for another purpose. This time it went, "You got $5, George? Can I borrow $3, Larry? How about $2, Dom?" Gene's sense of humor was quick and constant. He found life to be a ball, and nothing ever seemed to perturb him.

One time, it was the top of the fourteenth inning in Salt Lake City. The bases were loaded and the score was tied. Sowins was at the bat and the count was 3 and 2. Barczewski was sitting next to me on the bench in the dugout. The next pitch was over the plate, waist-high, and Ray hit the longest drive I have ever witnessed in baseball. (And that includes the time when I was with the St. Louis Browns, when Mickey Mantle hit one halfway up the light tower in April of 1953 off Bob Cain.) At Salt Lake, the base of the fence was 375 feet from home plate in right center field, but that fence was 25 feet high. The ball cleared everything, and about halfway between first and second Ray started into his "Cadillac Trot." Barczewski said, "Look at Sowins 'Cadillac' around the bases. It will take him five minutes before he touches home." When Ray finally came into the dugout, everyone on the bench remained silent for at least a full minute after he sat down. Then, after giving him the silent treatment, we simultaneously let out a war-whoop that reverberated for minutes off the Wasatch Mountains. As we congratulated Sowins, I yelled to Dom, "How can a little guy hit a ball so far?" The Salt Lake paper later reported that only legendary minor-leaguer Joe Brovia had ever cleared that monstrous fence.

The radio announcer in Pocatello was a young fellow just getting his start in broadcasting. He would complain about the tough names that he had to pronounce: Swerderske, Barczewski, etc. Little did he know that the infield for Pokie the next year would be Swerderske at third, Lewandowski at short, Barczewski at second and Czaplewski at first. How would you like to rattle those names off on a double play, with or without two martinis?

Ray's favorite song was "Body and Soul." We had a favorite watering spot in Pocatello, a little place on the east end of town that was a restaurant/bar. We liked the place because it had an excellent musician at the piano. His name was Sam, like the piano player in *Casablanca*. When Ray and I would walk into the piano bar Ray would yell, "Play it again, Sam!" And Sam would stop whatever he was playing and start in with "Body and

Soul." He also played "Home on the Range," among many other songs, and we would sing along with him. It was through Sam that I learned the words to the second verse of "Home on the Range," which is, to my way of thinking, the most beautiful part of the song. Ray was a private person inclined to be moody and sullen, but he was always great to me.

We were playing in Billings, Montana, when the news came to us about the Duluth bus accident. It was almost eleven o'clock in the morning of July 24, 1948. Ray and I were both awake but still in our beds when Larry Swerderske, our third baseman, came in with the bad news. "I guess you guys heard?" Larry asked. "Heard what?" we asked. "About the Duluth bus accident," Larry said. "Five guys on the Duluth Dukes were killed and 13 were injured. Their bus was hit head-on by a truck."

The Duluth Dukes of the Northern League had a working agreement with the St. Louis Cardinals, and most of their players were in the Cardinal organization. Joe Becker, a former teammate of mine at Decatur, was on that team. I got the Billings paper and read that Joe had been injured, how badly I did not know. I found out a few days later that he had been severely burned. I visited him in St. Louis later on that fall. His injuries would necessitate numerous operations and skin grafts. His career was over.

Dead were the Duluth manager, George Treadwell, 42; Gerald Peterson, 23; Gilbert Trible, 19; Donald Schuechmann, 20; and Pete Lazar, 23. James E. Grealish, 36, the operator of the truck that struck the bus, was also killed.

J.P. (Jack) Halliwell, who had been the president of the Pioneer League since 1939, had engineered the expansion of the league before the 1948 season, taking in two more Montana cities, Great Falls and Billings. The All-Star Game was to be played at Great Falls in a brand new plant that seated 4,000.

I was selected to the All-Star team and made the long trip to Great Falls. It was chilly at times, even though it was July 28th. And there were 3,320 cold fans in the stands watching that game between the Northern and the Southern All-Stars. The Northern team represented Idaho Falls, Great Falls, Billings and Pocatello, while the Southern All-Stars represented Twin Falls, Boise, Salt Lake City, and Ogden. A funny-looking hitter on the South's team got two hits that night. He let the barrel of the bat angle down toward the ground with his elbows in close to his body. I remember saying to Al Neil, "I don't see how that guy ever gets a hit, Al." That crazy-looking hitter was Gil McDougald, who went on to become a Yankee great.

As I knelt in the on-deck circle awaiting my first All-Star at-bat, I went through a ritual I had started in the Three I League. I kept it going all through my playing days. I never asked God to let me get a hit, but I always prayed, "Dear Lord, give me confidence and determination." This short prayer always seemed to relax me and help me to concentrate.

I got the first hit of the All-Star Game that night in Legion Stadium, and the Great Falls Brewing Co. rewarded me with a case of beer to be picked up on my next trip to Great Falls. When I returned to Pokie after the game, which we won 10–3, what did my buddy Sowins say when I got off the bus? "Nice hitting, Mick." No. "Nice game, Mick." No. He said, "Hey Mick, I'll help you carry the beer back to the hotel when we get back up to Great Falls."

We did get the beer when we returned to Great Falls, plus another case. The '48 season was my beer-drinking season. I drank more beer that season than all the rest put together. My muscular little roomie, Sowins, did all right in that category as well. We invited several of the guys to come in and help us drink the two cases from the All-Star Game. As time moved toward the wee hours of the morning, it was just Sowins, Barczewski, and me, and the show going on across the way. Little did we realize at the time that we were way ahead of the X-rated movies of later years. The hotel in Great Falls was U-shaped, and we could see directly into the room across the hotel some 50 feet away. We were sipping beer, enjoying the cool evening breeze and watching a couple of semi-nude night performers in foreplay. Several hours elapsed and it was early in the morning when the action became heated. At that moment, the shades came down and the lights went out. Sowins immediately slammed his fist against the headboard of our bed, sending a crashing sound reverberating throughout the hotel. We gave up in disgust and went to bed.

Dom, Ray and I left a call for 8 a.m. that morning. Our bus was to leave for Billings at 9 a.m. sharp. We either didn't hear the phone or they didn't call us from the desk, because all I can remember is having the living stuffings shaken out of me by an extremely irate Frenchman, Roland LeBlanc, our manager. He went from my bed to a sleepy Sowins and Barczewski. LeBlanc, in his late twenties, went 215 pounds on a 6-foot frame. We found that Frenchmen from New Iberia, Louisiana, can really get riled. LeBlanc was shouting and shaking each of us, yelling, "You guys have just fifteen minutes to get your asses on the bus or you'll have hell to pay!"

We certainly didn't need all fifteen minutes. We hurriedly scrambled onto the bus in five. A haughty hand-clapping ovation came from our teammates as we boarded. Our bus left Great Falls and LeBlanc was still mad, but he did relent to our plea for breakfast. Halfway between Great Falls and Billings, the bus stopped for gas. LeBlanc's three bad boys rushed into the restaurant to get something to eat and when we exited from the restaurant … no bus. So we started to hitch a ride. We had tried to hitch for maybe thirty minutes in the hot sun, when along the highway came our yellow bus. It stopped and we climbed aboard. More laughter and derision came our way from LeBlanc and the entire team.

That evening he was still mad at us, but not enough to keep us out of the lineup. In the fourth inning Sowins hit one out over the right-field fence with a man on base, and in the 7th inning Barczewski crashed one over the left-field fence. In the 8th inning I hit an outside fastball over the right-field wall, winning for myself a new Philco radio. We won 4–1 and Sowins, Barczewski, and I were feeling very smug and happy. LeBlanc's bad boys had done all the hitting that night. The three of us stood in the middle of the locker room laughing arrogantly and making caustic comments to our jovial teammates. We were really proud of ourselves. Our bats had redeemed us. Over in the corner of the locker room was LeBlanc, grinning sheepishly. Deep down I could see he was feeling good—we had won—and all was now forgiven.

Before you get the idea that I was a hell-raiser, let me interject here that on every trip I ever took in baseball, my little pocket Bible went with me. I didn't read it faithfully everyday, but I read it more often than not. I felt better when I felt I was with God.

We finished our series in Billings and won the series, two out of three games. It was 11 p.m. and the bus was leaving at midnight for Pokie. We would not arrive until 2 p.m. the next day. There was a tavern across the street from the ballpark with 15¢ large schooners of beer, one-armed bandits and free hard-boiled eggs. I guess the whole ball club was in the place drinking cold beer and consuming eggs. Well, you know what I'm leading to. Several hours later, we started to hit the bumpy, mountainous roads. All the hard-boiled eggs and beer started sloshing around inside us, and it wasn't long before the sounds emanating from the boys on that bus could match the percussion part of Tchaikovsky's *1812* Overture. The aroma on the bus was—let's just say nauseating—and the windows were constantly going up and down like the horses on a merry-go-round. The heater didn't work, so there was a constant battle between those who couldn't stand the smell and wanted the windows opened, and those who were freezing from the rush of chill night air. On went the sounds until twilight, when a faint sound could be heard with decreasing rapidity from one segment of the bus to another. Larry Swerderske, from St. Louis, won the aromatic award with a staggering total of 31 wind-breakers. That record stood up all season.

Gene Sack had crawled up in the overhead luggage rack and was sound asleep through it all. Ernie Schuerman, our shortstop, and Red Mahoney, our best pitcher, were snoring loudly in the back of the bus, sleeping on a pile of eighteen duffle bags filled with soggy baseball gear, as eighteen ball players traveled southwest on a lonely Idaho Highway 20 toward Pocatello. Several hours later some of the guys were yelling at Bussie to stop and let us pee. Most of the guys were groggy with half-opened eyes as we got off the bus. There was a 3-foot-high stone guard wall at the side of the road. As I looked down the mountain, I could see a meandering pencil line of a river below. Then it hit me—My God! We must be at least 4 or 5 thousand feet above the river and anyone toppling over the wall would hurtle to their death. As I grasped the situation, I noticed my right pant leg started to feel warm, then damp. When I looked at my leg, I realized that Ned Sheehan had decided to turn to his left and direct his stream on my leg. "What the hell are you doing, Ned?" He looked at me with a twinkle and we both started to laugh. I'm glad I didn't carry out my first impulse to slap him hard on the back. I might have been peering over the wall to see if I could spot him in the pencil-line river below. As we got back on the bus, everyone knew there would come a payback time for Ned. Gene Sack was still asleep in the luggage rack and Schuerman and Mahoney were still both lying contentedly on the duffle bags as Bussie put the old school bus into gear. It was nearly dawn, but we would not arrive home until 3:30 in the afternoon. We would eat, shower and head to the ballpark for the 7:00 p.m. game. I have long legs and my kneecaps had been pressed against the seat in front on me so tightly that it would take until the fourth inning before I could feel my legs.

George Koby was a former high-school standout from Wellston, Missouri, a suburb of St. Louis. I knew him from our high-school basketball days. He had been in the Cardinal organization only a few years, but his blazing fastball and Greek-god-like physique gave him a can't-miss tag. He was with the Cardinals in spring training of '48 and was supposed to have a chance to make the parent club. George hurt his arm in spring training, though, and was on his way down, if not out of baseball. He had moved, in one season, from St. Louis to Columbus to Omaha to Pocatello, his last stop. George was a competitor, but more than that, he was a realist. He had nothing on his fastball, but he did have pitching experience and pinpoint control. He was able to compile an 8–2 record with us on those attributes. Plus, he had the support of a team that batted .305 for the season and scored 1,022 runs in 126 games. That was over eight runs per game, but we seemed to get fifteen runs whenever Koby worked.

He was pitching one night against Twin Falls, a Yankee farm club with good hitters like McDougald, Gus Triandos, and Red Jessen. The teams seesawed back and forth, and we were leading 12–10 going into the 9th inning. Then Twin Falls got three runs in the top of the 9th and beat us 13–12. Koby, who was leading the Pioneer League pitchers in win-loss percentage, had now lost his third game. He came into the clubhouse storming. It was the first time George had shown any emotion to this degree. He took his glove off and angrily threw it in his locker. The glove seemed to ricochet back and forth for at least five seconds before it landed with a thud on the concrete floor.

Everyone was stunned. This was not genial George Koby. This was some madman in disguise. The silence seemed to linger forever. Finally George blurted out, trying to quell his laughter, "When in the hell are you guys going to get me some runs!" The clubhouse rocked with laughter. Koby had acted out the whole scene. He knew he was washed-up, and that the only reason he was winning in Class C ball was because of his gritty performances and a team that got tons of runs for him. Koby had blended in humor, temporarily at least, to ease his anguish.

Another time, we were taking batting practice in Pocatello, and at the plate was "Sabu the Elephant Boy." That's what we called Ray Sowins after seeing his look-alike in a movie. Ray had already hit three or four balls over the fence, with kids outside the park scampering and fighting to retrieve them. Two little boys were sitting on the eight-foot-high fence in right field. From their vantage point, they could see their buddies acquiring baseballs. They were left out as they yelled in unison, "Hey, Mr. Sowins! How about hitting me one?" God may strike me dead if, on the very next pitch, Sowins didn't hit a line shot toward one of those boys, who was wearing a new ball glove. The boy stretched his glove as high as he could while still seated on the fence. The ball hit in the webbing of his glove and catapulted the youngster backwards, feet over head off the fence and out of the park. The other youngster still on the fence was looking enviously over his shoulder at his fallen buddy. The Pocatello Cardinals, who had all witnessed the event, were on the ground rolling in laughter with tears streaming down our cheeks. Sabu remained the only upright player, exclaiming stoically, "Hell, he wanted me to hit him one, didn't he?"

The lights in Idaho Falls in 1948 had to be the worst I ever played under in my eleven years of professional baseball. As you walked across that field with the lights on, you could see twelve or fifteen shadows of yourself. A pitch to home plate was almost impossible to pick up. We would kid each other about wearing miner's hats with the light in front to help us see the ball. I was batting one night against Ken Lehman, who was really quick, and I let two pitches go by. I told the umpire, "Those pitches sounded a little high to me." The umpire grunted, "I didn't see them either, Mick, but to me they sounded low enough to be a strike."

About the 6th inning Ned Sheehan, who used an open stance facing the pitcher, was hit by a Lehman fastball right between the eyes. I don't believe he ever saw the pitch because he never moved a muscle to get out of the way. A few innings later I went into the dingy clubhouse to see how

Ned was doing, and a priest was giving him his last rites. I cringed as it struck me that Sheehan was seriously hurt. Blood was streaming from both ears and he was semi-conscious. Ned Sheehan spent a week in the hospital with a fractured skull. He would suffer from headaches the rest of the season and play one more year before retiring from baseball.

In late July that year, we had a Field Events Night at our ballpark. Our opponents that night were the Salt Lake City Bees, and they also were our opponents in the events that took place before the game. We competed in races, throwing contests, fungo hitting, catchers throwing into a barrel, etc. The dumbest event was the one I got sucked into at the last minute. Marvin Milkes, our business manager, decided to get me into a race with a guy on the Salt Lake team. His name was Jack Bacciocco. We were both to start from second base in opposite directions. He was to touch first on his way to home plate, and I was to touch third and then home plate. No one thought of what would happen in case of a tie.

It happened. He touched first as I touched third and we both headed for home. I ducked instinctively at the last second and my shoulder crashed into his cheekbone, caving it in. I came out of it with a concussion and a bruised shoulder and thigh, but he was seriously hurt. For some reason he was not taken to the hospital and he lay there on the floor in the locker room—delirious, asking for his mom. It was sickening and I felt sorry for him. He required surgery on his cheek when he got back to Salt Lake City early the next morning and was out for a month. He played a few weeks at the end of the season, never to play again. What a silly way to end a career.

Dom had an especially good game one night. There was a scoreboard in dead center field with square openings that were filled with the number of runs scored each inning. Dom managed to line one right through a vacant opening for a home run. The ball rattled around in that wooden scoreboard for what seemed like a full minute. Dom beamed from ear to ear, yelling, "Hey, Mick! Did you see that one?"

It was nearing the end of the season, and Big Al Neil was still constantly going at his sleeve, tugging at it and looking at his batting average. Dom and I agreed he would win the batting championship. And he did, hitting .390 with 150 runs batted in. We won the Pioneer League pennant with a record of 77–49 for an excellent .611 winning percentage, and we drew 88,193 fans. I had a good season, hitting .372 with 143 RBIs. I had a lot of work to do in the field, where I made 23 errors for a low .979 fielding percentage.

We beat Idaho Falls in the first round of the play-offs 3–1 but we lost 4–2 in the second round. The play-offs had wound down to the end of September. I had to leave before they were over to get enrolled in college, which had already started. I said good-bye to the guys and to old "Pop" Bailey, our groundskeeper. The last person I said farewell to was Ned Sheehan, who in five short months was now practically bald.

The Pocatello team was a rare mixture of individuals, never duplicated again in my baseball years. There was a chemistry between the players—one of talent, camaraderie and human purpose—that meshed so appropriately that it would be hard to repeat. Because we all got along so well and had so many good times together, that group of people—that team—provided me with one of the happiest and most unforgettable experiences of my life. I'm sure it was that way for all of us. As Dom Barczewski put it a few years ago, "Ed, that team was just the right group of guys at the right time of our lives, and gave me the most fun I have ever had in my life."

Amen, Dom.

4

The Bird-Doggers

It was back to Daytona Beach in 1949 and spring training with the Columbus Red Birds. The club stayed at the Friendly Hotel, with its big white columns and spacious front porch. My wife and I spent a week in Hollywood, Florida, before the start of training, visiting my aunt and uncle, Lamora and Tony Mickelson. Uncle Tony, my dad's oldest brother, had been a civil engineer who a hand in laying out the city of Hollywood. After a week of sun and fun for Jo Ann, she was back to St. Louis. I hated to see her go and she did not relish the idea of leaving Florida for St. Louis in February, but we just didn't have the money for her to stay during spring training. The ball club allotted me $4.00 a day for meal money and provided me a place to stay at the hotel, and that was it.

Mike Natisin was back at first base after a super season at bat for the Columbus team in '48. I figured I would learn what I could and try to do well when I got the opportunity to play in place of him. I did learn, but aside from a few good games, I was unimpressive. I was not an early starter in spring training.

Barney Olsen, "Ol' Barn," was the life of the party as usual that year. Barney had played some major league ball, but at 33 he was on his way out. He was a real con artist and I enjoyed him immensely. Nobody, but nobody, could beat Barney at hearts, a card game played universally by ball players at that time. Barney played hearts the first few days of camp, but won so much money that the guys banned him from future play.

Olsen used to sit on the veranda with Hal Anderson, our manager, and his wife in the evening. He would chat with them for hours and I think both the skipper and his wife enjoyed Barney's company. Promptly at 10 in the evening, Ol' Barn would stretch, yawn, and say, "Good night Skip, Good night, Mrs. Anderson. This spring training routine is too much for these old bones, and I'm going to have to put them to bed now." And with that, Barney would go up the steps to his second-floor room, out the window, down the fire escape, and out on the town. I admired the way he pulled it off and never got caught. Some of the other veteran players tried to skip out after hours but were caught and fined. But Barney

Illustration by Ronnie Joyner.

Olsen was "Mr. Straight," the courteous gentleman, to Mr. and Mrs. Anderson.

At least one aspect of the game was changing ever so subtly. Blacks and Latinos were starting to come into baseball. Not in large numbers, but they were coming. I felt that it was just, but I knew that the new additions would make my job of reaching the majors that much tougher. I noticed especially one young fellow with Jersey City who looked good in a game we played in Sanford, Florida. He was well-built and had good speed and coordination. He looked like an athlete. His name was Monte Irvin. I wondered if he would make it. "Good luck, Monte," I thought.

Turns out Monte didn't need all that much luck. In 1951 he led the National League in runs batted in, driving the "Miracle Giants" to the pennant. He batted .458 and stole home in the '51 World Series. And now he's in the Baseball Hall of Fame in Cooperstown.

Spring training in '49 seemed to go by so slowly. I missed my wife and I wasn't playing much. When I did play, though, I was struggling with the bat. I was feeling down and lonely when the team broke camp on the 8th day of April, and I was sent to Columbus.... Columbus, Georgia, that is, not Columbus, Ohio, where the Triple A club played.

Columbus, Georgia, was a Class A team in the South Atlantic League, called the Sally League. I learned quickly that to survive in Georgia, you had better like hominy grits. Because, like them or not, you were going to get them for breakfast in Columbus. I checked into the Ralston Hotel in Columbus, ready to start my second full season in organized baseball. Kemp Wicker, our manager, was a former New York Yankee pitcher. The ball field for the Columbus team was spacious, with a center field fence about 420 feet from home. The right and left-center field walls were about 380 feet from the plate. Many minor league clubs had deep fences, probably to save baseballs. The grass in the Columbus outfield was well-kept and the infield was in good shape. But the stands were of rickety wood, and in some places one could pick up quite a few splinters.

One thing that haunted me, throughout my days of playing baseball in the South, were the shacks, filled with poor black families, often located adjacent to the ballparks. Columbus was no different. Just across the street from the ballpark entrance, black children and their parents were living in complete squalor.

I opened the season at first base against Macon, Georgia. It was a close game, but in the late innings, a throw from our shortstop, Wally Lammers, pulled me a shade off the bag. I tried to stay on the bag and stretch for the ball, but it hit the tip of my glove and bounded out for an error. It proved to be costly because Macon went on to score a run and win the game. The fans from Phoenix City, a poor neighborhood across the Chattahoochee River from Columbus, mostly sat down the right field line behind first base. And they never let me forget that error.

The fans in Columbus were different than any I would encounter. Some were the nicest, warmest, and friendliest fans I have ever met. They would invite you to their home to eat, and they couldn't do enough for you. But some were the most ornery, nasty people I have ever met. They seemed like vultures, just waiting to pounce when you were down.

Phoenix City, Alabama, was, at that time, one of the roughest towns

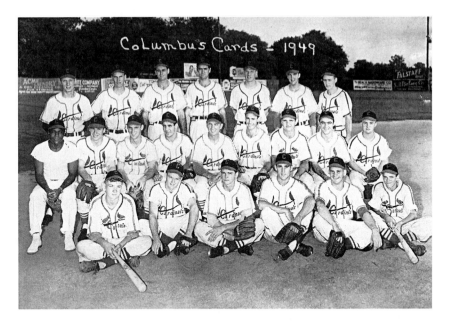

Columbus Cardinals, 1949. Left to right, back row: Bob Eisminger, P. Bryant, Ed Mickelson, Mike Clark, Jack Faszholz, Herb Moford, Wally Lammers. Middle row, left to right: Trainer "Doc" Folkes, Gene Faszholz, Mike Curnan, Lou Colombo, Mgr. Kemp Wicker, Roy Huff, Greg Masson, Ray Jablonski, unknown player. Bottom row, left to right: bat boy, Erv Schuerman, Don Stephens, Jim Clark, Dennis Reeder, and bat boy. From this group, four of us eventually went on to the big league: Mike Clark, Jack Fasholz, Ray Jablonski, and me. Kemp Wicker had been a Yankee pitcher. (Cosco Studios, John Cumbie, photographer. Used by permission of Main Street Baseball and the Memphis Redbirds.)

in the nation. We were told never to go over there alone and best not at all. There was one bar after another and one nightclub after another, with a sprinkling of prostitution houses. It was unusual if someone wasn't knifed or shot during any week of the year.

Most of the fans from Phoenix City came to the ballpark with one purpose in mind: To heckle a ball player. And as I said, they all seemed to sit behind first base. We came home once from a very successful road trip in June and had a small turnout for our first game back. But in July, when we returned after losing eight in a row on the road, the stands were almost filled with heckling fans.

I felt by the end of the season that, in their own sadistic way, those fans had warmed up to me. Some of those Columbus, Georgia, fans would have loved our Decatur team! Fear can be a great motivational factor, and with the heckling from behind me at first base I really had to focus. I reduced my errors from 23 to only eight all season, and only three at home.

The clubhouse in Columbus was small, but each of us had our own locker space. We also had a trainer for the first time. His name was "Doc" Folkes. He was great at rubdowns and helped me a lot with my sprained ankle and hamstring problems. Doc was black, and a former boxer who had fought during very difficult times for black athletes. He was really a lovable guy.

The trips in the Sally League were long, but nothing like those in the Pioneer League. The land was generally flat, not like the rugged mountain terrain out west. Several trips were right at 250 miles and would take us six or seven hours to complete. Our longest trips were to Charleston and Columbia, South Carolina; Jacksonville, Florida; and Savannah, Georgia. Our bus was first-class, nothing like Pokie's rundown school bus. There was carpeting on the floor, padded seats that reclined, and, thank God, the luxury of air conditioning, which was certainly needed in that part of the country.

The Columbus, Georgia, team was different than the other two I had played on up to that point. Decatur was a solid loser in '47 and Pocatello was a solid winner in '48. Columbus was average to the core. We would win some, lose some and some were rained out. The South Atlantic League was Class A, Decatur was Class B, and Pokie was Class C. The differences between the leagues were primarily in the quality of the pitching and fielding. The defensive play in A ball was starting to show some consistently good performances. And instead of having one or two pitchers per team with good stuff, there were now two or three pitchers who could throw good breaking pitches, sinker balls and, of course, fastballs.

We had two outstanding right-handers in Mike Clark, a wiry 6'3" hurler, and Jack Faszholz, a solidly built 6'2" guy with tremendous control and a sneaky fastball. Don Stephens and Dennis Reeder were both small, stylish lefties with good stuff, but they weren't as consistent as Mike and Jack.

I started the season alternating at first with a young lad named Henry Zich. We were both trying so hard to impress our manager that neither of us did much. Zich and I were hitting a little over .200 when the decision was made to send him to Salisbury, Maryland, in the Eastern Shore League. I still didn't get into the lineup regularly, though, as Gene Faszholz (Jack's younger brother) played first when Zich left. Finally, about the middle of June, I started to play regularly and hit over .300 for the remainder of the season, enabling me to bring my average for the year up to .259. I was proud of my RBI total of 81 after missing out on a third of the season on the bench.

Lou Colombo was our center fielder, and a good one. He had good speed and a good bat. He wasn't a power hitter but hit line-drive doubles and an occasional home run. Lou had one goal, and that was to save $500 to buy a car. Colombo was a trumpet player and he was enticed by a local nightclub to play after our ball games for some extra money. Lou played his horn into the early morning and would sleep until two in the afternoon, skipping breakfast. He would then eat two or three hamburgers and head for the ballpark, saving quite a bit of meal money. Lou scrounged for baseball shoes, because he didn't want to put the money out for a new pair. He borrowed my old pair of shoes to play center field. I used them for batting practice, but not in the games. The cleats were worn down and they were about two sizes too big for him. The toes curled up as he walked. Kemp Wicker, our manager, must have known what was going on because one night as Lou was going for a fly ball in center field he tripped, letting the ball fall for a triple. "Wick" blew up and hollered at Lou, "You better have a new pair of shoes for tomorrow night's game or you can pack your bags and head for Brockton!" Lou bought a new pair of shoes the next day.

Speaking of Colombo's hometown, Brockton, Massachusetts, I remember the time when Lou asked me, "Hey Mick, you follow boxing, don't you?" I said, "Yeah, Lou. I wouldn't miss the Friday night fights on TV for anything." Lou continued, "My brother, Al Colombo, is helping train a fighter in my hometown, the second guy he's trained, and when this guy fights, you'll see my brother in his corner. This guy is just starting out, but he's going to be a champ someday." I said, "Well, Lou, what's his name?" "Rocky Marciano," Lou responded. I said, "Sure, Louis, sure," as I thought, Who the hell is Rocky Marciano?

In the big leagues you have your cliques. Two guys go here, three guys go there, one guy that way, and so on. Not so in the minors, especially with the Columbus Cardinals. We were together. While on the road, we ate together, went to the movies together and bird-dogged together. Oh, how we bird-dogged together! Some ball clubs develop a characteristic of their own, and for the 1949 Columbus Cardinals, it was bird-dogging. Bird-dogging is baseball slang for voyeurism. It seems to be deeply ingrained in the genes of 19-, 20-, and 21-year-old ball players. Our bus rolled up in front of the Savannah Hotel in Savannah, Georgia, and I had no idea why there was such a rush to the front desk of the hotel. There was a great deal of excitement and anticipation. A muffled cheer went up when a pair of roomies got a third-floor room. I heard someone say, "Everything is okay now." I was wondering what was so special about the third floor. I would soon find out.

Savannah had a bad ballpark, poor lights, a bad infield and an outfield with holes in it. Charley Bishop was pitching for us that first night in Savannah, and he was something to behold. Charley was part Indian and he had a fiery temper. He was big, strong, and threw B.B.s. He was unique in at least one respect. He would wind up, throw a blur toward home plate and then charge off the mound as fast as he could, getting halfway from the mound to the plate as the pitch popped into the catcher's glove. Bishop had control problems. And he wanted to be on hand in case the umpire needed any help calling the pitch the way he thought it should be called—a strike. But Charley's strike zone never coincided with the ump's. His was from anything that didn't hit the plate to a foot over the batter's head. What a sight it was to see Charley throw the ball and then race toward the plate.

I was on an 0 for 23 hitting streak and I was depressed. But unlike my slump during college ball, I knew I could hit. I had my two previous seasons to fall back on for support. As long as I remained patient and didn't start pressing, I knew I would come out of it. "Just stay loose," I told myself. That night I got a couple of hits in our win, and I hit well the rest of the season. Everything looked good to me after I had come out of my rut. The shabby Savannah ballpark had suddenly turned into the gates of heaven.

A happy troop went back to the Savannah hotel that night. As I was eating in the coffee shop after the game I asked Roy Huff, one of the veteran ball players who had played in the league before, "What's so important about getting a room on the third floor in this hotel?" Roy answered, "Well Mick, it's not the room, it's the ledge." "What do you mean, Roy?" I asked. "Well, the ledge is about three feet wide and it goes around three sides of the building, except for the alley, and it's perfect for bird-dogging all the windows on the third floor." That night more than half of the Columbus Cardinals were out on the ledge of the Savannah Hotel, peeping into windows of unsuspecting guests.

We moved on to Jacksonville to play the Tars, a New York Giants farm club. As usual, most of the guys went to the afternoon movie. The picture, *It Happens Every Spring*, was one that I won't forget. I have seen it three or four times since then on late-night television. Ray Milland was the star, portraying a college professor who invented a scientific potion that made leather allergic to wood. He rubbed some of this magic potion on a baseball one day and pitched it to a batter. As the hitter swung at the pitch, the ball would jump six inches over the bat. Trick photography made the ball seem like it was a butterfly darting up to the plate, first this way, then that way. Milland used his invention to become an unbeatable big league pitcher, as he pitched his team into the World Series.

That night we went out to face the Jacksonville team, and everybody was still talking about the afternoon show. I was hitting fifth and our first batters in the first inning—Gene Faszholz, Lammers, and Colombo—came back to the bench shaking their heads muttering, "Holy cow, that guy's knuckleball dances up there just like the baseball in the movie." The next inning, Frank Gravino struck out and I was next to face this magic knuckleball pitcher.

I had hit against a few knuckleballers before, and I really didn't mind them. I stood further up toward the front of the batter's box, but this didn't help much, for the ball fluttered way up the plate. I blinked, swung, and missed. Several other pitches came in the same way. The action of the ball really did look exactly the same as those pitched by Milland in the movie. The guys in the dugout were in a state of confusion as an eerie silence prevailed. I topped a grounder to the shortstop later in the game, feeling I had accomplished something by merely making contact.

The knuckleballer that night was none other than Hoyt Wilhelm. He went on to pitch over twenty years in the majors and retire in his mid-forties. We faced Wilhelm several more times that season and finally beat him one night when the wind was blowing strongly behind his back. A knuckleballer's best friend is a wind in his face. That provides the pitch with some air resistance, and therefore more time for it do some fancy tricks. A strong wind at the back of a knuckleballer can spell disaster. Hoyt had to go to his fastball that night, and we jumped on it like bees on honey. Hoyt Wilhelm would go from that Jacksonville mound to Baseball's Hall of Fame in Cooperstown.

One Sunday in July, we were playing a double-header in Columbia, South Carolina. I must say that most of the ballparks in the Sally League were well-kept, and Columbia had one of the league's better parks. All of the clubhouses were small, dingy and usually architectural afterthoughts. I had hit my stride, and even though I wasn't burning up the league, I was managing to hit with regularity. I recall that double-header vividly and can see almost every ball I hit and where it went. I went 0 for 7 in those two games despite hitting every ball solidly. I hit six balls sharply on the ground, either in the hole between third and shortstop or through the box over second base. I thought they might all get through for base hits. It didn't work out that way, because Roy McMillan made six major-league plays, miraculously getting to each ball and throwing me out each time by a step. I began to wonder if major-league shortstops could possibly be any better than this guy. I didn't know then, of course, that McMillan would go on to play in Cincinnati for many years and would be touted as one of the best defensive shortstops in baseball.

It was back to the hotel to get our minds off a disappointing defeat. Wally Post, who would also go on to the Cincinnati Reds, beat us with an extra-inning home run. So we went back to bird-dogging. Is it possible that almost an entire minor league club can hide in one hotel room and not be seen by the neighborhood harlot? One of our young single guys had agreed to perform for us with the local prostitute, so we pitched in our money and manned our battle stations in excited anticipation. There were at least a dozen guys in the room—we carried eighteen on our roster. Some were under the bed, some were in the clothes closet, some hid behind chairs and some were behind a dresser. I happened to be above the clothes closet in what was probably a hat bin. The area was three by three feet, no more. How I got my 6'4" frame in that small space, I shall never know. The other incredible part was how I was able to remain there in a round ball position with my knees tucked under my chest for 45 minutes.

Anyway, there I was, with the night's losing pitcher, Mike Clark, standing in the middle of the room saying, "Get your head down, Mick, I can see you. Your feet are showing behind the dresser, put the rug over them. Close the closet door a little more, I can see your bright-colored shirt." And so it went. Each time the elevator stopped at our floor we became quiet as church mice, our hearts pounding rapidly. This went on for 45 minutes until we finally decided that our "lady of the evening" was a no-show. We disbanded to our rooms that night, but we were a determined crew and I really think we could have pulled it off.

Lou Colombo boarded our bus as we left Columbia with his usual brown bag which contained his toothbrush, comb, socks, and underwear. No suitcase. Lou traveled light. Under his other arm he had a brand new shoebox. As the bus started rolling into the outskirts of Columbia, Lou opened the box to reveal his new street shoes. He took off his old pair, put on the new and flipped the old ones casually out the window into a farmer's field. Like I said, Lou traveled light.

Bob Eisminger joined us in Columbus, Georgia. He was a veteran pitcher in his late twenties, having entered professional baseball in 1939. He had been in baseball for four or five seasons, then went into the service for several years, and then came back to baseball for three more seasons. He was informed of some tragic news soon after he arrived in Columbus. His wife, traveling by car from Camdenton, Missouri, to join him, had an auto accident and one of his small children had been killed. We were all stunned by the news, and we all agonized with him as he showered and let his emotions out after the game. I felt sorry for Bob, but also so helpless for not being able to do anything.

The players' wives have many advantages in baseball, but a constant state of instability may outweigh all the good points. Most of them had to travel by themselves with their children to join their husbands. The ones with school-age children had to wait until school was out and return before school started, which was before the end of the baseball season. A baseball wife had to be mighty flexible and understanding. If she was the type that wanted to get married and stay put, then she would have a tough time coping with all the problems that being married to a ball player presents.

Loneliness also prevails with the wives. Usually a wife would become close friends with a few others, and they would spend time shopping, sightseeing and listening to the games in the evenings. Then each would go to her respective apartment or house and the loneliness would take over until the next day, when she would try to think of something interesting to do for the day. Road trips could become long and lonesome for those very supportive women.

I became rather close to Ray Jablonski that season. He had come to us in June and he had played four different positions by July. He played third, short, and outfield and was now the second baseman. "Jabbo" had a short, quick stroke and he could hit for power. He was an outstanding right-handed hitter and went well with the outside pitch, but he had a mediocre arm and just average hands as a fielder. This was to be Jabbo's trademark throughout his professional career. His bat got him to the major leagues, but where to play him was a problem.

Jabbo was quiet and intense. He worked hard at his profession and was real down to earth. I would walk into Ray's room frequently to find him washing out his socks and underwear and hanging them out to dry. He was no different than the rest of us in his frugality, because the going rate for a Class A ball player in 1949 was between $250 and $450 a month. Maybe a few players were making more than that, but not many. I was making $400 a month, which was $100 per month more than I made at Pokie. Ray certainly wasn't the only one that washed his clothes while on the road.

My wife joined me in June. Erv Schuerman, our shortstop, with whom I had played in Pocatello, had asked me if I wanted to share a house with him and his wife. It was a spacious home with a large living room, dining room, kitchen and two large bedrooms separated by a bath. My wife and I talked it over and although we liked our privacy, we felt it would be okay. At that time we didn't have a car of our own, but we couldn't live within walking distance of the ballpark because it was in a run-down section of town. Fort Benning is located right outside of Columbus, Georgia, and any apartment or home that was furnished and clean was scarce and quite costly.

The arrangement was for only a three-month period. With two women in the same house planning meals, etc., there are bound to be some problems, but things worked out rather well. The one thing that got to me before the season was over were the big meals prepared at the house after a ball game. At midnight we would sit down to a large dinner and I never really got accustomed to it. Jo Ann and I always lived by ourselves after that, having our biggest meal before the game at 3 p.m. and a light snack after the game.

Some minor league teams were doing very well at the gate around this time, but others were floundering. Teams below Double A generally found it difficult to make money. The real salvation was the concession stands. Concession money made the difference for many minor-league teams, keeping them in the black instead of the red. The concession stand at Columbus, Georgia, was located under the grandstand near the main entrance to the park. It served delicious hot dogs, and customers could choose from sauerkraut, pickle relish, chopped onions, catsup and mustard to go with them—all for 20 cents. You could make a meal out of one hot dog if you loaded it up with that good sauerkraut. Peanuts, Cracker Jacks and popcorn sold for ten cents. Ice-cold beer was 25 cents and soda was a dime. As far as ticket prices went, the grandstand seats were 90 cents, the bleachers were 60 cents, and children were admitted for 30 cents. On a Sunday double-header, which started at 3 p.m., 1,500 fans would eat and drink the Columbus Cardinals to a profitable day of baseball.

I was going very well now as the season moved into August. I was on second base one night, and was taking a lead toward third when the pitcher whirled and threw to the shortstop covering second base. I was surprised, but I could have gotten back easily by sliding. Instead, I only half-slid, half-stood up. I got back safely, but in the process I severely sprained my ankle. It was a dumb play on my part. I had played long enough to know that when you make up your mind to slide, you don't do it half-heartedly. That is how you break a leg. I was out of action for six or seven days.

A few days after my injury, we were playing Jacksonville in Columbus. My ankle was still swollen and heavily taped. I was called upon to pinch-hit with a man on base and the score 7–4 in favor of Jacksonville. I was a terrible pinch-hitter because I had to play regularly to keep my stroke. So I was as surprised as anyone when the ball sailed over the fence. As I rounded second base limping badly, the shortstop tagged me out. I was shocked because I was sure that the ball had cleared the fence. It turned out that the ball had hit a pickup truck parked behind the fence in left field and bounced back to the left fielder, Jim Thomas, who threw it to the shortstop.

When base umpire Charley Harris called me out on the play, our entire bench (led by Kemp Wicker) cleared out of the dugout and onto the field. Some of the people in the stands came out too. I went over and sat on third base for a few minutes, and then, unknown to anyone, I walked down the line and touched home plate. I went into the clubhouse, leisurely undressed, soaked my ankle in hot and then cold water and returned to the dugout some twenty-five minutes later. I saw an irate Jack Aragon, the Jacksonville manager, chin to chin with Ed Boell, the plate umpire. Boell had reversed Harris' decision after he had gone out to the left field fence to talk to a youngster who had been sitting on top of his truck just in back of the fence. Boell told him, "Tell the truth, son, what happened?" The boy replied, "The ball hit a truck and bounced back into the outfield." With that, Boell called the hit a home run.

The argument between the manager and umpire now concerned how a guy could get a home run and not touch home plate. I would have told them if anyone had asked, but nobody asked. Boell stood his ground, though, and kept the decision a home run. Jack Aragon then proceeded into the dugout and bashed his hand against the concrete wall. The home run stood, but Jacksonville won 7–6. The next evening it rained and the game was called off. Jacksonville was about to leave early to return home. Aragon was sporting a cast on his right hand with wires coming out of every one of his fingers, meeting a metal ring that encircled his hand. He had broken almost every bone in his hand.

Frustration is a constant companion in baseball, and sometimes the feeling becomes overwhelming. Cliff Ross was a hard-throwing lefty, a phenom with Columbia, and I had faced him before in the Pioneer League when he was with Ogden, Utah. He had gotten me out on strikes four times in one night in late August during a game in Columbus. It was my most humiliating game at bat. At about 4 a.m. that morning, with the midnight supper still churning in my stomach, I had replayed each of those four strikeouts hundreds of times in my mind. My anger and frustration suddenly turned to rage. Jo Ann was sleeping peacefully at my side. I took my fist, and with one blow against the wooden headboard, sent the house rattling. My wife jumped a foot out of bed as if she had heard a gunshot. "What was that!" she exclaimed. "Four strikeouts," I grunted.

Many of the old Southern hotels have transoms over the doors. One such hotel was the Partridge Inn in Augusta, Georgia. One night there, three of us were put on duty for the Columbus Cardinals. At 1:30 in the morning, we had our hotel room door ajar, and we were scurrying up and down the hall in our Jockey shorts checking out the open transoms. We were in luck that night. The performance going on, as we stood on our orange crates looking through the transom, would have put some of the present-day blue movies to shame. The three of us were so engrossed that we didn't hear the elevator stop and its door open and close. What a sight we must have been to that young couple getting off the elevator. They were dressed in formal attire. We were in our under-drawers. I jumped off the orange crate and ran toward the open hotel room door with one of my bird-dogging buddies in close pursuit. The third fellow in our party was not so fleet of foot. In his exuberance to escape, he plummeted down into the orange crate! He came down the hall hippity-hopping with the embarrassed couple close behind.

We did the only manly thing we could do at the time. We closed the door on him. Our buddy was in the hallway as the young couple passed him in his Fruit of the Loom outfit. The conversation that followed went something like, "Nice evening." "Oh yes, a little warm though." As soon as the couple passed, our buddy banged on the door. The two of us inside were by this point in hysterics, and we let him enter. He blurted out, "Why the hell did you close the door on me?" I responded with something inane like, "We thought it would be a good chance for you to meet some new people!"

Jack Faszholz was one of my favorite people in baseball. He was a soft-spoken, easy-going guy, who in his own quiet way was one of the true leaders on our team. Jack was an athlete, a man who could have excelled at any sport. He was 6'2" and weighed right at 190 pounds. His chief pitches were a good fastball (though not blazing), a curve and a slider. His stable temperament, poise and pinpoint control had made him a hurler of extraordinary merit. On the night of August 5 in Augusta, Georgia, Jack became the first 20-game winner for Columbus since Ed Weismann in 1939.

Faszholz attended Concordia Theological Seminary in St. Louis during the off-season and was studying to become a minister. Jack lived by his convictions, and all the ball players respected him. He was always in the middle of a conversation on the bus or in the hotel lobby, for he was a good listener. He brought out the best in people by being supportive of them and by reinforcing the good qualities in each person. Jack wasn't a judgmental person. You got the feeling that he minimized your faults and maximized your strengths. It felt good being in his presence. Despite his religious convictions, Jack wasn't a "goody-two-shoes." He was in on some of our escapades, but when he thought we were getting out of line he would let us know by removing himself quietly.

Faszholz had nicknamed me "Junior Bear" after a cartoon character we had seen at a movie house. A group of us had gone to the afternoon movies one day, and after the feature picture the cartoons came on. One of them was about some bears, including one named Junior Bear. Jack yelled out, "Hey! That's Mick. Mick, you're Junior Bear!" The nickname stuck, and for the remainder of the season I was Junior Bear to the entire team.

The nickname seemed to be a show of friendliness and acceptance by my teammates. The '49 season was a painful one for me emotionally, though, because for practically the whole season, some of the fans and some of the press were on me pretty hard. It felt good to know that my teammates cared. I had learned to hang in there during bad times, the early months of the season. I was proud of myself because I had turned what could have been a disastrous season into a respectable year.

The stands at Golden Park in Columbus were far from the best. They were made of wood, and the years had not been kind to them. They were splitting and coming apart, and there were little open spaces where once wooden knots existed. The 7th inning stretch had become a ritual for our ball club. That was the time that our bench was deserted, except for the guy batting and the on-deck man. Each night, during the home half of the 7th inning, fourteen or fifteen players would at once decide that they needed to relieve themselves, get tape out of their locker, change a sweatshirt or find some other idiotic reason to go back into the clubhouse. They would scatter in all directions underneath the stands, looking up to see what could be seen.

We closed the season in Jacksonville, the hottest town in the league. The temperature, like Houston and Beaumont in the Texas League, was always in the 90s and occasionally it topped 100 degrees. Add to the heat a suffocating humidity, and you had one rough environment for a ball game.

Charley Bishop and I celebrated the closing of the Sally League season by enjoying a slight breeze on the roof of the Seminole Hotel, twelve stories above the ground. I could see very clearly numerous naval vessels docked in St. John's Bay, which led out a few miles east to the Atlantic Ocean. It was 1:30 a.m. And as I was enjoying the breeze and the early morning scenery, Charley said, "Hey Mick, let's go over the side and see what's happening." I thought I knew what he had in mind, but I certainly didn't think that he was serious. A metal ladder about eighteen inches wide went from the roof 12 floors above the ground to a two-foot-wide ledge on the 10th floor. The ledge went all around the building.

I said, "Charley, are you serious?" He said, "Hell, yes!" as his leg went over the side of the building, his foot stepping carefully on the first metal rung. Before I knew it, Charley was descending, rung after rung, and was about to reach the concrete ledge. I could feel the blood rushing to my legs in a tingling fashion. The cars looked like play toys on the street below. Charley reached the ledge and was standing erect with his stomach and chest pressed hard against the building. His arms were extended from his shoulders straight to each side with his palms touching the building, and both feet were pointed out. I watched for a moment, but left him inching his way along the ledge, looking in windows as he went, 10 floors above the street.

The team ended the season in 4th place. We had won 80 games, lost 73 and tied one. Our .523 winning percentage put us 15-and-a-half games out of first place. We lost to Macon in the playoffs four games to three. It was nearing the end of September, time to return home and go back to college. It had been one of those not-too-good, not-too-bad years for us.

I wished I could have driven in 100 runs, because that might have meant a promotion for the next season.

This was the end of my second full year in baseball. Was I really making any progress? Was it even worth the time invested? I had just had my 23rd birthday and I was nowhere near the major leagues. The thought of giving it one more year is always in the back of your mind. I was angry and frustrated early in the season because I wasn't playing regularly. I had driven in over 80 runs in just two-thirds of a season, and had hit .300 from June 1st on. Why didn't the Cardinals give me a shot from the beginning of the season? I was becoming aware that the Cardinals had decided that Steve Bilko was their first baseman of the future. He was touted as the next Jimmie Foxx. I tried not to let it get to me, but I felt that no matter what I did, Bilko was their man.

5

Be a Good Soldier

My season at Columbus, Georgia, in Class A ball was not spectacular. I had hoped it would get me a good shot at Double A ball, but the chances now didn't look so good. Unlike many players, I liked spring training. And for the next season, I really wanted my wife to go with me.

The calisthenics, running in the outfield, pepper games, batting, and infield practice were actually appealing to me. Spring training meant getting away from the snow, sleet and otherwise inclement weather across the Midwest in February and March. Looking forward to spring training became a ritual for me every year soon after the Christmas holidays. I still am overcome with that vagabond feeling every February just before the baseball camps open.

Needless to say, I was quite disappointed that spring when I received my contract for the same salary, $400 per month, to play in Lynchburg, Virginia, in the Class B Piedmont League. My effort to negotiate a contract for more money was futile. I was to report to the Cardinals' minor league base at Albany, Georgia, with the Lynchburg team in early March of 1950. This meant that I would not take Jo Ann with me because the Cardinals camp at Albany was a large compound housing most of the organization's minor league players. Some 24 or 25 teams trained there on 12 diamonds and on a minor league field on which the Albany, Georgia, team played its games.

Numerous major league teams had gone to a compound-type training base. The Brooklyn Dodgers were one example. Branch Rickey had moved the Dodgers after they bought a training base from the Navy at Vero Beach, Florida. The Dodgers established barracks-type living and sleeping quarters, mess halls, recreational facilities and baseball diamonds to meet the needs of over 30 minor-league teams. Almost 500 players were training at Vero Beach for the 1950 season, including the major league team.

All the Cardinal minor league teams below Double A were in Albany, Georgia. The big-league Cardinals team trained in St. Petersburg, Florida. The two Triple A teams—Rochester, New York, and Columbus, Ohio,

Illustration by Ronnie Joyner.

were in Daytona Beach, Florida. Houston, the Double A team, stayed right at home in Houston.

That left over 450 ball players training in Albany that year. Some of those minor-league teams quartered at the Georgian Hotel. We were staying there in this rickety hotel, sleeping on army cots in large rooms. I slept on the second floor with 10 or more guys in one large room. I felt like I was back in the service again. We were given $3 a day for meal money and a few dollars a week for laundry.

Whitey Kurowski, the Cardinal great World Series hero and excellent third baseman, was our manager. Each manager was responsible for his team. The schedule would be posted at the end of the day with the field number and time the field was to be used by each respective team. Half of the squads in camp used the fields in the morning, the other half in the afternoon. Morning practices started at 10 a.m. and were over at about 12:30 p.m. Then another team would immediately take the first team's place on the field.

Sliding pits with sand were available to teach that skill—no more bed sheets in hotel hallways. We did a lot of running, a great deal of batting practice, practiced cut-off plays, backing up bases and base-running, and played pepper. Pepper games were a part of spring training everywhere, and I guess they always will be.

The 12 fields were numbered and so were the players. My number, as I recall, was 132. It was not conducive to making one feel at home. Whitey

Kurowski knew his baseball, though, and was easily able to gain rapport with his players. We respected him, and this made it much easier for him to impart baseball techniques to his players.

Our guys felt lucky because we generally practiced in the morning. The Albany camp had one large training room with only a couple of trainers to handle 450 players. By contrast, the major-league camps carried about 45 to 50 players and had a trainer with several assistants. The major league training room was always filled with patients, whereas the minor league training room, which could accommodate many more players, was generally empty. I don't know how to account for this, but my guess would be that the young minor leaguers did not know how to avail themselves of the training services offered. In the lower minor leagues, very few teams had trainers.

In a game as competitive as baseball, just an ingrown toenail can make the difference between a good season and having your style of play hampered for weeks. In a five-month season, a few bad weeks can mean a mediocre season. Harry Walker, who managed the Rochester team I would play for in 1952, put it this way: "Ten or twelve additional hits during a season can make the difference between a .270 and .300 hitter." I am not trying to say that major leaguers were pampered and minor leaguers were not. But I feel that all players deserve good trainers and proper care for injuries.

In the major leagues, trainers are competent. And in the higher minor leagues then, there generally were competent trainers. At that time in the lower minors, treatment was either non-existent or incompetent—the trainers were bus drivers first, everything else second and trainers last, with no technical knowledge or medical skill. I wonder how many good, young ball players might have had their careers saved or lengthened by proper care and rehabilitation of an injury.

Our workouts that spring in Albany ended in the early afternoon. This meant that we walked back to town, had a sandwich and headed for the hotel or a movie. The afternoons were often spent playing hearts for a penny a card. It didn't take long to see all the movies at the three movie houses in town.

I never really cared for card playing as so many ball players did. But I did enjoy the card games that spring with Joe Carroll, Ted Lewandowski, Chuck Shields and me. We would play almost every afternoon and into most evenings. Toward the middle of April we broke camp, each club heading for its home town and a few workouts on the home field before opening night.

We had a few days in Lynchburg, Virginia, before our opener. The ballpark was a good one and the field was in excellent shape. Lynchburg had an excellent physical plant for Class B baseball. We played an exhibition game with the Rochester Red Wings one night in our park as they headed north. I got to see Jack Faszholz and some of the guys I knew who had moved up to that Triple A club. It was about time then for the April 28th opener with Portsmouth, Virginia.

In the evenings just before the season started, Chuck Shields and I would frequent the local pool hall. Chuck and I went there two or three nights in a row, and played 8-ball or rotation. I would beat Chuck about as often as he beat me. As we played one night, a couple of Chuck's shots went plummeting across the room, disrupting a game in progress at the next table. I noticed the men at that table were playing for money. These men each got a little pill with a number on it and were playing for sizeable sums. They were playing Kelly Pool, where if you sank the ball that coincided with the number on your pill, you won all of the money.

Later in the week we went back to the pool hall, and Chuck said to me, "Ed, I think I'll go join those guys in a game of Kelly Pool." I said, "Chuck, they will eat you alive. Those guys are pros." Chuck shrugged off my advice and sauntered over to their table. They seemed eager to get him into the game, remembering previous nights when his inaccurate shots caused the cue ball to fly off the table with myself in hot pursuit. "Sure," they said, almost in unison, "glad to have you play." One of the fellows, who was very thin and older than the other man, shook the leather box that contained the pills. He passed one to each player. I settled back to watch my buddy get slaughtered.

Chuck had been unlucky in his draw because he had been given a high-numbered pill. But as it became Chuck's turn to shoot, a metamorphosis took place. It soon became apparent that he would not be the one who got slaughtered. As he stepped up to take his first shot, a look of confidence now sparkled from Chuck's eyes. His hands suddenly became nimble and relaxed. In the manner of a skilled brain surgeon ready to make his first incision, he looked over the position of the cue ball in relationship to the other balls. I sensed at that point that I was about to see something spectacular.

For the next 45 minutes, Chuck Shields was infallible. He just did not miss. Every shot was like Willie Hoppe at his best. The countenance on the faces of these two men changed from looks of, "Hey, we got a sucker!" to "My God, who is this guy?" Chuck quickly amassed $125 in those 45 minutes and was excluded, now and forever, from all games played in that pool hall in Lynchburg. What a con job he had done on them, and me!

Chuck returned showing little emotion except for a sly grin as he said, "Hey Big Ed, let's play some rotation." Still spellbound, I said okay. He racked the balls and asked me in a manner that really didn't come across as bragging, "Ed, did you ever see a guy break and run all 15 balls?" I said, "No, Chuck, I haven't." By then, I was ready to believe Chuck could do anything he said he could. He responded, "Well, you're going to see it now." He broke and ran all the balls as I leaned heavily on my stick, never to raise it for a shot. Chuck knocked in the last ball and we exited from the pool hall. I was in awe of what had taken place. Too bad Chuck couldn't hit a baseball like he could play pool, because that optical illusion called the curve ball ran him right out of the league—about as quickly as he had put down those three amazed onlookers back in the pool hall. I believe it was Ted Williams who said, "The hardest skill in sport is to learn to hit a round ball with a round bat, the ball being thrown at speeds in excess of 90 miles an hour from a distance of 60 feet, 6 inches."

The Piedmont League suited me well. The bus trips were not too long, the ballparks were in good shape and the outfield fence in Lynchburg was perfect for my batting swing. I hit to left-center and right-center. I had learned to wait on the ball and hit the outside pitch to right field or through the pitcher's box. This meant many of my long drives were caught by the center fielder, but it also enabled me to hit the curve ball and fastball away through the box or to right field.

The outfield fence in Lynchburg was 355 feet all the way around from left field to right field, and I was certain that a lot of my drives would find their way over the wall in center field. And they did.

We got off to a good start on opening night with Ted Lewandowski, our shortstop, showing the way with several key hits including a home run. We beat Newport News that night before 3,000 people in Lynchburg.

We went on the road to Portsmouth and then to Norfolk after the opening series. Both cities are situated on Chesapeake Bay, adjacent to the Atlantic Ocean. It was in Norfolk that I participated in a game that started in semi-fog. By that I mean that the infielders and outfielders were distinguishable, but a high fly or pop-up would be lost momentarily in the fog. As the game moved on, we got a big lead and the fog lowered to about 10 feet off the ground. It was getting thick and heavy.

In the fourth inning, a pop fly was hit down the right field line behind first base. I ran for the ball having no idea where it was in the fog and ran under a guy-wire smaller than a little finger. The wire was coming down from the light standards and was pegged in the ground about 20 feet from the wooden pole. I felt something tip the button on my cap, and my hat flew off. I missed the ball entirely (it landed nowhere near me) and I went to retrieve my cap. A cold chill went up and down my spine when I saw what had knocked my cap off. I thought to myself, "Thank you, Dear Lord," for if I had been a little bit to my left as I ran toward the wire, I would have been carrying my head in my hands instead of my cap.

The umpires wanted to call off the game at the end of four innings, meaning that it would have to be replayed. Whitey Kurowski gave it the old college try as he grabbed a fungo stick and went out on the field and hit a fly ball to one of our infielders, exclaiming to the umpires as the ball quickly disappeared in the murky fog, "See, watch him catch it!" The ball came back down to earth, only being seen in the first 10 feet of its ascent and the last 10 feet of its fall. The ball very narrowly missed Kurowski's head—by inches. The umpire's voice bellowed almost instantaneously, "This game is cancelled!" Thank God, I thought.

Hooray! My wife arrived in Lynchburg in the first week of May and we had a brand new 1950 Ford. Her father had helped her negotiate a deal, trading in our second-hand car. We paid $1,500 at the time for a two-door, six-cylinder car. Her mother, Vesta Menzel, and sister, Pat, had traveled with her across country from St. Louis to Lynchburg. During the winter I had taught Jo Ann to drive, and driving cross-country through the mountainous terrain for close to 1,000 miles was quite an accomplishment. Jo Ann's mother and sister accompanied her for moral support and safekeeping.

A pattern that would repeat itself on several occasions went into operation that night of May 7th as we played Roanoke, Virginia, in Lynchburg. The pattern was that I hit well when my mother-in-law was in the stands. That night I went 4 for 5, driving in five runs as we won 15–4.

My wife, mother-in-law, and sister-in-law should have headed south as they came across country. On the 19th of May, we were playing Norfolk in Lynchburg. I was leading the league with a .393 average and I felt that this would be a great year. Kurowski called me into his office after the game. Generally when the manager calls a ball player to his office, it means the kiss of death. But I had no reason to be apprehensive. I really felt sorry for Whitey as he told me with sincerity, "Mick, I hate to see you go, but Frank Kellert is being sent down from Houston and he says that he will only play for Lynchburg. You know he had a good season last year."

I interrupted, saying, "But Whitey, how can they do his to me? I'm leading the league!" "I know, Ed," Whitey said, "but that's what the front office wants. And you're going to Montgomery, Alabama, in the Southeastern League."

What else was there to say? He wanted me to stay, but the front office had some money invested in Kellert and didn't want to lose it.

I reluctantly said my goodbyes that night and telephoned Joe Mathes, the head Cardinal scout at that time. Mr. Mathes had been present when I signed in St. Louis, so technically he had signed me. I said, "Joe, what the hell is going on? I'm leading the league in hitting and I'm being sent out!"

I don't remember the full conversation, but Joe had been down that road many times before, and I hadn't. So I knew that I wouldn't win any argument I might start. I do remember him saying, "What's the matter? Don't you think you can hit in that league?" I jumped at the bait and responded, "Joe, I can hit in any league." That's exactly what Mr. Mathes wanted to hear, as he said, "Well, son, be a good soldier and go to Montgomery and show me."

I felt like I had been hit by a sledge hammer. Rage and indignation welled up in me as I fought back the tears. I thought, "Joe, how could you do this to me, you son of a bitch?"

My wife and I hated to leave Lynchburg. Our apartment was on the second floor of a large older home and our landlord, a widower, was a kindly old retired gentleman. Jo Ann came home from grocery shopping one day and there he was, mowing the lawn in a dark suit, white shirt and a tie. We assumed that he had been shopping and had decided not to change his clothes. We later found out, though, that he dressed that way every day no matter what job he was doing around the house.

Lynchburg would have been a good town for practicing stopping and starting your car on hills. The older section and downtown was very hilly, and I was planning on helping Jo Ann become more proficient at that part of her driving, but I never got the chance. It seems like players always got sent to another club after they had been to the grocery store and stocked up on groceries for a week. Our case was no exception. We had no choice, though, so Jo and I packed and headed for Montgomery, Alabama. I was seething with hurt and anger for the remainder of that season. I HAD SOMETHING TO PROVE!

I played my first game against Pensacola in the Montgomery ballpark on the 22nd of May. I hit a home run and a double in a 7–6 losing effort. That night started a hitting streak that lasted the entire remainder of the season. Everything I hit seemed to be hit well. Even the outs were line drives. In my first 57 at-bats, I had 30 hits for a .526 average. And after 101 at bats, I had 48 hits for a .475 average. Tom Riddle of the Associated Press picked up the story and wrote, "Even if Big Ed Mickelson never gets another hit, fans around the Southeastern League will be talking about him for a long, long time. And if the husky Montgomery Rebel first baseman continues his hitting, he's a cinch to rewrite the Class B record book." He continued, "What's so amazing about the 23-year-old St. Louis Cardinal farm-hand? 'A near .500 batting average since joining the Rebels May 22nd,' answers any Montgomery rooter. After hitting his 11th and 12th home runs in his first two times at bat in Anniston, Alabama last Saturday night, Mickelson has collected 60 hits in 122 trips to the plate. Another single and he would have been exactly on the .500 stripe."

I was really going great and had to chuckle to myself with some satisfaction one night when I went hitless and got headlines in the Montgomery newspaper. What an unbelievable season it was to be. Montgomery moved slowly from fifth place to first place. We had a good club. Charlie Metro was our manager and he was tough. You just didn't fool around with Charlie. He was an infielder/outfielder and had played some major-league ball. Charlie didn't like pitchers, all pitchers. He disliked the ones on his own team, too, and he gave them a going over if they weren't doing well. It didn't seem to be what they needed because, for the most part, our pitchers were shaky at best all year.

Charlie had been instrumental in inventing a batting tee. It had an adjustable rubber hose contraption set on a heavy metal base. The hose could be adjusted by loosening some clamps, extending it upwards for high pitches and downwards for low pitches. The batter could set the batting tee on the outside of the plate and drive the ball into a netting. You could tee up a lot of balls and get a good deal of batting practice from it. I felt it especially helpful for me in grooving my swing. I had a problem of hitching, which meant that I dropped my hands. I found that the tee did a lot to help me eliminate this fault. I had suddenly learned the strike zone after three years in professional baseball, and was beginning to lay off bad pitches and concentrate on hitting the good ones. This made all the difference in the world for me.

Arnie "Yogi" Riesgo was my roomie. He was dark and swarthy, a little pudgy but a good catcher. Yogi was imperturbable. Nothing ever seemed to ruffle him. I was fortunate to have so many good roomies throughout my playing days. Most were outstanding human beings, and Yogi was certainly one of them. The Yog was a stable, perceptive person. He was good at helping me keep my feet on the ground. He let me know that everything was going my way now, but that there would still be other days when I would have to hang in there.

Yogi's wife, Lita, and Jo Ann got along beautifully, and we went to the movies, picnicked and did all sorts of things with the Riesgos. Frank DiPrima, our second baseman, and his wife, Martha, also joined us in our off-the-field activities. Yogi became my closest friend at Montgomery. I guess what I felt most from Yog was his support. He was there when I needed him, and vice-versa. It feels good to know that someone is really pulling for you. That's the feeling I got from Yogi and it sure helped.

The ballpark at Jackson, the state capital of Mississippi, was my ballpark. Every player, if he plays long enough, has a favorite ballpark. Jackson turned out to be mine. I rarely played a game there without getting at least two hits. I don't know for sure, but a conservative guess was that I hit about .700 in the games we played in that park.

Needless to say, as a visiting player, I wasn't too popular there. One night a pop fly went up and I went after it in foul territory. The stands were very close to the first base line, and a screen had been erected in front of the stands to protect the fans from line drives. I looked up as the ball was coming down, and I had my glove raised as high as possible against the screen. The ball just nicked the screen and caromed off and hit me in the mouth.

I had a partial plate with three removable teeth in front. The ball had split my lip and knocked the teeth loose. I went to the mound, bent over, and started to spit out blood and teeth. Some of the fans were laughing and clapping as I was spitting out teeth. Our strong, left-handed pitcher, Hamilton "Red" Graham, said, "Hey Ed, those fans are having a ball at your expense." I said, "Red, screw 'em. At least I've got the last laugh. Those teeth I'm spitting out aren't mine."

I got a new partial plate out of the Montgomery Ball Club, and I made a resolution that I would never have false teeth on anything but a partial plate. With a permanent plate you could lose good teeth along with those false ones.

One of my favorite people on our team was Jim Barkley, a native Montgomerian. I thought that Jim should have been our best ball player. He had all the tools: Speed, a good swing and a strong arm. He was also a little older than the rest of us, a very stable person. But Jim always seemed tired, and I felt like he never fulfilled his potential that season. I later found out the reason for his puny batting average. Jim had decided that this would be his last year in baseball, so he would rise early in the morning to work on the construction of his new home. Most of the work he did himself. It was no wonder that he was worn down as the season progressed. His batting average finally dipped to .230. Jim was working in the hot sun all day and trying to play ball at night.

Jay Van Noy was our right fielder, and he was a heck of an athletic specimen. Jay was about 6'1" and he weighed about 195 pounds. He had played college football back in Utah. Jay was a Mormon and a very clean-living gentleman. He had all the tools to go all the way. He would get a try-out with the Cardinals a few years later, but he just didn't pull it off.

The Montgomery Rebels were honored when three-quarters of their infield played in the Southeastern League All-Star Game on July 10, 1950. Ralph Franck, our shortstop, Frank DiPrima, our second baseman, and I were all chosen.

My wife and I were enjoying Montgomery. We lived in a two-story house at 907 Montgomery St. owned by a dear old lady named Mrs.

The 1950 Montgomery Rebels of the Southeastern League. Our manager, Charlie
Metro, had played major league baseball. He was credited with inventing the bat-
ting tee, which is still being used today. Charlie is numbered among the famous
"managers by committee" for the Cubs. Top row, left to right: Jim Beavers, Ralph
Clements, Bernie Gerl, Dick Ryan, Ed Mickelson, Dick Loeset, "Red" Graham, Jay
Van Noy, Roy Glaser; bottom row, left to right: "Goose" Gosselin, Frank DiPrima,
Yogi Riesgo, Delton Childs, Ralph Franck, Mike Rivera, Jim Barkeley, Charlie
Metro. (Albert Kraus Inc. Photographers.)

Brower. She was in her early eighties and was just as sweet as could be to
everyone. Her daughter, Mrs. Clay, also lived in the house, and mother
and daughter took their quarters on the first floor. We had use of the garage
to park our car. The second floor was all ours and it had a living room,
bedroom, kitchen, and a bath.

Those old Southern-style homes were spacious with high ceilings.
Our place was completely furnished for $50 a month. The people in Mont-
gomery were really nice to my wife and me. They were just about the
friendliest people I have encountered on my baseball journeys.

Mrs. Clay's daughter and husband lived next door. They went fishing
in the evenings, and when they found out that Jo Ann liked to fish, they
asked her to go with them when we were on the road. Jo Ann has fished
a lot with her dad through the years and was used to baiting her own hooks

with minnows or worms, but they used catalpa worms. She said, "That was a different story—they were just too gooey and messy!" Needless to say, her friend was a gentleman and did the baiting for her. We had fish to eat quite often.

In July, my parents and Jo Ann's parents traveled to Montgomery to visit. When they arrived we were playing in Selma, Alabama. Selma is only fifty miles from Montgomery, and we came home each night by bus. The ballpark had very deep fences. I don't remember the dimensions, but the left-field fence seemed miles from home plate. I didn't think about it at the time, but I hit two home runs that night, and after the game when I saw my parents and in-laws I said, "Well Vesta, I did it again while you were in the stands!" Both homers were hit as well as I could possibly hit a ball. Too bad she couldn't have attended all my games.

Preston Langston, of the Langston Finance Company, had arranged with George Williams, a Montgomery tailor, to furnish each Rebel ball player with a pair of tailor-made trousers for every home run he hit in our new Municipal Stadium. It was a beautiful ballpark. In my short stay with Montgomery I hit 21 home runs, 12 of them at home. When I returned to college that fall I had numerous pairs of trousers and a new suit for both me and my wife, thanks to the generosity of these businessmen.

One time that year, we were playing in Pensacola and I was called out on a high strike. I argued vehemently with the umpire but called him no names. I started back to the dugout as the umpire went about his business cleaning off the plate. As I turned to head back, I bent over and picked up a handful of dirt. In my anger I threw the dirt behind me, and it scattered all over the plate the umpire had just finished cleaning. He thought I had intentionally dusted the plate and ejected me from the game. This would be the only time I was ever kicked out of a ball game, and it was a cheapie.

Meridian, Mississippi, was trying something new for that 1950 season. It was very hot in the Southeastern League and the team appeared in baseball pants that resembled Bermuda shorts. The pants were cut off just above the knee, allowing a little air to circulate. I don't think the guys really wanted to wear them, but they appeared that way for the remainder of their games that season. Their attendance increased somewhat as a result of the shorts, for some people were interested in seeing grown men play ball in these funny cutoffs and knee socks. But baseball has long and lasting traditions which are hard to break, and Meridian went back to the normal attire for the '51 season.

We hit a little slump at the end of the season and finished in third place, just three-and-a-half games out of first. We won 77 games and lost 54 for a .588 percentage. Pensacola won the league with a .612 percentage, going 82 and 52. Neb Wilson led the league with a .354 average, 35 homers and 153 RBIs. "Jungle" Jim Rivera had a great season for Pensacola, hitting .338 and driving in 135 runs. Jim would soon go to the St. Louis Browns and then on to the Chicago White Sox, where he would play many years of outstanding major-league baseball.

I ended up with a fabulous season. I had gone to bat 300 times, had 125 hits, and ended with a .417 average that would have led the league if I had had sufficient times at bat. In 82 games played, I had driven in 102 runs on 33 doubles and hit 21 home runs.

We played Pensacola early in September in the playoffs and lost to them four games to two. Charlie Metro came in after we lost the last game of the playoffs and stated that the St. Louis Cardinals wanted me to report immediately to finish out the season! Arnie "Yogi" Riesgo, my friend and roommate from Tucson, Arizona, was in the hotel room with me that night when I called home to St. Louis. My wife had left Montgomery a few days before the season's end, and as I broke the news to her, tears of joy started to roll down my cheeks. I was very happy and thankful, and I thought at that moment that the years of frustration were now worth it.

I took the train east to join the Cardinals and met them in Brooklyn. I walked into Ebbets Field, the Dodger ballpark, that Saturday afternoon in mid-September, 1950, carrying a $1.75 gym bag with my baseball shoes, glove, jock, cup and sweatshirts inside. I left my suitcase at the Knickerbocker Hotel after going from the train by cab to the hotel, and then to the ballpark.

The Cardinals were already in the clubhouse dressing for the game, and I was feeling awkward and out of place. The gate that led to the clubhouse was locked. A maintenance man finally appeared but would not let me in. It took more than just a few minutes to convince him that I was really supposed to join the team. Actually, if the truth was known, I really was not convinced I should be there either.

In the clubhouse, the Cardinals' long-time equipment manager, Butch Yatkeman, gave me a uniform with number 34 on the back—a real scrubbini number! A scrubbini is a scrub who is a long way from being a regular. That fit my status with the ball club perfectly. Stan Musial was playing first base. I asked myself what I was doing there, playing against guys like Jackie Robinson, Preacher Roe, Pee Wee Reese, Roy Campanella, Gil Hodges and Duke Snider, not to mention playing on the same team with Musial, Red Schoendienst, Enos Slaughter, Marty Marion and Harry Brecheen.

I shagged some fly balls during batting practice and before I knew it, the game was under-way. It felt strange sitting in a major-league dugout wearing a major-league uniform. I really couldn't grasp the reality of the

National League of Professional Baseball Clubs

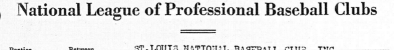

Parties

Between .... ST. LOUIS NATIONAL BASEBALL CLUB, INC., herein called the Club, and .... EDWARD MICKELSON ....

of #7704 Arthur Av-Richmond Hgts.. herein called the Player.

Recital

The Club is a member of the National League of Professional Baseball Clubs, a voluntary association of eight member clubs which has subscribed to the Major League Rules with the American League of Professional Baseball Clubs and its constituent clubs and to the Major-Minor League Rules with that League and the National Association of Baseball Leagues. The purpose of those rules is to insure the public wholesome and high-class professional baseball by defining the relations between Club and Player, between club and club, between league and league, and by vesting in a designated Commissioner broad powers of control and discipline, and of decision in case of disputes.

Agreement

In consideration of the facts above recited and of the promises of each to the other, the parties agree as follows:

Employment

1. The Club hereby employs the Player to render, and the Player agrees to render, skilled services as a baseball player during the year....... 1950................. including the Club's training season, the Club's exhibition games, the Club's playing season, and the World Series (or any other official series in which the Club may participate and in any receipts of which the player may be entitled to share).

Payment

2. For performance of the Player's services and promises hereunder the Club will pay the Player the sum of $..5000.00 ...., as follows:

In semi-monthly installments after the commencement of the playing season covered by this contract, unless the Player is "abroad" with the Club for the purpose of playing games, in which event the amount then due shall be paid on the first week-day after the return "home" of the Club, the terms "home" and "abroad" meaning respectively at and away from the city in which the Club has its baseball field.

If a monthly rate of payment is stipulated above, it shall begin with the commencement of the Club's playing season (or such subsequent date as the Player's services may commence) and end with the termination of the Club's scheduled playing season, and shall be payable in semi-monthly installments as above provided.

If the player is in the service of the Club for part of the playing season only, he shall receive such proportion of the sum above mentioned, as the number of days of his actual employment in the Club's playing season bears to the number of days in said season.

If the rate of payment stipulated above is less than $5,000 per year, the player, nevertheless, shall be paid at the rate of $5,000 per year for each day of his service as a player on a Major League team.

Loyalty

3. (a) The Player agrees to perform his services hereunder diligently and faithfully, to keep himself in first class physical condition and to obey the Club's training rules, and pledges himself to the American public and to the Club to conform to high standards of personal conduct, fair play and good sportsmanship.

Baseball Promotion

(b) In addition to his services in connection with the actual playing of baseball, the Player agrees to cooperate with the Club and participate in any and all promotional activities of the Club and its League, which, in the opinion of the Club, will promote the welfare of the Club or professional baseball, and to observe and comply with all requirements of the Club respecting conduct and service of its teams and its players, at all times whether on or off the field.

Pictures and Public Appearances

(c) The Player agrees that his picture may be taken for still photographs, motion pictures or television at such times as the Club may designate and agrees that all rights in such pictures shall belong to the Club and may be used by the Club for publicity purposes in any manner it desires. The Player further agrees that during the playing season he will not make public appearances, participate in radio or television programs or permit his picture to be taken or write or sponsor newspaper or magazine articles or sponsor commercial products without the written consent of the Club, which shall not be withheld except in the reasonable interests of the Club or professional baseball.

Player Representations

4. (a) The Player represents and agrees that he has exceptional and unique skill and ability as a baseball player; that his services to be rendered hereunder are of a special, unusual and extraordinary character which gives them peculiar value which cannot be reasonably or adequately compensated for in damages at law, and that the Player's breach of this contract will cause the Club great and irreparable injury and damage. The Player agrees that, in addition to other remedies, the Club shall be entitled to injunctive and other equitable relief to prevent a breach of this contract by the Player, including, among others, the right to enjoin the Player from playing baseball for any other person or organization during the term of this contract.

Ability

(b) The Player represents that he has no physical or mental defects, known to him, which would prevent or impair performance of his services.

Condition

(c) The Player represents that he does not, directly or indirectly, own stock or have any financial interest in the ownership or earnings of any Major League club, except as hereinafter expressly set forth, and covenants that he will not hereafter, while connected with any Major League club, acquire or hold any such stock or interest except in accordance with Major League Rule 20 (e).

Interest in Club

Service.

5. (a) The Player agrees that, while under contract, and prior to expiration of the Club's right to renew this contract, he will not play baseball otherwise than for the Club, except that the Player may participate in post-season games under the conditions prescribed in the Major League Rules. Major League Rule 18 (b) is set forth on page 4 hereof.

This is my first major league contract. It is an interesting read. Note the minimum salary for the time. What a difference the years have made. Further back in my contract the word "chattel" appears in reference to the ball player.

situation. I kept looking down at my chest to see if the two cardinals were perched at either end of the bat, if I was really wearing a St. Louis Cardinals uniform.

A few days later in a game against the New York Giants at the Polo Grounds, we were getting walloped 13–0. The bases were loaded with Cardinals, and Eddie Dyer yelled, "Hey Mickelson! Get a bat." I always wondered what I might do in my first time at bat in the major leagues. How many times had I fantasized my first at-bat ending with a home run. Larry Jansen was pitching for the Giants, and he was on his way to a 19-win season. He threw me two balls outside. But the next pitch, I will see in my dreams for the rest of my life. It was a hanging curve ball over the middle of the plate, and I froze. "Strike one!" the umpire cried.

I told myself that I would swing if the next one was in there. It was, and I foul-tipped a fastball. On the next pitch, I committed a cardinal sin as a hitter. A batter is never to let the third strike go by if it is close. It was close, and I let it go by. The ump yelled, "STRIKE THREE, YOU'RE OUT!" That shot the hell out of my fantasies.

Three days later, we were in Boston to play the Braves. It was the 22nd of September, and when I got to the park, I heard that Stan the Man was confined to his hotel room with a temperature of 103 degrees. I saw my name on the board to play first base. I was wondering if Eddie Dyer, our manager, would finally go over the signs with me. And he called me off to the side and did just that. When he realized that he wasn't getting through because I was too preoccupied with nervousness, he said, "Kid, forget all the signs I just gave you. Just remember, when the third base coach touches his sleeves, you're taking, and when he tugs at his cap, you're bunting."

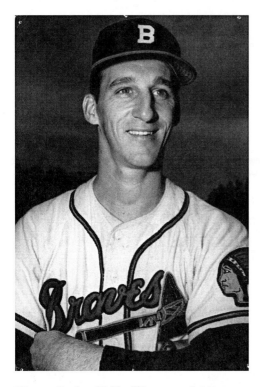

Warren Spahn, Hall of Famer, and 363-game winner, ca. 1957. I used this story with many a young pitcher over the years, including Ken Holtzman, another left-hander, when he was a high school pitcher. He, like other pitchers, was having trouble after losing a game. I said, "Kenny, Warren Spahn won 363 games. How many games do you think he lost?" Kenny shook his head; he didn't know. When I told him Spahn lost 245 games, his jaw dropped. (National Baseball Hall of Fame Library, Cooperstown, New York. Used by permission of Patricia D. Kelly, Photo Archivist.)

We took hitting and infield practice, and I was sitting in the dugout before the start of the game. I was thinking, this is my first big-league start, and I should feel great. But I was feeling about as nervous as I possibly could. Red Schoendienst came over and sat next to me and said, "You'll be okay, Mick, everybody gets nervous before the first game. But as soon as the game starts, you'll get over it. You'll see, you'll be all right." I said, "Thanks, Red," and to this day, I still consider that to be one of the kindest gestures ever offered to me. Red knew what I was going through, and he took the time to come over and sit down with me and let me know that he cared. It says a lot about the character of the man. A Hall of Famer as a ball player. A Hall of Famer as a man.

My first time at-bat, against the great Warren Spahn, I hit a single to left field. But we only got one more hit that day. Eddie Kazak got the other in a 5–0 loss on Spahn's two-hitter, his 21st victory of the season. I started again a few days later in Chicago and went 0 for 3 as Paul Minner beat us 2–0. I played in one more game at the end of the season, and we won behind the excellent pitching of Gerry Staley. I had gone 1 for 10 at the plate, which is nothing to brag about, but I did handle 40 chances in the field without an error. It was quite an experience and, everything considered, I had to feel good about the 1950 season. I had played for three different teams and batted .404 for the season.

6

The Lost Season

I used to cringe when I would listen to old-time baseball players talk about how good the players were in their day, and how poor the caliber of play was in my time. I swore that I would never do that, but here I go anyway, breaking that promise. It irritates me to see players brought up to the major leagues these days after hitting just .240 or .250 and driving in 50 or 60 runs. This just did not happen in the '40s and '50s. A phenomenal year in the lower minor leagues might get you into the higher minors, but unless there was a real need at your position, you could spend your life in the minors. I can attest to that. It happened to me.

I hit .393 at Lynchburg and .417 at Montgomery, and the Cardinals knew exactly where they wanted me to play next season—Houston, Texas, in the Texas League, which was Double A ball. Stan Musial played first base for the parent club, Mike Natisin would play that position for Columbus, Ohio, and Steve Bilko would play the same for Rochester, New York. I was to play first base for Houston under one condition: I would have to beat out Jerry Witte, who had 30 home runs there the previous year.

What I'm saying is that after the season I had in 1950, the Cardinal organization was definitely impressed, but needed my services about as much as they needed a hole in the head. I was not much different than the 26 aspiring first basemen in the Dodger organization who were trying to move out a young and productive All-Star, Gil Hodges. The contract I got from Fred Saigh, the Cardinal owner at the time, expressed more explicitly their need and appreciation for my services. I jumped from $400 a month to $600 a month. I've often wondered if I had hit .500, would they have given me another $100 per month raise?

So I was to make $3,000 for the '51 season, which is about $141,000 by today's standard. I had been attending Washington University in St. Louis under the G.I. Bill of Rights, and during the winter of 1950–51 Congress changed the ruling regarding the use of this benefit. The new rule stated that if you terminated school at the end of a semester, with the exception of summer vacation, you would lose the remainder of your benefits. That's what would happen to me if I went to spring training and

Illustration by Ron Joyner.

missed the second semester of the 1950–51 school year. The amount of time I had left to finish college was one year. With tuition, sustenance, books, materials and other miscellaneous fees, it would cost me roughly $2,500.

I told Mr. Saigh, "If I play for the $3,000 you have offered me, and terminate my schooling the second semester, I would lose $2,500 for schooling and be playing the season for $500." I also said, "You owners will give a big bonus to someone who hit .400 in sandlot ball, but you won't give me $2,000 extra to defray the loss of my schooling if I report to spring training."

The Pirates had just signed a player named Paul Petit for $100,000 in '51. But Mr. Saigh didn't budge, and I didn't go to spring training. He would not raise my contract to the $5,000 major-league minimum salary. This indicated to me that the Cardinals had no immediate plans for to get a shot at major-league ball.

So I stayed at home for the spring of '51 and continued the second semester at Washington University. This would enable me to come back in the fall and graduate at the end of the fall semester. I really wanted to go to the major-league camp with the Cardinals, but I believe I would have played in a couple of games that spring and then moved on to Houston anyway. But by staying home, the Cardinals may have listed me as being unmotivated.

When the spring semester was over at Washington U., I did go back to the minors. But of my 11 seasons of professional baseball, that '51 season had to be the worst. On June 8th, I reported to Joe L. Brown, the general manager for the New Orleans Pelicans, an affiliate of the Pittsburgh Pirates. I was being sent to New Orleans because the teams in the St. Louis organization were filled with established first basemen. The Cardinals were grooming Bilko, the burly first baseman, to take Musial's place at first base. Stan wanted to move back into the outfield. New Orleans needed a first baseman, and the team had gotten off to a poor start and was mired in last place. The Pittsburgh Pirates were also looking for players, and the Cardinals, I believed, were looking ahead to sell me to Pittsburgh if I did well. Joe L. Brown, the son of comedian Joe E. Brown, seemed tickled to have me with the ball club.

Joe Brown and his staff were very helpful to Jo Ann and me in procuring housing. They gave us numerous leads. And since we were unfamiliar with the city, the office manager drove around with us, checking out the prospects. We rented a house owned by a minor-league baseball player. We liked the house very much, and with its living and dining area, two bedrooms, kitchen, bath, and a little screened-in porch, it was quite a nice place to stay.

The house was completely furnished for $85 a month. This was the most we had ever paid for lodging, but it was very comfortable. It didn't have air conditioning, though, and according to the natives it was one of their hottest summers in years. We made use of the little porch, trying to keep cool. Two of the other players on the club also rented homes of players that were in another league that year.

I worked out a few days with the club, for this time had to substitute for the spring training that I missed. No one can ever tell me that spring training is not important. The sharpness and instinctively quick reflexes are honed in spring training. Not to a fine edge as they become later in the season, but to a degree that enables a player to start the season playing with respectability. I was nowhere near that sharpness as I stumbled through the remaining weeks of June playing first base for New Orleans.

One of the first games that I participated in should have given me an indication of the kind of year it would be. A freakish hurricane blew in from the Gulf of Mexico, driving with it much rain, wind and millions upon millions of mosquitoes. We started the game that night playing in a strong wind, and by the time the game was nearing its completion the wind had picked up to hurricane force. The players, talking among themselves, wondered why the umpires had not called the game. In the eighth inning, the light standards were swaying to and fro. A sheet of metal, four by eight feet, came hurtling down from the roof of the stands, just missing the home plate umpire, catcher, and batter. The umpire, pale-faced and without hesitation, ruled the contest over. We ran to the clubhouse for sanctuary as heavy rains began to fall.

The next evening, we played on a water-soaked field. Our companions that night were the mosquitoes. I could count at least one hundred of those little pests on the shirt and pants of my uniform. It was unbelievable. My teammates in the outfield looked like castoffs from the French Foreign Legion, with white bath towels draped over their heads and hanging over their faces. The towels sufficiently covered their ears, cheeks, and necks from the unwelcome guests, and their baseball caps held the towels in place. Bug spray did no good.

It really was not funny at the time, but you just had to laugh as each player on the field swatted, scratched, or made some kind of continuous movement with both his arms and legs, trying desperately to fend off the little demons. But there were just too many of them. All you could do was stand there and be eaten alive. It was even more humorous to look into the dugout. Each player had a towel over his face and legs and, despite the very hot humid night air, wore a warm-up jacket. In unison, the men on the bench would part the towel covering their faces as the pitcher released the ball. They would follow the proceedings until the play was completed, and then quickly close the opening in the towel between pitches.

The next day, the New Orleans radio station announced that the ballpark was being fogged and would be void of mosquitoes for the game that night. It went on to mention that the ballpark would be the only place in New Orleans that would be free from mosquitoes. Needless to say, we packed the stands that night. How could they call a game off because of mosquitoes?

My wife and I went to Lake Ponchartrain one afternoon a few days after the hurricane, and we saw a deserted beach. We couldn't imagine why no one was there, for it was a popular spot and was always crowded with people. We jumped out of the car and I dashed onto the sandy beach, plunged into the water, and swam out to a raft. I pulled myself out of the water, and as I lay back on the wooden slats, I noticed my wife was making a quick retreat back to the car. I looked down at my legs and they were both so thickly covered with mosquitoes that I could barely see my skin. I dove back in the water and swam to the beach and ran all the way to the car. My wife and I laughingly exclaimed at the same time, "Honey, I guess we know why no one is at the beach today!"

The Southern Association was Double A ball, and had some good teams and some large Southern cities in the loop. Besides New Orleans, there were Birmingham, Nashville, Memphis, Atlanta, Mobile, Little Rock and Chattanooga. I had moved from a bus league to the train and Pullman league. It was starting to feel a little like the big time. I kept thinking, "Just one more good season and surely I'll be there—the major leagues!"

My wife was having a good time in New Orleans. She enjoyed traveling and meeting people, and she was always the kind of person who is interested in learning new things and seeing new places. She was to have one of her most pleasurable summers in New Orleans that year. The wives of the players were young and most of them were without children. While the players were on the road, the wives spent their time going to the beach, playing card games, curio shopping and sightseeing in the French Quarter. The cemeteries also were very interesting, with the burials above ground because of the low sea level in New Orleans.

The away games were broadcast by radio, and seven or eight wives would gather at someone's house to play cards and listen to the game. Their favorite was solitaire. Jo Ann said it was a wonder someone didn't end up with a broken arm or hand the way the wives were slapping their cards on the aces. When you get eight people playing that game, there are a lot of arms crisscrossing.

The French Market was of particular interest to Jo Ann and several of the other wives. After the radio broadcast of an away game, they would frequent the place for French coffee (strong), or American coffee (lots of cream), and hot doughnuts.

After three or four weeks of play, I was struggling, hitting just .260 or .270. I really wasn't too disappointed, though, because I knew it would take some time to get into shape. I felt my timing at bat beginning to improve and I was sure it was just a matter of time before I would start hitting.

We were playing a series in Little Rock early in July. Neither team took infield or batting practice because a light drizzle was falling. Little Rock had a tarpaulin on the infield and at home plate. Most fields below Double A did not have protective coverings on their field, but from Double A on up all the fields were protected. The rain came down ever so lightly as we started the ball game and it continued throughout the early innings. The field, especially the dirt infield, became sloppy. In the fourth inning I singled to left. The next batter hit safely to right field, and as I ran from first to third, my left ankle gave way in the slosh, and I felt shooting pains. I played out the rest of the game as my ankle slowly ballooned to twice its size. In retrospect, it should have been examined and X-rayed on the spot to see if any bones were broken. But, in fact, nothing was done. The ankle was taped and I played for a week, barely able to hobble around.

Back in New Orleans, Joe Brown had me see an orthopedic surgeon who took X-rays and told me that ligaments were torn. The doctor put my leg in a cast from toe to hip and said, "Ed, you will be out of action for at least six weeks. If you would have kept playing on that ankle for another week or two, you could very easily have developed an arthritic ankle." I was beginning to feel like this would be a lost season. It would be the middle of August before I would play again, and by that time there would be only a couple of weeks to play anyhow.

I spent the time off fishing the rivers, lakes and bayous of New Orleans. I enjoyed the fishing and the fun times that Jo Ann and I had in New Orleans, but there was a constant gnawing in my gut that I only had a short life span in baseball, and this accident could put me back another year or two in progress.

One day as I went out to do some fishing, I stopped in a local restaurant/bar to get a Poor-Boy sandwich, which is composed of cheese, ham, beef, salami, lettuce, tomato, pickles, pepperoni and other assorted goodies all placed inside a large piece of French bread that has been sliced length-wise. A Poor-Boy is a meal in itself and defies most people when it comes to opening the mouth wide enough to bite down on it. The lad fixing my sandwich asked me in his deepest New Orleans drawl, "Do you want mainize on it?" I asked, "What's that?" "Mainize? Do you want mainize on it?" A young man standing beside me became my interpreter, saying, "He means mayonnaise." I then was able to reply with understanding, "Yes, give me my-nize on my sandwich."

The New Orleans Pelicans were having a miserable season. Rip Sewell, the old blooper-ball pitcher, was our manager. We had a fair ball club, but we were short on pitching and could have used another good hitter ... or two, or three. Frank Thomas was having a good year for us, and he was on his way to the major leagues. Frank was a big raw-boned lad. He could hit the ball with tremendous power, run, and throw well. He had a good attitude and worked hard at the game.

Jim Piersall was in the Southern League with Birmingham at that time. He was one of the most publicized athletes in the minor leagues because of his zany antics. It was the season before his breakdown in 1952, and he seemed to be written up in the press weekly. I didn't see Jim do anything, but stories about him were told around the league. I had heard that once when he was called out, he pulled out a pistol, backed the umpire up to the screen and pulled the trigger. Fortunately water streamed out onto the umpire's face. I didn't know what to think of the stories, but I was quite shocked when I read about his breakdown the next year.

The Birmingham team had more than one unusual personality, though. George Washington Wilson was hitting a ton that season. He was an excellent minor-league hitter and had fine seasons wherever he played. It was said of George that he frequently communicated with the front office by letter or telegram telling them that the Red Sox (Birmingham's parent club) were missing a bet if they didn't call him up to finish out the season. He certainly had the credentials to back him up. In Birmingham, a ball player got some piece of wearing apparel for every extra base hit in the home ballpark. George Washington Wilson was one of the best-dressed ball players in baseball at the end of the '51 season. He had over 80 extra base hits, and he probably got half of them at home.

Bobo Newsom, who had seemingly pitched with almost every team in the majors, was pitching for Birmingham that year. Bobo was in his early forties, but he could still throw hard and he had good control. Bobo was quite superstitious and very eccentric, though. One thing that set him off was to have paper torn up and sprinkled in the pitcher's box. This got him more upset than you can imagine. So naturally I had to shred up a bunch of paper and drop it in the hole in front of the pitching rubber between innings. When Bobo went out to pitch the next inning, he went berserk. It was as if he had seen a rattlesnake. He shouted profanities toward our dugout and declared that he would clobber the person responsible. No one responded, but Bobo pitched from that inning on with a vengeance. All the paper trick had done was stir up "Ol' Bobo."

He also had an unusual wind-up that whirled his body around as he looked out toward center field before he unwound and delivered the ball homeward. It was eerie standing in the batter's box and looking at the pitcher's back momentarily before the pitch. Who says you have to keep your eye on the plate? My hat's off to Bobo Newsom, one of the most traveled ball players of all time—a real competitor.

Nashville had one of the craziest parks in baseball. The right field fence was very close to home plate. The distance was, roughly, only about 250 feet down the line, and the fence did not angle out fast in right-center. There was a screen stretching at least 30 feet from the ground to the top, but for someone who could loft the ball to right field, it was an easy fly ball for a homer. In 1948, Chuck Workman of the Nashville Vols hit 52 homers for a league record while driving in 182 runs.

What happened to Charley Workman after that? He was promoted to Triple A Minneapolis where, in 1949, he hit 41 homers, batted in 122 runs and hit .294. He had 21 assists in the outfield (second highest in the league) while making only five errors all season. And after hitting 93 home runs and driving in 304 runs in two seasons, Charlie Workman found himself back in the minor leagues in 1950. Do you think those credentials would give him a shot at the major leagues today?

The right-field fence in Nashville made many left-handed hitters pull the ball. The hillside going up to the base of the fence was as ridiculous as the fence itself. In a very shallow right field, the ground started to slope upward until it reached the fence. The hillside rose sharply from ground level to a height of about 10 feet. It was difficult to climb, obviously, and it sure did help if the outfielder was part mountain goat. A level space was dug out near the top of the hill, which served as a platform for the right fielder as the pitcher delivered the ball.

It was quite a sight indeed to see Babe Barna, who had played some major league ball, try to navigate that hillside. Babe weighed around 230 pounds, mostly above the waist. He was a strong, rotund player, but one needed the grace of a ballet dancer to play right field in Nashville. The Babe took a lot of jockeying from the other players about his hilltop fielding. One night, when he toppled headfirst while coming in for a short line drive over the second baseman's head, he looked like a barrel rolling to the bottom of a hill. The ball skipped by him and up the hill, and he staggered up after it, stumbling and fuming. But generally, if a right fielder charged the ball, caught it cleanly and made a quick throw to first, a one-hop line drive to right could make for a relatively easy out.

I made it to all the cities in the Southern Association with the exception of Chattanooga. I thought that Birmingham, with that steel and concrete ballpark, was by far the best park in the league. Overall, the playing fields and lights were much better than anything in the lower minors. The caliber of play was good, with every club having two or three regulars with major-league experience. The baseball played in the higher minor leagues in the early 1950s was outstanding. Of course, it didn't match the major leagues, but with many returning war veterans from the 1940s hanging on, and a steadily increasing influx of African-Americans and Latinos, the competition was keen. There were a lot of minor leagues in 1951—some 58 of varying classification. So in some ways, it was easier to find a place to play then. A player with little experience but some raw talent could start out in D ball and, hopefully, improve and work his way up.

Another difference between the 1950s and the present is that a player having problems in Double A or Triple A could be sent down and come back at a later date. A player now must make it quickly, or he is often released. There just aren't as many leagues available to ship ball players here and there to find a niche for them until they can work out inadequacies. The Eddie Stanky and Solly Hemus-type players, who were not naturals, in all probability would not even be signed in today's baseball market. The

Max Patkin was a very busy man. He made appearances at almost every minor league team during every season. He was a great dancer too. Check out the movie *Bull Durham*, where he dances with Susan Sarandon. Date of photo is unknown. (National Baseball Hall of Fame Library, Cooperstown, New York. Used by permission of Patricia D. Kelly, Photo Archivist.)

super athletes, with great tools already apparent, are the players signed today.

The average time spent in the minors before making it to the big leagues was much longer in the '30s through the '50s. And once a guy did reach the majors, he did a lot of sitting before he got a chance to play. I believe that today's players, overall, are better because they are bigger, stronger and faster, better schooled in high school and college in the fundamentals. The team trainers have scientific knowledge. The medical treatment is superb. Players do not have to get an off-season job to support themselves and can spend the entire winter keeping their bodies in shape.

Max Patkin, the "Clown Prince of Baseball," came to New Orleans in 1951. I had already seen him in every season I had played in the minors. Patkin was laughable even before he went into his antics. He was a tall, turkey-necked stringbean with a long, hooked nose and dark beard, who dressed in an oversized baseball suit with outrageously baggy pants. Max was double-jointed and a terrific contortionist. It seemed as though he could touch his chin to the ground while bending over from the waist. He would stand like that while looking in to home plate from the coach's box. Then Max would whirl his arms and legs, tying himself up in a knot, and the people in the stands would be in stitches.

He was putting on his show on one night for the Pelican fans, and the people were enjoying it. But he was dripping wet with perspiration. I had a great view while playing first base, and I finally said, "Hey Max, do you feel all right?" He replied, "Yeah, I'm okay. I'm just tired. I've been breathing all day."

Max was a 50-year tradition in the minor leagues, and he earned every penny he ever made.

Another showman who played mostly to minor league audiences was Jackie Price. He drove around the outfield in an army jeep at breakneck speeds, chasing fly balls that he had shot heavenward with a special-made bazooka. He could shoot a baseball so high that the spectators could lose track of it, then jump in his jeep, ride under the ball and catch it in his glove-hand while remaining seated. He often ended his act by shooting a ball from his bazooka a mile over the center field fence.

The '51 season was, for me, a disaster. I could rationalize it by saying that I only played 35 games, and some of those I played hurt, and all without the benefit of spring training. Knowing why, though, still didn't detract from how bad that season was. Climbing to the majors was like climbing a ladder. The 1950 season had enabled me to climb two or three rungs at once, but the '51 season had caused me to slip down a couple. I will always second-guess myself about not going to spring training. It may have been a big mistake. The injury in Little Rock was just one of those things. I shall always remember the kindness of Joe L. Brown and the Pittsburgh organization. The fans in New Orleans were patient with me and deserved better. I just wished I could have been at my best for those fine people.

I played out the last three or four weeks of the '51 season with nothing spectacular happening, and the club going nowhere in the league standings. The day after the last game, my wife and I packed our belongings and headed the car for St. Louis. It was the middle of September and time to enroll again for college.

In professional baseball, people look at cold-blooded statistics. For me, they would say 1950 was a flash in the pan and that I couldn't hit in Double A ball. Little consideration would be given to my lack of spring training, starting the season in June and missing six weeks with torn ligaments in my ankle. The bottom line was: I hit .235, and that just stinks. That winter, for the first time in my life, I felt depressed for an extended period of time. I felt like I had blown my chance by not going to spring training.

7

Around the Horn

In the winter months our home was a two-story flat in Richmond Heights, another suburb of St. Louis. My parents, who were co-owners, lived upstairs and we lived downstairs. Jo Ann and I enjoyed our apartment-like living. We had a large living room, dining area, small kitchen, bathroom and two bedrooms. When it was time for the baseball season, we were always lucky to find someone we knew to rent our place to. A couple of times it happened to be players that were with the St. Louis Cardinals. My wife and I were very comfortable during those fall and winter months. We enjoyed settling down to a life less nomadic and adventuresome. It felt good to stay in one place for a while and savor the delights of a more tranquil way of life.

I returned to Washington University and enrolled in the fall semester. This was my sixth fall on that campus. I had seen undergraduates come and go, but I was still striving to get my degree. I would end my studies for my Bachelor of Science degree in physical education that semester if all went well. I enjoyed my studies. But I have to admit, the long time-span on campus had produced a feeling of boredom — and an anxiety to get it over with and finally obtain my degree. I had started college in the fall of 1944, spending each fall sitting in college classrooms. I felt it was certainly about time to graduate.

Christmas of 1951 came and went, and I was getting excited once again to begin spring training. To my surprise, the Cardinals had put me on their roster. I was to head south for the first time to St. Petersburg, Florida, with the big team. I guess they actually did understand why the '51 season went so poorly for me. I finished my final exams near the end of January and completed all the courses I needed for graduation in June of '52.

Kurt Krieger, who had pitched for the Columbus Redbirds the previous season, called and said, "Ed, I am going to drive Mr. Saigh's brother's car to spring training. Do you want to ride down with me?" That sounded great to me. So about the middle of February, Kurt drove up in a Ford convertible loaded down with luggage in the trunk and back seat. We found

Illustration by Ron Joyner.

room in the back seat for my suitcase and baseball gear. I bid goodbye to Jo Ann and left the cold weather behind, speeding southward toward the Promised Land, sunny Florida. Kurt and I felt like a couple of big-time major leaguers, riding in our convertible with golf clubs visible in the back. Of course, no one knew the car and clubs didn't belong to us. And it was a great way to cut down on expenses.

After staying in a small motel in a small Georgia town that first night, we were back on the road for St. Pete's. Kurt was at the wheel and we must have been cruising at eighty miles an hour as we approached a rise on a two-lane highway. As we reached the peak, we saw a farmer pulling a hay wagon with a team of horses about a quarter of a mile down the sloping roadway. Kurt hit the brakes. And despite the weight of the luggage and the speed of the car, we were able to stop just a few feet from the rear of the wagon.

And it's a good thing we were able to stop. Another car was approaching us quickly in the other lane, so we couldn't have swerved to the left. And the shoulder to the right of our lane was narrow, with a ditch close by that would certainly have toppled our car if we had entered it. This narrow escape was the only eventful happening on an otherwise peaceful journey. The southern pines of Georgia arched over the road from both sides, as spring flowers were starting to bloom and trees were just beginning to bud. Spring was just starting in the lower Southland, and our spirits rose that second day on the road as nature came alive. The sight of spring somewhat negated the gloom we both had felt the first day leaving our loved ones behind.

Kurt Krieger was a fine gentleman and a family man, typical of most of the ball players I knew. He was a religious person who always tried to see the good side of people and situations. He died in 1970, and I must say that I was proud to have been a part of his life. He left a wonderful wife and some fine children.

The Bainbridge Hotel was an old established spring training headquarters for the St. Louis Cardinals in St. Pete. The hotel had been their training headquarters since the 1920s. After Kurt and I got our luggage out of the car, I got my room key and went up to unpack my bags. I roomed that night with Mike Ryba, a Cardinal coach who had quite a career in professional baseball. Mike had been a journeyman player. He had the ability to play many different positions, but was a catcher by trade. Mike once had the distinction of playing every position on the field during a nine-inning game. But his greatest claim to fame might just as well have been his loud snoring, which shook the room that night.

The next morning, the pitchers and catchers arrived early for the first day of spring training. There were only a few early-bird infielders and outfielders, mostly aspiring rookies like myself. Eddie Stanky, the newly appointed Cardinal manager, had made a short talk advising pitchers to be cautious the first few days, not to throw too hard and to dress warmly. He was a stickler for long-sleeved wool shirts. He felt that this was a protection against the cool spring breezes that might tend to stiffen a pitcher's arm.

Stanky impressed me very much with his baseball knowledge and his intensity and devotion for the game. I admired not only his ability to teach the fundamentals of the game, but also the intensity he manifested. Stanky seemed to be full of sincerity at one meeting when he said, "These things should be of utmost importance to striving young baseball players: First should come your family, then your religion, and then baseball." There are some people that you either strongly like, or strongly dislike. Eddie Stanky had that kind of personality—no gray. I liked him.

Al Lang Field, the Cardinals' spring training home, was rich in tradition. It was, for many years, a major league training base. Babe Ruth, Ted Williams, Stan Musial, and most greats of baseball had trod on that stadium's dirt and grass. I felt no small degree of awe and respect to be training on that field. The clubhouse, though far from spacious, was adequate enough. Old "Doc" Weaver was in charge of the training room. He would give the ball players the best of care, fixing up their minor injuries, sore arms, aching muscles and the like. Dr. Middleman, the team physician, gave us our physicals and flu shots, and remained with us during most of spring training. Each player had his own locker space in the clubhouse, and shoes were shined and sanitary socks were washed for us each day. In the lower minor leagues, you shined your own shoes and washed your own underwear and socks, so I certainly appreciated having those things taken care of by somebody else.

Al Lang Field seated about 5,000 fans and had a press box at the top of the stands. There were lights for night games, but the Cardinals didn't play a single game at night that spring. Lighting was the one thing that really distinguished minor-league playing fields from the major-leagues fields. There was just no comparison between the lighting systems. Minor-league games are almost always played at night, with some of the batters wishing they could wear a miner's helmet so they could see the ball!

The major league clubs in 1952 had a new innovation called "Iron Mike," which was used in batting and bunting practice. This machine was powered by a gasoline combustion engine and took the place of a human pitcher, the iron arm mechanically rising and slinging a ball rapidly toward the batter. Stanky became quickly disenchanted with the machine. So it was relegated to the deepest part of right-center field, where it was used exclusively, but extensively, for bunting practice. Stanky, a good bunter in his own right, had everyone spend hours bunting as Iron Mike, a tireless worker, threw pitch after pitch.

Around the end of February, the main contingent of the St. Louis Cardinals started arriving. They were a proud crew. Several of them had played on the 1946 World Championship team. Stan Musial, Enos Slaughter, Red Schoendinst, Red Munger, Gerry Staley, Harry "The Cat" Brecheen and Terry Moore, who was now serving as a Cardinal coach, were some of the veterans from '46.

I learned a great deal of baseball that spring. A major league camp is fun and businesslike. One thing I learned that really stuck with me was that these baseball greats were very down to earth, as were most major leaguers. I remember asking Mr. Strehlman, my 12th-grade physics teacher in high school back in 1943, if we could listen to the World Series game during class. He said, "Okay, as long as you work quietly." As we turned on the radio, the announcer, Mel Allen, said, "And Billy Johnson, the Yankee third sacker, has just doubled to left." As I came out of the clubhouse in the spring of 1952, Billy Johnson said, "Hey, Ed, how about coming with me to see the pros play some golf?" I said, "Sounds great, Billy, let's go!" "Mize will be here shortly to pick us up," he said. In a few minutes, a car stopped in front of the ticket office and Billy and I got in. Billy said, "John Mize, I want you to meet Ed Mickelson." We both said hello, and there I sat, riding with one of my favorite hitters from Cardinal Knothole Days, when they'd let kids sit down the left field line for free. John Mize, a Hall of Fame hitter, and Billy Johnson, a former Yankee great that I'd followed on the radio in high school, were sitting right there in front of me. They made me feel at ease. They were glad to have me with them, and we enjoyed watching Jackie Burke lead the way in the 1952 St. Petersburg Open.

Most of the great ball players were like that. Musial was that way for sure. He talked to everyone, and he enjoyed life and enjoyed people. He was not pretentious. I can't say that for all the players. Some were loud, haughty, and downright obnoxious, but those were certainly a minority.

Wally Westlake, who had come over to the Cardinals with Cliff Chambers, was a very likeable guy. He was the Walt Whitman of the team—an outdoor, fisherman type. He would talk to anybody for hours on end about fishing and hunting. Wally saw everybody as an equal, but there were cliques on any major league team. The great variances in age, interest and financial status, plus old allegiances, tended to create various groups. This was so different than in the minors, where everyone seemed to hang together.

Training would now move into high gear with the regulars finally in camp, and soon the spring training games would start. Although this was the start of my sixth year in pro baseball, it was quite a thrill for me to take the field each day with so many great players. Musial had been asked hundreds of times what his greatest thrill in baseball was, and the reply that I have seen quoted again and again by him is: "Just putting on a major league uniform each day was my biggest thrill in baseball." Sounds trite. But when that is what you have aspired to and you finally reach it—well, that's pretty much the way I felt wearing that Cardinal uniform and being among those players.

Kurt and I spent time walking the beaches those early weeks of spring training, each hoping in our own way that fate might deal kindly with us. The weather and surf were great and we enjoyed the time in the sun. Meals were taken at the Bainbridge Hotel and we just had to sign the checks, which were then paid for by the parent club. The Cardinals also gave us laundry money, but it was still tough to keep from digging into your own pocket during spring training.

I had a new roomie after the first night in St. Pete—Red Munger. He was one of the nicest guys I have ever met, and he was a bit of an enigma to the Cardinals. Red had been with them for several years and had made his mark as a major-league pitcher. He once possessed a blazing fastball and a better than average curve, but he never achieved the greatness that others had predicted for him. He was an affable guy and an easy person to get to know. Red didn't make me feel like I was a minor leaguer rooming with a big-time major leaguer.

He followed a routine that he hardly ever broke. After supper he would go up to our room, get out several Wild Western paperback books and read in bed for the rest of the evening. Munger was great for chewing tobacco as he read. He lined the wastebasket with a newspaper and let it serve as a spittoon. He would get up every morning and take the trash basket down the hall and empty the newspapers into a large container. This bit of housework was done to avoid any confrontation with the housekeepers. Red was a family man, and every night around 10 p.m. he would phone Houston, Texas, and talk with his wife and family. You read a lot about the rounders in baseball, and certainly there are some of those, but most of the married men I knew in baseball were like Red Munger and Kurt Krieger—family people.

The routine at spring training was: Up at 8 a.m., breakfast and then to the ballpark at 10 a.m. The games started at 1 p.m., and it was about 5 p.m. before the players arrived back at the hotel—famished. By that time my stomach had usually shrunk so that I couldn't eat half of what I thought I could. So the ice cream parlors or the hamburger joints were often visited right before going to bed.

The Cardinals clubhouse was always full of fun and laughter. The new guys were starting to get to know the veterans and the team seemed to be developing a chemistry of its own. As a young rookie I held back some. I believed it was better to keep my mouth shut and learn all that I could. Toward the end of spring training, when the inter-squad games were over and we were about to start the exhibition season, I felt ready and eager to play, but I had a sort of anxious feeling inside. Everyone else was so relaxed and I felt different. One day, I was in a lavatory stall when Stan Musial entered the stall next to mine. It was private and I had a captive audience. I asked, "Stan, do you get nervous or anxious before games?" He was both generous and gracious in his reply: "Ed, if you don't get nervous or edgy before a game it is probably time to quit." I can't tell you how much relief I felt in those words. I thought, "If Stan Musial gets nervous before a game, I guess everyone does so I must be o.k." I respect Stan for his honesty and help toward a rookie!

We started our exhibition games at St. Petersburg against the Yankees with Mantle, Berra, Woodling, Reynolds, and Rizzuto. I got to play and managed to get a hit. I was wondering why the Cards were giving me a chance after the poor season I had at New Orleans. I also wondered why J. Roy Stockton, the former sports editor of the *St. Louis Post-Dispatch*, was writing so many nice things about me. I played the whole game against Detroit the next day, getting two hits and driving in two runs. I got headlines from Mr. Stockton in the St. Louis paper. But that was all I got to play. In retrospect, I feel safe in saying that the Cardinal front office was grooming Steve Bilko for first base, thus my early departure from the spring training lineup, a fine example of the politics involved in baseball. I played some "B" games after that but no more varsity games. I began wondering what I had done wrong. So did some of the sportswriters and broadcasters. Harry Caray, the radio play-by-play announcer, had laid me out publicly the year before on his late afternoon sportscast for not reporting to spring training. He had now come to my defense and questioned why I was not given an opportunity to play after looking good in early games.

While I was bemoaning my fate, an accident occurred on March 24th that made me realize just how lucky I really was. Jim Dickey, a left-handed batter, lined a pitch thrown by Bob Slaybaugh directly back to the mound. The ball hit Slaybaugh in the right eye, and the eye actually popped out of the socket. I was standing at first base and I actually heard the impact and saw Bob double up and gasp. The trainer and doctor rushed to his assistance and he was taken immediately to the local hospital. Nothing could be done to save the sight in that eye, and a false eye was made. Believe it or not, Slaybaugh actually went courageously on to pitch for Omaha that season. A guy really has to want to play baseball to go on after an injury like that.

Spring training sped by rapidly, and much of my time was spent playing pepper with a St. Louisan named Earl Weaver. Neither of us had been getting into the lineup, so we kept busy during the ball games by playing pepper hour after hour. Earl had good hands and appeared to me to be a good infielder with a lot of enthusiasm toward the game. He was a product of Beaumont High School in St. Louis, which had produced close to 20 major-league baseball players. Their high school coach, Ray Eliot, was a marvel at teaching fundamentals to high-school boys. It's a shame that coaches like Eliot do not receive some sort of remuneration from baseball for the molding of hundreds of lives, and the development of so many careers. Despite the personal liking that Eddie Stanky had taken to Earl, he left before we officially broke camp. I think that Eddie saw a lot of himself in the "spunky Weaver kid," and seemed upset by the job of sending Earl on his way. I was delighted to see Earl become a major league manager in later years, and his Baltimore Orioles do so well, winning pennants and doing battle in the World Series several times.

When we broke camp in '52, I was still with the Cardinals as we went from whistle stop to whistle stop, playing our way back north to St. Louis. Well, I should say as they played their way back, because I watched all the games from the bench. I kept myself occupied in the best way that I could. At one game in Raleigh, North Carolina, as we played the Phillies, I kept track of the pitches thrown by Wilmer "Vinegar Bend" Mizell. He could throw as hard as anybody, but he had trouble finding home plate. He also had the problem of being over-coached. It seemed as though everyone wants to be helpful when a youngster who throws as hard as Mizell can't get the ball over. So Wilmer had a multitude of advisors telling him such things as: "Bend your back," or "Don't kick your leg up so high," or "Pick up a blade of grass on your follow through," or "Look at the target at all times."

And so it went. Everybody was shouting something different at the same time, all under the guise of being helpful. How can you think of all those things at once and still pitch well? You can't! And on that day, Mizell certainly did not pitch well. I stayed in the game mentally by counting Mizell's pitches. He was seemingly 3–2 on every hitter, and I had counted 123 pitches thrown by the sixth inning. Some nine-inning games take fewer pitches, so Vinegar was struggling. He eventually got straightened out and helped win a World Championship for the Pittsburgh Pirates in 1960. I am sure he got a lot of free advice on how to run the government, too, in his later days, for he became a representative to Congress from North Carolina. Hopefully, though, his pitching experiences helped him to discern the good advice from the bad.

When we got back to St. Louis, I was told I had been optioned to Houston. JoAnn and I packed our bags and headed south to Texas. As we traveled in our car toward Houston, I was wondering why the Cardinals were sending me there. Jerry Witte, a former major leaguer who had hit 38 homers and drove in 95 runs for Houston in 1951, was still there as the first baseman. Witte had hit 50 home runs for Dallas in 1949, and he was a big name in the Texas League. I played as soon as I got there and went 1 for 3 in my first game. Art Routzong, the business manager, called me to his office after the game and told me I was to report to Columbus, Ohio, to play with the Cardinals' AAA team. Again, I was wondering why I was sent to Houston to play one game. Upon our arrival in Columbus, JoAnn and I headed directly to the clubhouse where I met Johnny Keane, the team manager. The conversation with Johnny was brief as he told me I was to report to Rochester, New York, to play for the Cardinals' other triple AAA team. JoAnn and I were getting very frustrated with the Cardinals' management. I had to keep in mind the word chattel in my contract because at that time a ball player had no recourse. I rationalized the situation by telling myself that I was going to the next level to the big leagues and if I did a good job I might get a shot at the majors.

Why was I sent all the way from St. Louis to Houston to play one game? Why was I now being sent to Columbus, a higher classification than Houston? You can go crazy trying to answer questions like that in

Rochester Red Wings, 1952. These guys ended the season winning the International League play-offs and the Little World Series. It was arguably the best minor league team in baseball that year. Nearly everyone had or would have major league experience. Bing Devine was our general manager. He next went on to be general manager of the St. Louis Cardinals and built them into World Series teams, 1964, 1967, and 1968. The Mets benefited from the same expertise, winning their first World Series in 1969. Bing is still very active with the Cardinals as a special assignment scout. Back row, left to right: Johnny Bucha, Larry Ciaffone, Pete Riggan, Dan Whalan (trainer), Rip Repulski, Jack Crimian, Steve Bilko; middle row, left to right: Bob Habenicht, Ed Mickelson, Lou Ortiz, Fred Hahn, Fred Martin, George Condrick, Fred McAlister, Jack Faszholz; front row, left to right: Don Richmond, Jack Collum, Cot Deal, Harry Walker (manager), Ray Jablonski, Will Schmidt, Lou Kahn (coach). (Used by permission of Rochester Red Wings.)

baseball. Especially since when Jo Ann and I got to the clubhouse in Columbus, manager Johnny Keane told me not to unpack, because I was going to Rochester, New York, also a Triple A ball club.

On April 22, 1952, I signed my contract with the Rochester Red Wings as an option from the St. Louis National Baseball Club, Inc. Vaughn P. "Bing" Devine, the business manager of the team—and later general manager for the St. Louis Cardinals for many years—signed as the authorized official for the club. So in less than one week, I had been with four different clubs within one organization. Talk about going around the horn! But I still had one more stop to make that season.

I felt pretty good about being with Rochester. The season in New Orleans wouldn't really hurt that much if I could pull it off in Triple A. After all, I told myself, this is the highest I can go in the Cardinal organization besides the big team. I was anxious to see if I could do well in Triple A.

Jo Ann and I always seemed to be fortunate in finding nice places to live. We moved into a house on 907 Bay Street and had the entire upstairs to ourselves. It was furnished comfortably and had a living room, bedroom, large kitchen and a bath. Our landlady lived downstairs and owned the house. She treated us as if we were her own children, and we felt the same kindness and warmth toward her. After we left, my wife corresponded with her for fifteen years until her death. We always wrote messages about our family at Christmastime, and she would let us know how she was doing.

Rochester was in the International League, which had started operation in 1884. There were some excellent cities in the league in 1952: Montreal, Ottawa, and Toronto in Canada, and Buffalo, Syracuse, Baltimore, Springfield and Rochester in the States. All were good-sized cities and gave me the feeling of approaching the big time. The ballparks were not new. But they were, for the most part, made of steel and concrete with individual seats in the grandstand. The seating capacity of most parks was between 15,000 and 25,000.

The scorecards in Rochester and throughout the International League were big league. The up-to-date batting averages of the visitors and the Red Wings were inserted daily in the scorecard, which was sold for a dime. The batteries (pitchers and catchers) in the league were shown for each team. The scorecard also showed the prices for concessions. Cigarettes, beer, and hot dogs were a quarter. Soda, peanuts, popcorn, coffee, ice cream and Cracker Jacks were a dime.

I started playing regularly for Rochester soon after my arrival and got off to a good start. The difference between 1951 and 1952 was getting back to spring training. I was ready to play in '52. After my first 10 games with Rochester I was hitting .324. But my old nemesis, Steve Bilko, had injured his right arm playing for the Cardinals and was sent down to Rochester. He had hit 30 home runs there the year before, and as I worked out before each game, I wondered how long it would be before Harry Walker, our manager, called me in to the office to tell me that I was going somewhere else to play. The only control I had concerning my fate was to continue doing my best and concentrate on playing each game as it came. As always, I knew that I had to make the most out of any opportunity I was given, even if Steve Bilko was always breathing down my back.

Early in May our car was uncoupled and put off on a side track while all the players were still sleeping. The preceding week, we had Don Cornell at our ballpark to sing a number of songs including his hit, "I'm Yours." He was the hottest vocalist in the country at that time. So with everyone still asleep at about 6:30 in the morning, Lou Ortiz, our fancy-fielding second baseman from San Diego, climbed out of his berth, stood in the center of our Pullman car and bellowed out his rendition of Don Cornell's hit song at the top of his voice. For some reason, the guys didn't wake up complaining. There were 20 ball players, a manager, coach, and trainer at 6:30 in the morning in Montreal, Canada, all laughing at Lou as he belted out his song, word for word, to the end.

As it turned out, we all could have used the extra sleep that morning, because we played one of the longest games in International League history that night. It was nearing the end of the ball game, we were winning and I was pulling an "Al Neil," figuring out my average for the night in my head. Ball players will deny it, but ask any player during or after a game how many hits he got in how many times at bat, and he can tell you. I was 3 for 4 that night and was feeling pretty good about our chances of winning. Montreal tied us in the ninth, though, and that was just the beginning. We got a run in the top of the 14th inning to go ahead, but Harry Walker, our player-manager, dropped a line drive hit right at him in left field. Harry was generally pretty sure-handed, but this one had just popped out of his glove. And Montreal came back to tie in the bottom of the 14th. Fred Martin, who had pitched a good deal of major-league baseball and was no spring chicken, pitched 14 innings that night before he finally got some relief. We went on to lose the game in the 19th inning.

It was almost 1 a.m. when we entered the clubhouse at the end of the game. We were an unhappy bunch as Lou Ortiz, a handsome lad, tried to cheer us up by giving us an encore of his early morning wake-up song. My 3 for 4 at the end of nine didn't look so good as I wound up going 3 for 9, hitless in my five times to bat in extra innings.

Montreal is a great city steeped in tradition. It is a bilingual city with French and English spoken about equally as much. We stayed at the stately Mount Royal Hotel, designed in a manner of the parliamentary buildings in England. The steakhouses were terrific and the other restaurants were excellent as well. The weather was a bit nippy, but it felt good to wear a wool, long-sleeved sweatshirt under my baseball shirt. We would arrive at the ballpark about 5 p.m. There was an ice cream counter located under the stands, and many of us would order a cone before pre-game practice. I found it a lot of fun to try to converse with the ladies who worked behind the counter, because they understood very little of our English as we tried to order our cones.

The Montreal ballpark was a beautiful field with a seating capacity of 20,000. There was some signing of autographs in the lower minor leagues, but in the International League there were always kids waiting to get your autograph before and after the games. Montreal, Toronto, Rochester and some of the other parks came pretty close to looking "big league."

The Montreal team in 1952 was a Brooklyn Dodger farm club. Their manager was Walter Alston, who was later inducted into the Baseball Hall of Fame after a long career as skipper of the Dodgers. The entire Montreal outfield of Walt Moryn, Carmen Mauro, Don Thompson and Junior Gilliam eventually went on to the major leagues—although Gilliam was later moved to the infield, where he played for many seasons as a big-league second baseman. The infield included Don Hoak at third and Jim Pendleton at short. Each would become a star in the majors, with Hoak a big part of Pittsburgh's World Championship club in 1960. Joe Lutz was at first base for Montreal, with Gilliam and Wally Fiala sharing time at second. Pitching for Montreal were John Podres, Ed Roebuck, Mal Malette, Gil Mills, Dan Bankhead, Hampton Coleman, Bob Alexander and Tom Lasorda. Most of these pitchers made the majors, with Lasorda eventually following Alston's lead as a longtime Dodger manager who reached the Hall of Fame. Montreal had good catchers in Charlie Thompson and John Roseboro, another longtime Dodger regular.

I contend that in 1952 the Brooklyn Dodgers could have taken their top Triple A players from Montreal and St. Paul, as well as some Double A players from Mobile and Ft. Worth, and had a winner that year in the big leagues. For a manager, you could have your pick between Alston, Clay Bryant, and Bob Bragan. The team could have been made of players like Hoak, George Freese, or Bob Wilson at third, Pendleton, Don Zimmer, or Billy Hunter at short, Gilliam at second and Joe Lutz or Wayne Bedlardi at first. The outfield could have had fine players like Sandy Amoros, Dick Whitman, Gino Cimoli, Moose Moryn, Don Thompson, Carmen Mauro, and Al Gionfriddo. Tending home plate would be Thompson or Roseboro. Throwing the pitches would be Podres, Roebuck, Ron Negray, Ray Moore, Joe Landrum, and Elroy Face.

Can you imagine one club, the Brooklyn Dodgers, having that many fine ball players on just four of their 25 minor-league teams? Many of those players listed above went on to long careers in the majors and several even became big league all-stars. In 1952, players in the high minors were not only concerned about having a good season to move up, but just to maintain their status in Triple A or Double A.

But then, who in the Dodgers organization in 1952 could actually go up to Brooklyn to knock Gil Hodges off first, Jackie Robinson off second, Pee Wee Reese off short or Bill Cox off third? Who could come up and replace three outfielders in their prime like Carl Furillo, Duke Snider or Andy Pafko? Roy Campanella was Most Valuable Player in the National League in 1951 at catcher and would win again in '53 and '55. Who could take his job? Of all the young stars in the Dodgers' minor-league system that year, only one player got a chance to move up to the parent team in 1953. That was Gilliam to second base as Robinson moved to third. This meant that over 450 minor league ball players in Brooklyn's lower ranks had to mark time for another year in the minors. Most of the minor-league stars in that organization would languish on the vine until some other team saw what it needed, purchased them and brought them up to the majors.

Rochester, though, had a fine club too, in '52. Harry Walker, our manager, was a great hitting instructor. He was a fine hitter himself. Even though Harry was over 35 years of age, he still showed flashes of how he once led the National League in hitting. Walker had the idiosyncrasy of tugging at the peak of his cap, and he became known for this around the major leagues. "Harry the Hat" became his nickname. It was a nervous gesture, and in between pitches he would step out of the box and tug at his cap 10 to 12 times or more.

Harry was not a long-ball hitter, although he could hit home runs at times. He was a line-drive hitter, hitting for a high average. A left-handed batter, Harry went with the pitch. An outside pitch he would slap to left field and an inside pitch he would pull to right. He was a really tough out because he didn't strike out much. Even with the responsibilities of managing the club, Harry the Hat hit .365 in 115 games that year.

Harry had one fault, though. He talked incessantly. He was knowledgeable on many subjects but loved to talk baseball, and especially hitting. Harry talked all the time to anyone who would listen, and even to some who wouldn't. Even though he knew his subject well, I must admit that his incessant chatter made me more than a bit nervous at times.

Walker was an excellent instructor for certain types of hitters. He taught hitters to hold their hands high, swing down on the ball and try to hit the top half of the ball. A short, quick stroke was preferable. It sacrificed power for average, but this was Harry's style, and it kept him over the .300 mark wherever he played.

Sometimes he imposed his style on the strong, stand-up, long-ball hitters like Rip Ripulski, a 6-foot, 185-pounder from Minnesota. Rip had good speed, a strong arm and could hit with power. He was a stand-up, free-swinging long-baller but Harry had him hitting out of a crouch, short-stroking and chopping down at the ball. Before each pitch, The

Hat would yell at Rip, "Get down, get down. Get your hands up higher, higher!" It was working, because Rip was hitting well over .300, but you could see that Rip was uncomfortable in a style not his own. Rip had hit only a couple of home runs since Harry took over his swing, and most of his hits were singles. This went on for several more weeks before Rip's average slowly started slipping to just above .300, and very few extra-base hits were coming.

Harry Walker, 1946. He led the National League in hitting in 1947, hitting .363. If you wanted to be a line-drive hitter, his philosophy was, in my opinion, the best. Because I did want that, I listened and watched and learned an enormous amount. I use his techniques and mechanics to this day when I coach young players. (National Baseball Hall of Fame Library, Cooperstown, New York.)

One night in Rochester, Rip was having a terrible time. He had been hitting "Walker-style" for almost two months. Rip was becoming frustrated and Harry was becoming more vocal. Rip had struck out and popped out and was becoming irate with Harry the Hat, who was constantly yelling instructions. Finally, while at the plate with Harry yelling instructions to him, Rip stepped out and yelled, "Screw it, Harry! I'm going to hit my way!" Rip stepped back into the batter's box standing erect, bending his knees only slightly. The next pitch saw Ripulski take a long, fluid swing. The ball ended up in left-center for a double. Rip struck out more often after he went back to his style of hitting, and his average dipped, too. But balls now came rocketing off his bat and carried against and over the outfield walls quite regularly. Rip had two home runs during the first third of the season with 15 RBIs in 171 at-bats. True, he was hitting over .300, but if he continued at that rate, he'd only hit 6 homers and 45 RBIs for the season. The over .300 batting average would give him major league credentials, but just 6 home runs and 45 RBIs would not. So Rip went back to hitting his way and finished the season with respectable totals of 13 home runs, 24 doubles, 7 triples and 65 RBIs. The next season, he went up to the Cardinals.

Harry Walker had as much knowledge about hitting as any man I have met, and was respected as an outstanding instructor. But at that time in his life, it seemed to me that Harry tried to mold everyone to his style of hitting, and some guys just could not adjust.

George Toporcer, a utility infielder with the 1926 St. Louis Cardinals' World Championship team, gave a talk at the Ad Club luncheon at the Powers Hotel in Rochester. George was a native of Rochester and had become blind since his playing days. He was one of the first ball players to wear glasses while he played, and his eyes got much worse after leaving baseball. George was an inspiring speaker and was living a productive life despite his blindness. He was an encouragement to all that heard him that day in June.

We had another entertainer come to Red Wings' Stadium a little later in the season. He was short of stature with a hawk nose. This fellow was a warm, outgoing person and seemed to like baseball and the company of baseball players. He was nervous as he sat hunched over, looking at his shoes and swinging his feet back and forth under the dugout bench. A microphone was being set up for him to sing at home plate. The singer's name was Tony Bennett, and that night I was very impressed with his style and voice. Tony Bennett was just starting out in 1952 I was right in my prediction about his future. I thought to myself, "This guy has real talent." How I still love his singing of "I Left My Heart in San Francisco," which, of course, was a huge hit.

We played in Ottawa, Canada's capital, and now Philly's top team, Ottawa had replaced Jersey City. I enjoyed visiting the Parliament and the House of Commons buildings in Ottawa. The parts of Canada I saw were beautiful, amazingly impressive and astoundingly large. At the time the main cities were experiencing growing pains due to a population boom. Too bad the ballpark didn't match the rest of the country and its cities for beauty, because the stands and the playing field in Ottawa left much to be desired.

The day Bilko arrived with the team, May 20, we were playing in Buffalo. I had a good night with four hits in five times at bat in our 7–6 win. I would need to continue that kind of hitting to stay in the line-up.

Rochester was moving up from second place in the division as we went on into Baltimore and its spacious ballpark, with the longest dugout in organized baseball. This dugout started between home plate and third base and ended deep down the left field line. The stadium was built for football, not baseball, and 100 football players could sit buttocks to buttocks and not fill up the dugout bench.

After losing the first game to Baltimore 14–8, Rochester was 1½ games out of first place with 34 wins and 27 losses. I hit a triple and a home run in that losing effort. The next night we won, 8–1, as Ray Jablonski hit two home runs and I went 1 for 4. The next night we lost in the 12th inning, 3–2, and I was collared—0 for 5. I was hitting over .298 at that point, and I hadn't made an error in 40 games. I felt like I had made a contribution so I naturally felt a surge of resentment when I was told that I would be benched. Harry Walker had told me, in a diplomatic way, that he wanted more power in the lineup. I had hit only one home run and Bilko had hit 30 the year before. So I tried to understand what Harry was saying, that the St. Louis front office had made the call, but I could not dismiss the welling anger.

I knew that if Bilko stayed healthy and played up to par, I would not see much action for the remainder of the season. This could be another lost season for me. But I was finally in Triple A, I had started well and anything could happen in baseball. So I hoped I could stay with a good ball club and a bunch of great guys. Why ask to be sent out? I felt that there was nothing left for me to prove in the lower minors. Triple A was where I had to prove myself at that time. But when we got back to Rochester, Bing Devine, our general manager, called me into his office and told me that he was sending me down. That's when the dam broke. All the frustration with the St. Louis Cardinals organization ran through my mind: $2,000 bonus minus $500, Eddie Dyer's "I'll take you to spring training if you hit over .250," be a good soldier and go to Montgomery, play well in the first two games in spring training but never start again, bounce from Houston to Columbus to Rochester in one week.

I flew into a rage. I was trembling and tears filled my eyes. I cursed and shouted, "I know I can play at this level and I'm not going down!" In his book, *The Memoirs of Bing Devine*, he says I was intimidating and threatening. I am sure I was. Deep inside I knew the Cardinal front office had made the decision, but overwhelmed by emotion, I wanted to kill the messenger. For what ever reason and to his credit, after that meeting in June, he kept me at Rochester until the last three weeks of the season and then sent me to Triple A Columbus, Ohio.

As the summer went on in Rochester, Ray "Jabbo" Jablonski was coming into his own as a hitter. But Jabbo, whom I had known since our days in Columbus, Georgia, was still trying to find a position for himself. By the first of July, he had already played every position on the infield as well as the outfield. Ray had developed strong forearms and wrists. He wasn't a big man, only standing 5'10" and weighing 175 pounds. But he could hit the ball with power, either pulling it to left field or going with the pitch to right. Ray moved to the Cardinals in '53 and had a good season with the big-league club.

Little Jackie Collum proved that a small guy with guts and a good specialty pitch (for him it was the screwball) could make it in baseball. Jackie was sturdily built at 5'6" and was a real fighter. He had good control and a sneaky fastball, but it was his "scroogie"—screwball—and competitiveness that got this diminutive pitcher to the big leagues.

We had some other good pitchers on our team. Bob Tiefenaur had a great knuckler. When I wasn't playing in the games, I would go to the bullpen and help warm up the pitchers. I put on knee-guards, a mask and a chest protector to handle Bob's dipsy-doodle knuckler. Fred Hahn (my roommate), George Condrick, Willard Schmidt, Cot Deal and Fred Martin all showed good stuff. Jack Faszholz was our most consistent pitcher with 15 wins and 8 losses. Jack had great control, poise, and pitching know-how. The fastball, overhand curve and change-up made up most of the pitches thrown at that time. But the slider was coming on strong and would baffle many a hitter. Two of the greatest batsmen of all time, Stan Musial and Ted Williams, would publicly state that the slider was the toughest pitch to hit in baseball. Old-timers would ridicule the slider as a "nickel curve" because it only broke five or six inches compared to the overhand curve, which could break as much as two or three feet. What made the slider so devastating? It came in just like a fastball, but as the batter started his swing, the ball would break at the last split second. The hitter wouldn't have time to readjust. Simply, the slider fools hitters because it breaks so late and so sharply.

We played Toronto in a double-header on July 1st, and almost 13,000 fans paid to see it. July 1st in Canada is Dominion Day, something like our Independence Day, and the people of Canada celebrate this day with great respect for their country. I marveled at the number of planes taking off from an airport a few miles beyond the center-field fence. I talked with some of the natives, and they told me that it was common for local fishermen to fly north to the lake areas, fish for a few hours and fly back that night or the next day. I was amazed at the number of small planes taking off—it seemed like several hundred during our double-header. I had plenty of time to observe, of course, because I was sitting on the bench. Bilko played first in both games.

We had a battle every time we played Montreal that year. We lost the first game 7–2, but I got to play in the second game. Bilko had injured a leg muscle and I was back in the lineup. Every ball player sitting on the bench must want to play or he isn't worth his salt. But the only way a guy gets back in the lineup is because of an injury or a slump to the man playing ahead of him. You don't consciously wish the guy bad luck, but you do hope that you will get a chance to play. I kept in shape by running in the outfield, taking a lot of infield practice, and playing as much pepper as I could. But batting form and timing just aren't there unless you are playing every day. So I got collared in that second game as I went 0 for 3. We did win, though, and I felt good to be a part of it. I continued to play regularly until July 27th, when Bilko came back into the lineup.

We had a third baseman on our team who was an excellent hitter and a fine ball player. Don "Poopsie" Richmond was his name, and aside from Harry the Hat, he was one of our best hitters. He was also a very gifted fielder and it was hard to figure out why he wasn't in the major leagues. He was consistently above .300 in Triple A ball, and though his home run production wasn't too high, he hit a lot of doubles and triples. Richmond, like Harry Walker, had a unique idiosyncrasy while batting. He would often be bothered by the umpire positioning himself in front of second base. In the higher minor leagues there were three umpires, not four as in the majors. With a runner on first base, the umpire there would move to a spot between the pitcher's mound and second base. This would put him in a position to call double plays and still handle a call at first base. Don Richmond, when bothered by the umpire's positioning, would call time out and request that he umpire move a little in one direction or the other to get out of his line of vision. The umpire would oblige him and move a few steps toward third base or first. This seemed to satisfy Don, who would often hit the very next pitch for a base hit. We would all wait in the dugout for this nightly occurrence, and it rarely seemed to fail. Richmond would call time, move the umpire and smash a "blue darter" on the line for a single.

One of the toughest men I met in baseball was our catcher, Johnny Bucha. John was not a large man, only 5'9", 180 pounds, but he was really put together. He loved to receive the ball from an outfielder and block the plate, tagging out the oncoming runner. Bucha reveled in this kind of contact, and he guarded home plate with ferocity beyond description. I remember vividly a play that occurred in Rochester in a game against Montreal. Bucha received a throw from the outfield and braced himself to face the stampeding runner coming home. The runner neglected to slide and tried to barrel into John, who was crouching. Bucha flexed his knees, bent slightly at the waist, lowered his right shoulder and caught the unfortunate runner square in the gut. The runner's speed was used against him as Bucha catapulted him into the air. The runner was deposited in Rochester's on-deck circle, halfway between home plate and our dugout. That runner was Johnny Roseboro, who would eventually replace Roy Campanella in Brooklyn after his auto accident before the 1958 season.

On the 17th of August, I was again called into Bing Devine's office and told that I was to finish the season at Columbus, Ohio. Willard Schmidt and I were being sent to that Triple A team in the American Association team for Charley Kress and Al Papai. Devine felt that he needed Kress's left-handed power for the play-offs as well as Al Papai's pitching. I had to agree with the logic of his move—Kress and Papai would both help the ball club.

But that didn't change the fact that I was stung deeply by this move. I had accepted my job as a reserve player and I had made my contribution to the club with both the bat and the glove, doing whatever I could to help the team when I was not playing. While playing irregularly, I hit .270 and I led the league in fielding percentage, making only two errors in 500 chances for a .996 percentage. I wanted to finish out the season at Rochester because I felt like I was a part of that club and I believed that I could help them in the play-offs. A sudden surge of anger and resentment overwhelmed me, and I vented out that hostility on Devine, the future Cardinals general manager, with a barrage of curse words that stunned both the recipient and the sender.

I left the upstairs office quarters at Red Wing Stadium feeling anger, rejection, and pain. I found it difficult to say goodbye to the guys I had lived with all season—my teammates and my friends. I choked back the tears as I quickly packed my belongings, said my goodbyes and retreated to 907 Bay Street. I climbed the steps leading to our upstairs apartment and broke the bad news to Jo Ann. Tears streamed down my cheeks as I released the feelings that had then overwhelmed me. I kept telling myself that this was a part of the game. I had experienced it before and I would experience it again, but knowing it did not lessen the anguish.

We packed, left Rochester, and went to St. Louis. When we arrived, I dropped Jo off at home and headed for the Cardinals office. I was to finish the last three weeks of the season with Columbus on the road.

I stopped off at the Cardinal office to chat with Bill Walsingham, the Cardinal vice-president, and to get some expense money before joining Columbus in Kansas City. Before my meeting with Mr. Walsingham, I came to the full realization that the Cardinals would go with Bilko in the years to come, and if I were to play first base in the major leagues it would not be with the Cardinals. Mr. Walsingham was a gray-headed, distinguished-looking man, and he was very courteous and proper. The meeting started off in a low-keyed, matter-of-fact discussion pertaining to my travel arrangements and hotel accommodations in Kansas City. But before the conference ended, my pent-up wrath had surfaced yet again. I stated emphatically that I wanted out of the Cardinal organization.

Rochester defeated Syracuse in four straight games and polished off Montreal four games to two to win the International League playoffs. They met Kansas City, the American Association playoff champs, and defeated them in a seven-game series four games to three, winning the last three games in a row to clinch the Little World Series Championship. Each Rochester player netted $1,700 for the playoff games and Little World Series in addition to his salary.

I joined the Columbus Cardinals in Kansas City with three weeks left to play in the season. What had started out six years ago as a dream was now a reality—I was the starting first baseman for the Triple A Columbus Cardinals. Johnny Keane, the manager of the Columbus Red Birds, was a wiry, sharp-featured man who was very religious and had been managing in the Cardinal organization for years. He had seen many ball players come and go and he seemed to sense what I was feeling. He gave me the encouragement to do my best for myself and the ball club during those last few weeks. Keane was highly respected by me and everyone else who played for him as man who was fair, a real straight-shooter. It didn't surprise me that when he finally got a shot with the Cardinals, he managed them to the 1964 World Championship.

When I played for Keane at Columbus, we were mired in seventh place and going nowhere, but I hit .308 in 12 games. And I had completed an entire season in Triple A ball. It was reassuring to know that I could compete in this caliber of baseball.

8

Farewell Brownies

During the World Series, baseball's owners get together and trades are often made. When I came up with the Cardinals at the end of the 1950 season to play a few games, I must have impressed a tall, gangling shortstop on that team named Marty Marion—who in my opinion should be a member of the Hall of Fame. Marty was then the manager of the St. Louis Browns, and through his recommendation I was purchased by the Browns from the Cardinals for the $10,000 waiver price. It really made me feel good to be wanted after the rejection that I felt in the Cardinal organization.

The winter sped by as I continued my courses at Washington University in St. Louis, now working towards a degree in higher education. I assisted with coaching duties at University City High School, helping Stub Muhl in football and Lloyd Brewen in basketball. I met with Browns owner Bill Veeck in January and signed for $800 per month. My contract would increase to $5,000 if I made the team. That was the major league minimum. Bill Veeck was the most open and forthright baseball owner I had ever dealt with. He enjoyed the players. He joked with them and expressed a real interest in their affairs. Most club owners of that era appeared aloof to me, choosing to stay apart from the enlisted men, but not Bill Veeck.

He was flamboyant and outspoken, but a real sentimentalist. Gene Beardon, a miracle-working pitcher in the '48 season for Veeck's Cleveland Indians, was also at the signing. It became apparent that, for Veeck, Bearden's feats would never be forgotten. He would "carry" Beardon on the team, even though Gene had seen better days. In a game that seemed to lack caring, I was impressed to find an owner with such a big heart.

Jo Ann and I headed for spring training in 1953. After all those years, Jo was finally going to spring training with me. What a place to go—the Mission Inn in Riverside, California. The Mission Inn was an experience in itself. It took up an entire city block and patterned itself architecturally in a Spanish motif. The palm trees and the red tiled roofs set off the three-story structure with its enclosed patio and walkout porticos. Every evening at 6 p.m. the chimes atop the Mission Inn belfry rang out the tune,

THERE, THERE, LITTLE FELLA.

Illustration by Ron Joyner.

"When You Come to the End of a Perfect Day." We were captivated by the charm and elegance of the setting.

The large swimming pool in the center of the flower-bedecked courtyard was the first thing that caught your eye each morning as you looked down from the balcony outside each room. The well-groomed grounds and beautiful Spanish structures were breathtaking. The sky was a beautiful blue color except on cool mornings, when the stench and murky clouds from the smudge-pots blotted out the sun with a gray haze. Smudge-pots were lit to protect the orange trees in the field surrounding the Inn and much of the outskirts of Riverside. On clear days, the smell of orange blossoms wafted in the air.

My first recollection of Riverside was unpacking the car on the street outside the Inn, carrying our bags to our room and meeting Virgil and Vicki Trucks. Virgil had long been an established star in the major leagues, and I must admit I was still awed by big-league names. After introductions, he said, "Come on, Jo and Ed. Let me buy you a drink." We accompanied Virgil and Vicki to the bar across the street from the Inn. After a few drinks, Vicki and Jo struck up a friendship which would last all spring, both women swimming and shopping together almost every day. Shopping, though, was actually Vicki buying and Jo wishing.

Virgil Trucks was amiable and generous off the field, but the same Virgil with a ball in his hand and on the mound was a completely different person. Early in the season we opened against the Chicago White Sox and Jim Rivera hit a home run off Virgil. Incensed by Rivera's "lack of respect," Virgil told everyone on the bench, "The next time that son of a bitch comes to bat, I'm going to deck him!" He not only decked Rivera but hit him in the head, knocking Rivera's cap one way and "Big Jim" the other. To Rivera's credit, he was able to climb to his feet and trot down to first base—this before hitters even wore helmets.

Spring training in '53 started out with a daily ride of 12 miles from Riverside to San Bernardino, where the ballpark was located. The trip was made by car, and the players would drive themselves and a couple other players. Each driver would get reimbursed for his travel expense by the ball club. I always rode with Boris "Babe" Martin, a burly, hard-nosed catcher who grew up in St. Louis. He was the only remaining member of the Browns team that won the American League championship in '44 and played the St. Louis Cardinals in the "Street Car Series."

On our way to "San Berdoo" we would travel through the foothills of the San Bernardino Mountains. Babe had a penchant for saving gas. So when we went around the hillside taking a left curve, Babe would drive on the left side of the road. Every day for six weeks I took my life in my hands riding with Babe, as he took left turns on the left side of the road. Did we ever meet any oncoming cars? Well, we were surprised by a few, but we didn't hit any—or I suppose you wouldn't be reading this right now.

The pitchers and catchers opened spring training for the Browns on February 12, 1953. A few infielders and outfielders were among the 20 players who reported to manager Marty Marion at the San Bernardino training base. I was one of the early birds. The pitchers for the Browns that year were coach Harry Brecheen, Gene Bearden, Bob Cain, Don Larsen, Earl Harrist, Bobo Holloman, Cliff Fannin, Clarence Marshall, Satchel Paige, Duane Pillette, Marlin Stuart, Virgil Trucks and Hal White. Clint Courtney, Les Moss and Babe Martin did the catching.

The Browns had six first basemen on their roster: Roy Sievers, Dixie Upright, Dick Kryhoski, Gordon Goldsberry, Frank Kellert and me. Mar-

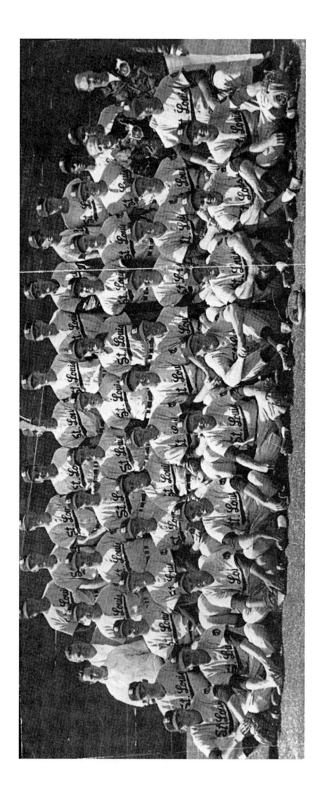

ion had been influential in drafting me and I sensed that, though he never said it, he wanted me to make the ball club. He gave me every chance to do well that spring, and I hit well and had good days in the field.

Two New York sportswriters were in camp with us for a part of spring training. They were Artie and Milt Richman. Artie was with the *New York Daily Mirror* and Milt was with United Press International. As youngsters in New York City, Milt and Artie were often shunned by the Yankees players when trying to get autographs. But when the Browns played the Yankees, the Richmans found that the players not only signed autographs but were willing to talk to them. Soon the two boys made friends with the team, especially Harland Clift, and were led into the clubhouse, hand in hand. Later they were frequent stowaways on the train trips to play Philadelphia. The players hid them in the upper berths when the conductor came through the train. They were smuggled into the players' rooms for the series.

Artie tells this story. During the 1944 World Series between the Cardinals and the Browns, Artie was called into the dean's office and was told he had to make a choice of attending the Series or continuing his education at Brooklyn College. Artie chose the Series and his beloved Browns. He has mandated that he be buried in his Brownie uniform with his cap on his head. Milt and Artie became lifetime Browns fans. They both visited us in San Bernadino, California, for spring training in 1953. Milt eventually became the sports editor for United Press International and is now in the National Baseball Hall of Fame for Writers in Cooperstown. Artie is now the oldest baseball executive, working full time with the Yankees as vice president.

We played the Chicago Cubs on March 21st in San Bernardino. Don Larsen, who would pitch a perfect no-hit, no-run game in the 1956 World

Opposite page: The Saint Louis Browns 1953 Spring Training Squad. Front row, left to right: Duane Pillette, Jim Dyck, Dick Kokos, Dan Baich, Harry Schwegman, Les Moss, Willy Miranda, Hal White, and Clint Courtney. Second row, from left: Don Larsen, Row Sievers, Bob Elliot, Billy Hunter, Coach Bill Norman, Manager Marty Marion, Coach Bob Scheffing, Pitcher-Coach Harry Brecheen, Cliff Fannin, Marlin Stuart, Bob Cain, Dixie Upright. Third row, left to right: Trainer Bob Bauman, Traveling Secretary Bill Durney, Hank Edwards, Vic Wertz, Mel Held, Bobby Young, Dick Littlefield, Babe Martin, Mike Blyzka, Neil Berry, George Freese, Satchel Paige, Clubhouse Attendant Art Peters, Johnny Groth, Assistant Trainer Bob Sackman. Rear row, left to right: Ed Mickelson, Frank Kellert, Don Lenhardt, Bobo Holloman, Pete Taylor, Bob Habenicht, Dick Kryhoski, Clarence Marshall, Rocky Ippolito, Virgil Trucks. For a team that lost 100 games, there were an amazing number of young players who went on to have good major league careers, and some of those went on to stardom. (From *St. Louis Commerce* magazine, April 8, 1953, courtesy Baltimore Orioles.)

An old postcard showing the Mission in Riverside, California. At the time, this was among the best hotels in southern California. Jo Ann and I were royally treated during our stay. It is still in business and looks to be a wonderful place to stay to this day.

Series for the Yankees, followed Virgil Trucks to the mound. Larsen was a tremendous athlete, tall and well-built. He could run, throw and even hit in super fashion. Pitching the last four innings that day against the Cubs, he hit a 400-foot home run off Bob Schultz for his second homer of the spring. In the ninth inning, Toby Atwell doubled to left and scored on Hal Jeffcoat's double with none out. Frankie Baumholtz, the runner-up in the National League batting race the previous season, struck out. Then Carl Sawatski was called in to pinch-hit. And as reported in the *Chicago Tribune* by Edward Burns, "Carl slammed a mile-a-minute grounder, but Ed Mickelson, an Ottawa, Illinois boy, came up with the smash far from the bag and Larsen was there to cover for the out. The game ended as Bob Ramazotti fouled out to Les Moss." I really felt great after that game. My teammates pounded me on the back and offered congratulations. Satchel Paige sauntered over to me after I had showered and sat by my locker. He shook my hand and said, "Kid, great play." I had hit several home runs that spring, but being congratulated by "Ol' Satch" was easily my most thrilling moment.

Satchel Paige has to go down as one of the immortals of baseball. At that time, Satch was over fifty years of age. He was tall, raw-boned and very thin. The program had him listed at 6'3½" and 190 pounds. The height was correct, but I doubt that Satch weighed much over 175. The

"That's Right! That's Leroy (Satchel) Paige, two-generation wonder boy of the Browns' pitching staff, catching! Satch just thought he'd show the boys how it's done during a training season lunch-hour gag at San Bernadino, CA. And that blur just in front of Satch's mitt is the ball, sailing right by rookie first baseman Dixie Upright. Satch knows how to play all positions." (From *St. Louis Commerce* magazine, April 8, 1953, courtesy Baltimore Orioles.)

team roster listed his birth date as September 22, 1908, in Mobile, Alabama, meaning Satch would turn 45 years old that season. But most every ball player has two ages: His baseball age and his real age. Most guys deduct a year or two, but with Satch it probably amounted to five or six. He had gone 12–10 in 1952 for the lowly St. Louis Browns, finishing 32 games. A winning record in the major leagues for a pitcher over 50 is a phenomenon. It was a thrill to be in spring training with the likes of Vic Wertz, Harry Brecheen, Marty Marion, Virgil Trucks, and Clint Courtney, but to be on the same field with Satchel Paige, the future Hall of Famer, was something I could only have dreamed about.

During one spring-training game, I was playing first behind Satch. A man got on base, and I went over to hold him on. Satch had all kinds of moves. That time he came off the stretch to his belt, and without moving his front foot or looking at me, using only his great wrist action, he flipped the ball under his left raised forearm to me at first. He threw the ball with such quickness that he not only picked the runner off, but nearly picked me off as well. Luckily, I caught the ball and tagged the runner. The umpire called him out. Then realizing what he had seen, he reversed his call and yelled, "Balk!" Meanwhile, Satch was doubled over in laughter.

FLAVOR CHAMPION OLD JUDGE COFFEE

KXOK DIAL 630 BROWNS SPONSORED BY FALSTAFF BEER

WRIGHT Flash TRADES HIGH

Bank Financing

YEAR'S GUARANTEE ON USED CARS

You Can't Go Wrong with WRIGHT Flash

6111 DELMAR DE. 6111

Stag BEER SUGAR-FREE As Beer Can Be!

GRIESEDIECK WESTERN BREWERY CO. BELLEVILLE, ILL. — ST. LOUIS, MO.

Coca-Cola "What You Want Is A Coke"

"COKE" IS A REGISTERED TRADE-MARK.

Budweiser. LAGER BEER

ANHEUSER-BUSCH, INC. . . . ST. LOUIS, MO. NEWARK, N. J.

FLAVOR CHAMPION OLD JUDGE COFFEE

Salomon Hannegan, Portnoy & Assoc, Inc. LIFE INSURANCE

Morton R. Bearman / Martin S. Kosberg
Donald L. Carpenter / Sig Lippman
Adolph M. Friedman / Joe Oxenhandler
Robert Ginsburg / R. Jayce Portnoy
Mrs. R. E. Hannegan / Sidney Solomon, Jr.
Mrs. Bert E. Klausner / Robert W. Weddell

AMBASSADOR BUILDING • GA 0925

"a hit!"

PEVELY POLAR ECLAIR CHOCOLATE COATED ICE CREAM BAR

"get 'em from the vendor!"

Rawlings BASEBALL EQUIPMENT FIRST CHOICE FROM SAND-LOT TO MAJOR LEAGUES

THE FINEST IN THE FIELD

NEXT BEST TO A SEAT AT THE PARK
CONVERT ANY TV SET
INSTALL IT YOURSELF
Be Ready For Browns' Games On WTVI
Newberry RADIO COMPANY
MOTOROLA ALL-CHANNEL TUNERS $49.95
3401 S. KINGSHIGHWAY PL. 6300

Sold At Sportsman's Park . . .
"EL REY" Pure Ground Beef Patties
GENERAL MEAT CO. :: St. Louis 7, Missouri

This score card is from the first home series between the Browns and the Yankees in 1953. Note the Yankees roster. How many Hall of Famers do you find? Now check out the Browns. There are 8 Yankees (Rizzuto, Mantle, Berra, Mize, Ford, Crosetti, Dickey, Stengel) and 1 Brownie (Paige). That is about how the score went too, when the Yankees played the Browns.

Satchel Paige had millions of stories to tell about the years and travels in the Negro Baseball Leagues. Occasionally, and without provocation, he would start talking about his adventures. If you were fortunate to be in earshot, you were in for a real treat. The pitchers nearby would gather around him and hearty laughter would prevail. And then just as quickly as he began, he would stop. We'd all have to wait for another day and another tale.

One day that spring, Satchel gathered the pitchers and asked them if they had ever seen anyone hit the inside and outside corners of a matchbox with a pitch. These veteran and even World Series pitchers scoffed at such an idea. While they put the matchbox on the plate, Satch warmed up as the unbelievers stood back to watch. He threw ten pitches, calling "inside" or "outside" before each pitch. Unbelievers became believers, as most of his pitches missed their assigned spot by just an inch or two. Only one pitch missed by as much as three inches. Incidentally, Satch was born in 1902, according to his son. That made him nearly 51 at the time of this story. Imagine him in his prime, throwing 100 miles per hour with pinpoint control.

One beautiful spring evening after supper, I ventured into Satch's room. He spent endless hours at the typewriter, evidently going to great lengths to answer each of the thousands of pieces of fan mail that he received from every part of the country. I spent a quiet hour with Satchel Paige as he typed away. We chatted ever so infrequently, but I sensed a great depth of character in a man who thought deep thoughts. He had seen so much of life traveling in the Negro and Winter Leagues, playing baseball almost every day of the year, in all sorts of places and in all kinds of conditions. In the soft light of his room, I remember thinking how old he looked and how peaceful and gentle he seemed to be. Satch called only a very few of the players by their first names. He was like Babe Ruth in that respect. Except for two or three of the veterans on our team, everybody was "Kid" to Satch. So as I left his room, Satch said, "Goodbye, Kid." I don't think he ever really knew my name. There had been so many places and so many people that whisked across the screen of Satch's memory. To him, almost everybody had become "Kid."

My last recollection of the great Satchel Paige was a game played in Detroit against the Tigers. I had been called up to the Browns at the end of the season and was playing first base. I had doubled to right-center field and was feeling good about getting a chance to play. Pat Mullins, a long-time Tiger favorite, had just announced that he would retire after his last few games for the home club. He hit a slow roller to me at first base, and the ball went between my legs and into right field. It clearly should have been called an error, but a benevolent hometown scorer gave Mullins a hit on the ball. Satch gave up a few more hits and some runs, and was eventually replaced. I felt badly about my misplay and felt responsible for his departure. So I sought him out after the game and said, "Satch, I'm really sorry for not coming up with that ball. I should have had it." Satch gazed upon me for a long time, and I was expecting a real chewing out. Not from "Ol' Satch." Instead he said, "Don't mind about that, don't you worry about it, Kid." As I left him and entered a cab for the ride back to the hotel, I thought about how many hundreds, even thousands, of good and bad plays had been made behind this all-time pitching great. Satchel had his own philosophy of life, and he had certain rules that he lived by. But the one I found to be most helpful was his statement, "Don't look back—something might be gaining on you!"

During the spring, we just had to sign checks at the Mission Inn for our food. We received no meal money but as long as we didn't overdo it, we could eat well there. The wives received no compensation. So when I ordered, I got the large helpings. I also added a few extra things for my wife, so we didn't have to spend too much out of our own pocket. The meals at the Mission Inn were excellent and the atmosphere was plush. We had a large bedroom with a sitting room off the bedroom, plenty of closet space, a large dresser and a large bathroom. As you stepped out of the room on the third-floor veranda, you could overlook four sides of the Inn, which enclosed the pool and gigantic courtyard. The flowers, ferns, bushes, trees and lawn were immaculate, and the large swimming pool was strategically located in the center of the courtyard. It truly was a beautiful sight.

The St. Louis Browns occasionally made arrangements for the wives to visit the Hollywood filmmakers. Buses were provided and the wives made it an adventurous all day trip. Jo Ann was quite excited to see Gordon McRae, one of her favorites, in action. On another outing, most of the players, their wives and Browns staff appeared on the quiz show called *Truth or Consequences* with Ralph Edwards. We were called the Brown family, and the contestant had to have us over for dinner if they had to pay the consequences of not telling the truth during the questioning. As we waited, I spotted Boris Karloff in his small dressing room. The door was ajar and I stuck my head in to tell him how much he scared me in a movie from my youth called *The Walking Dead*. He invited me in and we chatted ever so briefly until he was summoned to the stage. While we were behind the curtain waiting to be the consequences, Mr. Edwards questioned a young married couple. I could hear Mr. Edwards say, "… and for your consequence you will invite the Brown family for dinner." The curtain opened and there we stood, all 60 members of the Brown family, ready for dinner. Needless to say, we did not go to their home for dinner. The television promoters fed us all at a very exclusive restaurant, the young couple included.

Soon after, we broke camp and headed north. But on our way, we would play the Cubs in one of the most interesting places I had ever played ball—Alpine, Texas. A wealthy rancher was holding the exhibition game on his ranch. I don't remember exactly how big his spread was. But we got off the train in Alpine—about 180 miles southeast of El Paso and 45 miles east of the Mexican border at the Rio Grande—and traveled 25 miles by car before reaching the ranch. The beautiful setup was high atop the very rugged plateau country. We were at 6,200 feet in elevation. In the distance some five or six miles north of us was the ballpark, nestled in a peaceful valley. You could see for miles in each direction. All of the land around us was owned by this one rancher.

The ballpark was used by the Alpine semi-pro team, which was operated by our wealthy host. The field was in beautiful shape and the stands held several thousand people. In this spacious Texas country, only little towns dot the map, separated from each other by 20 or 30 miles. At game time the stands were filled, and after the ball game, both teams were treated to a real tasty Texas barbecue. Several hundred people enjoyed the food and the occasion was quite festive. I ate heartily and consumed several steaks until someone told me I was eating antelope meat. For some reason, the thought of eating antelope prejudiced my gastric juices, but that didn't stop me from sampling the delicious cakes, pies and assorted desserts made for the occasion by the local women.

I had been playing well, and I had the feeling that Marty Marion was pulling for me to make the ball club. But toward the end of March, while running in the outfield, I felt something pop in the arch of my left foot. A shooting pain radiated immediately from that area. For the next six weeks I could not bear much weight on that foot, and I ran with a noticeable limp. X-rays at first showed nothing. As I limped around, I got the impression that some people started to think I was "jaking." A "jake" in baseball is one who feigns injury so he will not have to play. This angered me to no end. Why would I not want to play? X-rays taken several weeks later at Barnes Hospital revealed a hairline crack, or what is referred to as a stress fracture. Bob "Doc" Bauman, a splendid trainer for the Browns and a wonderful humanitarian, had diagnosed my injury even though the doctors were baffled. He began treatment and showed great care and understanding.

Bob Bauman was one of the finest sports trainers in the business. He knew his work and studied constantly. He would treat ex-ball players and friends at his training headquarters at St. Louis University, where he had been the trainer for many years. He helped all of these people free of charge, rendering long hours of treatment and loving care. Doc Bauman was honored in April 1978 at the Chase Park Plaza Hotel in St. Louis by over a thousand well-wishers at a testimonial dinner. I was proud to be one of the many in attendance that night. Trainers like Doc Bauman can mean a pennant to a contending team. His presence and know-how aided our club in preventing injuries and speeding up recovery time markedly after injuries occurred. He was a wizard in fostering rehabilitation of injured arms, legs

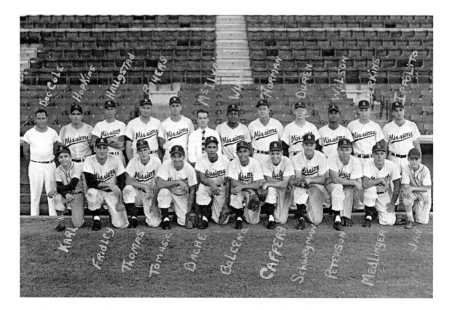

San Antonio Missions, Texas League, 1953. Tow row, left to right: Trainer Doc Cole, Charlie Hopkins, Phil Haugstad, Russ Bowers, Ed Mickelson, general manager Stan McIlvain, Charlie White, manager Bill Norman, Ryne Duren, Wilson, Perkins, Esposito; front row, left to right: bat boy Karl, Jim Fridley, Bud Thomas, Andy Tomasic, Bache, Bobby Balcena, Jim Caffery, Harry Schwegman, Peterson, Irv Medlinger, bat boy Jan. (Used by permission of San Antonio Missions.)

and egos. Hundreds of former college sports stars were at that banquet, attesting to Doc's healing touch. And many baseball players, present and past, also sang his praises. Stan Musial, Red Schoendienst and Bob Gibson were there, to name a few of the many who acknowledged Bob's expertise in lengthening their careers.

Six weeks after I hurt my foot, Marty called me to his office and told me I was going to San Antonio in the Texas League. I knew it was coming. I hadn't started a game and couldn't run since I'd been hurt. I was moving much better on it, but my chance at the big leagues had passed me by while I was hurt. And I had to accept the move to San Antonio.

Jo Ann and I left the next day and rented a little cottage from a loveable Texas couple, the Bennetts. Our little cottage was clean, cozy and had a nice screened-in porch. It nestled under some large trees in the backyard behind the Bennetts' home. Despite not having air conditioning, our window fan kept us cool during the dry San Antonio heat.

The San Antonio Missions were not a good ball club. We had our good games and our bad games, but we certainly were not as hopeless a group as that Decatur team. We had two African-Americans on the ball club in San Antonio: Charley White, a catcher, and Harry Wilson, a pitcher. This was my first experience playing on the same team with black players during the regular season, as opposed to a few weeks in spring training. Charley White was open, humorous and easy to get to know and like. He later went on to catch in the majors. Harry Wilson was quiet and reserved, and I never really got to know him well. But he was always pleasant despite his aloofness.

We had a great center fielder in Bobby Balcena. Bobby was 5'6", 175 pounds, a muscular guy who could really go get the ball. He was a good hitter, too, hanging around .300 all year. He was quite a player and a great guy to be around. Bobby was the best defensive center fielder I ever played with. In fact, at that time there was not a better defensive outfielder in all of baseball, as far as I was concerned. He went on to the major leagues and played briefly with Cincinnati.

Ryne Duren was an interesting young man who played for the Missions in that '53 season. I doubt I have ever seen anyone throw a baseball harder than Ryne. He wore very thick glasses—so thick that they were likened to the bottom of a glass milk bottle. The first game Ryne pitched after I got to San Antonio, he walked the bases loaded. I wondered why our manager didn't take him out. And I soon found out, as Ryne struck out the next three batters. He was temperamental, though, and was always fighting to control both his temper and his fastball.

His outbursts were something to behold. Ryne could be pitching well, striking out batter after batter, until he would just lose control—of his pitches and his cool. As he started to walk batters, he would become angrier and angrier with himself until he was absolutely seething. Finally, Jim Crandall, our manager would come out to the mound and wave in a new pitcher. Ryne would stalk off the mound and head for the dugout. As I looked in from my position at first base, I would see every San Antonio ball player clear off the bench and head to the clubhouse. No one would be on the bench when Duren arrived in the dugout, for Ryne would then go berserk. Towels would start flying out of the dugout onto the field. Bats, buckets and anything else he could get his hands on would soon follow. But one thing you could say for Ryne was that the scale of his temper equaled the velocity of his fastball.

On July 24th, 1953, we played a double-header in Tulsa. We had won the day game 2–1 as Phil Haugstad, a former Dodger, pitched us to victory over the Oilers. That game was called on *Mutual's Game of the Week*, which was broadcast nationwide. Each week, the Mutual Broadcasting Company would carry a minor-league game across the nation. That night Ryne was on the mound against Tulsa. In the fourth inning, Mike Lutz was batting for Tulsa and was hit on the forearm by a Duren fastball. The

Jo Ann Mickelson with Bill Borst, founder of the St. Louis Browns Fan Club, in September 1982. Jo Ann was the only wife present at the founding meeting of the St. Louis Browns Fan Club. The brownies created an award in her name after her death to symbolize the value placed upon the support given them by their wives. Our daughter, Julie Pedroley, accepted the award in her mother's honor.

popping noise was like a rifle shot heard round the park. Ryne had broken the arm of one of the strongest men in the league with an errant fastball.

I do not remember the park where we were playing but it was the second game of a double header. In the Minor Leagues at that time, the second game was only seven innings. We were in the fifth, and Ryne Duren was pitching a no hitter. I spotted a beautiful young lady sitting four rows above our first base dugout. When I bent over into my fielding stance, I was not looking at the plate. I was looking at her, and then focusing on the plate, just when the ball was delivered. Eventually, I continued my ogling a little too long, and when I glanced back toward the plate, the pitch had already been delivered. The ground ball headed my way, just to my right. Consequently, I got a late jump on the ball and dove, missing my glove by inches. The play was not that noticeable, but I knew if I had been focusing on the plate, I would have gotten a better jump and made the play. Duren went on to finish the game with a one hitter. Fifty years later I told Ryne the story when he turned up at the 2003 annual St. Louis Browns Dinner. He said that he did not remember the play or the one hitter.

Bill Norman relieved Jim Crandall as manager on the 9th of July. Jim was a likeable guy. But we were mired in last place and Bill ("Willie Card") Norman had come to San Antonio with one purpose in mind: "Get the Missions out of the coal hole." Bill was very close to Bill Veeck and was a knowledgeable baseball man. He had spent much of his 46 years of life in professional baseball. Bill loved baseball and beer, and not necessarily in that order. As far as I could judge, he was a close second to Harry the Hat as far as his ability to chatter constantly. Walker could talk on any subject, but Bill Norman talked only baseball. He called everybody "Laddie Buck" and made only one rule in our first pre-game meeting. He wanted no milk drinkers on his team. "You don't win pennants or get out of the coal hole with milk drinkers," he'd say. "Everybody drinks beer." No drastic changes occurred under Norman's tutelage, but we started to show some improvement.

The Texas League is a killer because of the intense heat and high humidity in most towns. Houston and Beaumont were the hottest towns with extreme humidity. Dallas, Ft. Worth, San Antonio, Tulsa, Oklahoma City and Shreveport had high temperatures as well, often exceeding 100 degrees. Most all of the games were played at night and the hotels were air-conditioned, but the heat took its toll anyhow. The Texas League was always known as a pitcher's league, with few batters ending the season over .300. My contention is that the combination of heat, humidity and talented pitchers finally wore the hitters down.

A very funny incident occurred on August 16th during the last trip of the Oklahoma City Indians to San Antone. Tom Tatum, their manager and a long-standing Texas Leaguer, was nearing the end of the line. On this particular day, Tommy was chipper and singing to himself as he taped the lineup card to the top of the dugout. I was fielding grounders at first base and yelled in, "Hey Tommy, what are you so happy about?" He said, "Well Mick, it's a beautiful day and the season is about to close, so I put my old bones in the lineup today." Down the left field line Duren had begun his warmups for the game. Tommy, who had moved to the other end of the dugout closer to me, asked, "Who is that pitching for you today, Mick?" I said, "Duren." "That's what I thought, but that guy warming up doesn't have any glasses on," said Tom. "Yeah, I know, Tommy," I said. "Duren has another one of his wild ideas today. He wants to pitch without his glasses." I had hardly gotten the words out of my mouth before Tommy Tatum was racing to the other end of the concrete dugout, sparks flying from his metal cleats, to grab the lineup card from the wall to remove his own name. All the while he was muttering aloud, "I'm not going to get myself killed this late in the season." Duren had that effect on people.

"Charlie White Night" at San Antonio Mission Stadium came with some good news and some bad news. The good news: Charlie White was presented with a brand new 1953 auto by the Negro Chamber of Commerce. The bad news: Charlie responded rather poorly, going hitless in four times at bat, dropping a pop foul for an error and grounding to the pitcher with the tying and winning runs on base in the ninth inning. It seemed to be a perennial pattern for a player to have a bad game when given a night in his honor.

"Willie Card" made good on his promise as manager. He got the San Antonio Missions out of the coal hole, but it took a double-header sweep of the Beaumont team on the last day of the season to do it. Duren won the first game, striking out 12 to raise his league-leading total to 212. In the second game, everybody chipped in as we got 15 hits and won 6–4. Bill Norman was elated and the beer flowed like wine, as Laddy Buck had just climbed his mountain. Bill Norman went on to manage the Detroit Tigers in the major leagues, though ever so briefly, and later passed away suddenly. I've never met a man who loved the game of baseball more than he did.

I was called up to play with the Browns at the close of the season, and I met the team on September 10th in Boston. From there we went to Philadelphia, New York, Chicago, Detroit and then back to St. Louis. I started a couple of games and I got to pinch hit in several others. The season was quickly coming to an end.

The Brownies first came to St. Louis in 1902, winning 78 and losing 58 for a .574 winning percentage under manager James R. McAleer. In 1922, the Browns finished second with a .604 percentage, their highest percentage ever for an entire season. The season attendance record was also set in that year when more than 712,900 fans saw the Browns play at Sportsman's Park. In 1939, the Brownies reached an all-time low with a .279 winning percentage—they went 43–111 under Fred Haney, who stayed on to manage them for two more seasons. The '44 Browns, though, surprised everyone, winning the pennant with 89 wins and 65 losses with Luke Sewell at the helm. The Browns clinched the American League pennant on October 1, 1944, before a club-record crowd of 34,625.

The Browns had many outstanding stars during their more than half century in the American League. None shone any brighter than George Sisler, who hit .420 in 1922 and had a lifetime average of .340. In 1920, George pounded out 257 hits—a major-league record that would stand until 2004—and stole 51 bases. But the old-timers who saw him play said his superb hitting and speed took a back seat to his fancy fielding. Through the years, the Browns had to sell off their best players to the wealthier teams in order to remain in operation. This kept them from ever becoming a contender year-in and year-out like the Yankees or Red Sox, who could buy the players they needed to stay in the pennant race. Besides Sisler and Rogers Hornsby, who were two of the all-time greatest, the Browns had Ken Williams, who set club records with 155 RBIs and 39 homers in 1922, and Urban Shocker, who won 27 games in 1921, George "Rube" Waddell, who struck out 232 batters in 1908 and Buck "Bobo" Newsom, who started 40 games in 1938, among others. One of them was Pete Gray, the one-armed outfielder who played for the Browns during World War II. Pete held his own as a player and was quite a drawing card in the 1945 season. Another Brownie notable was Ned Garver, the only pitcher to win 20 games for a team that lost 100 games. I recently asked Ned how he managed to win all those games in 1951 for a team with such a bad record. He said, "Ed, I lost two more games that season one-to-nothing!"

Bill Veeck, the one-time Browns owner, was an entrepreneur with a flair for the ridiculous. He had staged numerous crazy promotional nights in the minor leagues at Milwaukee. The conservative major-league owners ostracized him because they felt that the circus atmosphere he created was too undignified for a baseball game. Today many of his innovations are in vogue.

Probably the most bizarre of Veeck's promotions was the use of Eddie Gaedel, a midget, as a pinch-hitter on August 17, 1951, against Detroit. This was Gaedel's one and only at-bat in a major-league uniform. Bob Cain of the Tigers walked Gaedel on four pitches, and after the game the American League banned midgets from future play. Jim Delsing, who had a solid 10 years in the major leagues, is unfortunately remembered most often for being the only big-league player to pinch-run for a midget.

On September 27, 1953, in St. Louis, bags and boxes were packed for traveling and shipping, and players were thinking and talking of off-season activities. The sky was azure blue and a few fleecy white clouds wafted gently overhead as 3,174 fans ventured to see the Browns play their last game of the season. Billy Pierce was pitching for the Chicago White Sox, with future Hall of Famers Louis Aparicio at shortstop and Nellie Fox at second base, and the incomparable "Minnie" Minoso in left field. Our starter was a veteran pitcher, Duane Pillette. In the third inning, Johnny Groth hit a double to left center field and I singled to left field, driving him home. In the 7th inning "Jungle Jim" Rivera of the White Sox homered on top of the right pavilion, tying the game. The score remained tied until the top of the 11th when the Sox scored a go-ahead run.

With two outs in the bottom of the 11th, Jim Dyck, our third baseman, hit a lazy fly to center field to end the game at 3:44 p.m. The Browns had lost 2–1 and would never play in St. Louis again. And I had become a trivia question, "Who drove in the last run for the St. Louis Browns?"—because on September 30th, the Browns were sold for $2,475,000 to a syndicate in Baltimore, where they moved and became the Baltimore Orioles.

9

Gaedke's Gardens

Jo Ann and I pulled out of the driveway on a cold, gray February day in 1954. Her mother and father, Vesta and Art Menzel, were with us. Our 1950 blue two-door Ford was loaded down. We were traveling west to San Diego for a few days of fun before spring training. On our way we encountered some snow around Flagstaff, Arizona. The scenery was magnificent. We shot some movie film of Art and Vesta romping in the snow and of a deer we saw darting through the fir trees. The next morning when we got up, it was near zero degrees Fahrenheit, but it was a dry cold and not penetrating like the St. Louis weather we knew. When we got in the car to leave I said, "Guess what I have on to help keep me warm?" I answered my own question, "I left my pajama pants on." Art said, "So did I."

We arrived in San Diego and stayed for several days at the Caribbean Motel. It was out on a point and adjacent to the ocean. We relished the warm days, pleasant sunshine and good fishing. My father-in-law loved to fish and was enjoying himself out on the jetty trying for a big one. He then wanted to try some deep-sea fishing, so we made some reservations on a charter boat going out of San Diego. The next morning we got up at 4 a.m., had our breakfast and headed for the pier with great enthusiasm. We would be fishing for rock cod, a deep-running fish that was excellent eating. The rock cod's eyes would bug out when brought to the surface because of the pressure change. I was enjoying the boat ride to our fishing spot while talking to a real estate man from San Diego. We were both fantasizing about having property in the San Diego area for speculation when the seasickness hit me.

It was about 10 a.m. and I had been popping chocolate-covered peanuts to assuage my hunger. I ran to the restroom to throw up and was sick from 10 a.m. until we arrived back in port at 4:30 p.m. I felt fine as long as I lay down, but when I got up I became nauseated. As I lay there, Art kept pulling in rock cod and haughtily showing them to me. I got up once to join in when I had a fish on my line, but before I could bring it in I had to lie down quickly again. That fish story would always bring Art and me some hearty laughter whenever we recalled it through the years.

MOONIE TO THE RESCUE! MOONIE TO THE RESCUE!

Illustration by Ron Joyner.

Jo Ann and I spent some time with my Aunt Jo and Uncle Jack Harris in Van Nuys, California, before reporting to Yuma, Arizona, with the Browns-turned-Orioles for spring training in '54. We enjoyed their company and especially their good humor. My Uncle Jack was a great baseball fan and very interested in my progress. Jo's folks spent time visiting relatives in Los Angeles. Her dad flew back to St. Louis and Vesta went with us to Yuma. The way I hit when my mother-in-law was around, I should have kept her all season. Before we had gotten too far into spring training, Jo and her mother headed the blue Ford back to St. Louis to wait and see where I would be playing in the coming season.

Baltimore had decided to train out west, and though the uniforms were different, the players who started spring were essentially the same that finished the previous season in St. Louis. The following ex-Brownies were present that spring with the new Baltimore Orioles: infielders Vern Stephens, Billy Hunter, Jim Dyck, Bobby Young and Dick Kryhoski;

catchers Clint Courtney and Les Moss; outfielders Vic Wertz, Dick Kokos and Don Lenhardt; and pitchers Duane Pillette, Don Larsen, Bob Turley, Dick Littlefield, Marlin Stuart and Harry Brecheen.

The Flamingo Hotel and Yuma were not of the high caliber of the Mission Inn and Riverside, California. The Flamingo was on the highway a few miles out from Yuma and really was more of a motel than a hotel. The ballpark in Yuma was in pretty good shape. The ball traveled a long way because of the dry air, which also had humidity below 10 percent. My roomie, Howie Fox, a pitcher, had recently been traded from Cincinnati. We both complained of early-morning nosebleeds because of the dryness. Yuma is a place where you can get out of the shower and be dry before reaching the towel.

The spring of '54 was good for me because I got regular playing time. Dick Kryhoski was hit on the forearm with a pitch and suffered a broken bone. I played frequently after his injury and was hitting over .300 and driving in runs when the bad news came. Eddie Waitkus, a first baseman, had been purchased for $40,000. He was a great fielding first baseman who had played for the Phillies in the 1950 World Series against the Yankees. Eddie was later shot at close range in a Chicago hotel by a deranged female fan. The police found three scrapbooks owned by the woman, and all were filled with pictures of Waitkus. I've heard that the movie *The Natural*, starring Robert Redford as Roy Hobbs, was based on this shooting.

Anyway, Waitkus' arrival meant that I was gone. It was the most devastating thing I had to face in baseball to that point. I really felt that I belonged because the other players seemed confident in me, and I felt confident in myself. Soon after Waitkus was purchased, Bonneau Peters, the president of the Shreveport Sports, bought me for $7,500 from the Orioles. I went home to St. Louis, picked up Jo Ann and our belongings and set out to have my very best year in baseball.

I was back in the Texas League, the first time I had been in the same league two seasons in a row. Some players spent several years playing for the same team. Now, for the first time, I would be familiar with the towns and ballparks in a league as well as some of the players. It gave me a feeling of confidence, especially because I had a good season in that league the year before. The season opener found us playing in Shreveport before an opening night crowd of 5,214. We won 4–2 as Harry Heslet hit his first of 30 home runs that season. I went 0 for 4, one of the few games that season in which I wasn't a contributor. Shreveport was great to me. I loved the people, their staunch support and warm friendly attitude toward the players. Don't believe it when a player says that he doesn't hear the fans, or that the fans don't affect his play. He does, and they do. I contend that every ball player is, to some degree, affected by fan reaction.

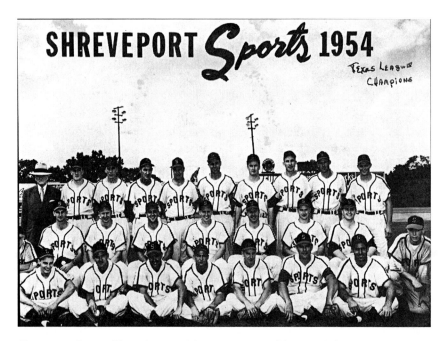

Shreveport Sports, Texas League Champions, 1954. Top row, left to right: Bonneau Peters, president; Jim Martin, catcher; Joe Piercy, pitcher, Fred Martin, pitcher; Harry Heslet, right field; Ed Mickelson, first base; Bob Smith, pitcher; John Andre, pitcher; Jim Willis, pitcher; Mel McGaha, manager. Middle row, left to right: Billy Raus, bat boy; Eve Joyner, left field; Jim Ackeret, third base, Doyle Lade, pitcher; Don Spencer, second base; Arnie Atkins, pitcher; Bob Van Eman, center field; Billy Muffett, pitcher. Front row, left to right: Joe Koppe, shortstop; Bob Nichols, catcher; J.W. Jones, catcher; Jake Jacobs, pitcher; Al Joe Hunt, infield utility; Dave Cyrus, pitcher; Ed Barr, center field; Glenn Hall, bat boy. The Sports were composed of experienced minor league players, including some with major league experience. (Used by permission of Texas League.)

Our third baseman, Jim Ackeret, was a rugged, steady ball player. There was nothing flashy about him. He was just a pleasant, broad-smiling guy who was there when you needed him with a base hit or a good play. He was the type of guy who made you feel better by just being around. Joe Koppe, our shortstop, had a tremendous arm and great fielding range. It seemed like he could make all the plays, plus he was a hustler. He went up to the big leagues later on. Don Spencer, our second baseman, was usually quiet and reserved, but he was steady and he provided us with a lot of laughs—especially when the moon was full.

In left field we had Harry Heslet, a veteran of Texas League play. Harry was slow of foot and hurt us at times defensively, but he was a major-league hitter who provided the Sports with about 30 homers and 100 RBIs pretty consistently. Eddie Barr played an excellent center field for us all year but never really found himself with the bat. Bob Van Eman hit well and played well defensively when we needed it in the outfield. Ev Joyner had a fabulous year, hitting .328 and playing excellent in the outfield.

John Andre, who wound up with twenty victories that year, was one of our better pitchers. John had great stuff and pitched excellent baseball for us. Bill Tremel, who went to the Cubs in the middle of the season, and Freddie Martin came in on many occasions to save games for John and the rest of the staff.

Freddie Martin is one of my all-time favorites. He was in his late thirties at the time but was able to rise to any occasion. Freddie broke me up when he would walk into a game bouncing on his tiptoes as if walking on eggs. He would give that sly grin of his, throw his sidearm sinker for a double play with the bases loaded, and tiptoe to the dugout, getting us out of one jam after another. I gained enormous respect for the man as a player and as a person. Fred Martin was one of the toughest and coolest competitors I have ever seen operate in stress situations. Years later, as pitching coach for the Chicago Cubs, Fred taught Bruce Sutter the split-finger fastball, making him one of the most dominant relievers for a decade.

Jim Willis, Otis Jacobs, Arnie Atkins, Joe Piercey, Doyle Lade and Billy Muffett, a future big-leaguer, rounded out our pitching staff, with lefty Bob Smith coming on strong for us as the year went on.

J.W. Jones did most of our catching. J.W. was quiet and a real gentleman, but as tough as nails behind the plate. Jim Martin did a good job replacing J.W. on occasion at the catcher's spot. Bob Nichols was a utility catcher, and the utility infielder was my roomie, Al Joe Hunt.

Mel McGaha, our first-year manager, did a superb job of running the team. He also filled in more than adequately at several positions in the infield and outfield, as well as at catcher.

This crew lacked the overall talent of several other teams in the league, but we fought and scratched and picked each other up. The *Shreveport Times* advertised that 1,364,000 people lived within 100 miles of town. And baseball fever seemed to infect a good portion of them during that '54 season. The Shreveport papers were big on the Sports, their Texas League entry. The sports sections had headlines on all of our games, plus write-ups of all the other Texas League games. Jack Fiser wrote for the *Shreveport Times* and Otis Harris for the *Shreveport Journal*. Both were also sports editors for their papers and were excellent journalists. Jack Fiser, who also had a sports program at 5:15 p.m. and 10:15 p.m. on radio station KWKH, really put the monkey on my back.

Jack wrote in the *Journal* on May 21st, "Could it be true that as Ed

Mickelson goes, so go the Shreveport Sports? As every fan knows, the Sports' 1954 record to date falls into three distinct periods: The one from opening day to April 18th, when the team won 11 of 12. The one from April 19th to May 20th, when they lost 18 of 21. And the subsequent comeback, during which they won seven out of eight.

"If you'll break down Mickelson's batting performance, you'll find that it coincides almost exactly with that of the team. During the getaway streak, Ed walloped the ball for a .500 average by virtue of 23 hits in 46 at bats and batted in 20 runs and hit four homers. During the collapse, he got only 18 blows in 86 trips, batted in only seven runs and hit no homers.

"Since the club quit losing, guess what Edward has contributed? Just 14 hits in 27 at bats, four more round-trippers and eight RBIs for a phenomenal .519 average."

I had put great pressure on myself after being sent down from Baltimore. I personalized the articles that were being written about me, and I began to feel very much responsible for the plight of that ball club.

I think what prompted Jack Fiser's comments were the night I had in a double-header on May 20th that preceded his article the next day. I had my best night in baseball, going 3 for 3 in the first game while driving in four runs, and 3 for 4 the next game, driving in four more, with three home runs that night.

On the night of June 10th at LaGrave Field in Ft. Worth, Harry Heslet hit three home runs and drove in seven runs. I hit a bases-loaded homer in the 1st inning and another homer in the eighth for five RBIs. Heslet and I quite often had big games together, as we batted in 239 runs between us that season.

We won our ninth in a row on the 18th of June and Ev Joyner was starting to come on as a hitter. He was extremely fast and hit slashing line drives, which accounted for his 47 doubles. Lou Colombo's long-ago comments from 1949 in Columbus, Georgia, about Rocky Marciano were brought to mind that night. The Rock defeated Ezzard Charles in 15 rounds at Yankee Stadium, becoming the heavyweight boxing champion of the world.

We were to open a crucial series against Houston, a team that I felt to be the best in our league, with Ken Boyer, Don Blasingame, Bob Boyd, Hal Smith, Larry Jackson, Luis Arroyo, Bob Tiefanauer and Willard Schmidt all going on to the major leagues. Houston drew well over 300,000 fans that season in the then-fastest growing city in the United States. The Houston players loved the town. Many of them got good jobs and stayed there. Buff Stadium, a beautiful ballpark, held over 10,000 fans. And 6,200 people were in the stands to watch this important series begin. We were leading the league with Houston only 4½ games behind us.

We had taken batting and infield practice and were waiting for the playing of the National Anthem. As both pitchers were warming up, a golden glow appeared, ever so slightly over the left field fence. A few minutes later, you could easily discern this glow coming from one of the biggest and fullest moons imaginable. All of our players and even our manager Mel McGaha heaved a sigh of relief. It was as if we had won the game before we played it. Everyone was laughing and giggling, and Koppe yelled at Spencer, "Moonie, do you see that full moon?" Ackeret said, "My God, we'll take them tonight." These were intelligent young men, many with college educations, believing to a man that we would win because the moon was full and Don "Moonie" Spencer's celestial powers would take over for us.

That first night of the full moon, July 10, 1954, in the second inning with one man on, Moonie Spencer hit a home run as we won 2–1 behind the pitching of Jim Willis. Next was a Sunday day game. Without the benefit of the full moon, Moonie lost his effectiveness, and we lost 4–3 in 11 innings. The next game at night Moonie doubled in a run in the 9th inning and McGaha hit a 2-run homer behind him to win the game 6 to 5. In the final game of the series Moonie's home run won the game.

In baseball, you don't try to figure out the exploits of a guy like Don Spencer under a full moon. You just accept it because you lived it, saw it and felt it happen. So gamblers beware, there is more to a game than who's pitching or catching or injured. You also have to consider the planets, the stars and the moon. God bless you, Moonie, wherever you are.

We took time out that summer to watch the Major League All-Star Game on television. And it gave me a chance to relax and reflect on some earlier years in baseball as I watched Ray Jablonski play for the National League All-Stars. As I rooted for Ray, my old roommate from Columbus, Georgia, I wondered if he was still washing out his clothes by hand.

The Texas League All-Star Game was played in Ft. Worth on July 23rd. My wife had her first plane ride. Jo Ann's cousin Dorothy lived with her husband Harvey Ferris in Ft. Worth. So Jo Ann and a couple of other wives flew over for the game, with my wife remaining for a visit with her relatives. I was representing the South as their first baseman.

Ken Boyer played third base, Don Blasingame was our shortstop and Howie Phillips was at second. Heslet and Joyner from the Sports joined Ed Knoblach in the outfield. John Andre, Ryan Duren, Willard Schmidt, Dave Hillman, Gene Jansce and Bob Smith were our pitchers. Dick Rand and Jim Fanning caught for us.

It was a great evening in Ft. Worth's LaGrave Field. 6,177 fans saw the game as a total of 29 hits filled the night air. But Willie Brown and Les Fleming hit solo homers and Buzz Clarkson hit two more, leading the North to a 9–8 victory. I had three hits and enjoyed the evening very much.

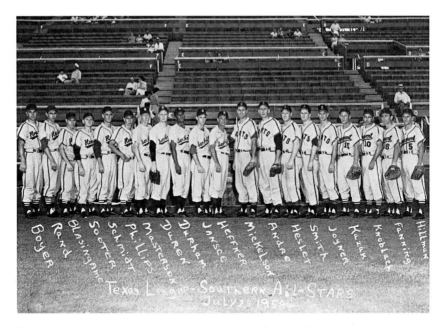

Texas League All-Stars, July 23, 1954. Several of these players went on the major leagues: Boyer, Blasingame, W. Schmidt, Duren, Mickelson, B. Smith, Kazak, Fanning, and Hillman. Both teams were given nice Elgin watches for playing in this game. Our watches all had "Texas League All-Stars" on the face. Mine still ticks right along when I remember to wind it. (Used by permission of Texas League.)

We all received Lord Elgin watches with "Texas League All-Stars" inscribed on them. I have become attached to that watch and have kept it all these years.

Bonneau Peters was to have a "night" in Shreveport in August of 1954. He was in his 17th year as president of the Shreveport Sports, a conservative, forthright man and very outspoken. Mr. Peters let you know exactly how he felt about things. On his night, 3,683 fans turned out to pay homage with gifts and many kind words. The country was just starting its social movement toward civil rights and racial equality, though Bonneau Peters had openly stated that no black would ever play on his team. Most clubs in the league had black players, but not us. Our black fans sat in a section down the right field line demeaningly referred to by some as the "coal hole." To me, our black fans were just like any other good baseball fans and were highly supportive of the Shreveport Sports.

Bonneau Peters was gruff at times but was basically a kind man. He would do anything for you if he liked you. He was well thought of throughout the Texas League and especially the Shreveport area. Unfortunately, he never changed his stand regarding black players.

One of my favorite black players was Buzz Clarkson. Buzz was too old to make the big time because he was already in his early forties in 1954. But what a hitter he was—and must have been in the Negro Leagues in his youth. He stood 5'10" and weighed about 190 pounds, with tremendous shoulders and a large upper torso. One night he hit a ball at Joe Koppe, our shortstop, during a game against Dallas at Shreveport. Koppe leaped for the ball, just missing it with the tip of his glove. The ball kept rising, and it sailed on to clear the 10-foot-high wall in left-center for a home run. Buzz was a great ball player. He hit .326 and drove in 126 runs for Dallas that season. I believe he would have enjoyed many years of major-league success if he had not been denied the opportunity to play at an earlier age because of his color.

One time in Shreveport, our entire club attended a barbecue after a Sunday game. One of the wealthy local oilmen invited the team out for food, fun and frolic. Huge trees served as umbrellas, blotting out the late afternoon sun, and a breeze helped to make the evening tolerable. We were treated to a feast of chicken, beef, corn on the cob and cold drinks. The players and wives were having a fun time, eating and enjoying each other's company, but I was bugged by something during the festivities. Just outside the owner's bedroom window, an oil well was pumping with a methodical rhythm that never stopped: KA-CLANG, KA-CLANG, KA-CLANG, never varying its pace. I asked our host how the devil he could sleep with all that constant noise. "Ed," he responded, "if that noise ever quits, that's when I won't be able to sleep."

One of our biggest fans in Shreveport was Mrs. Louise Curry, an elderly lady who was confined to a wheelchair by an arthritic condition. She never missed a home game. Although she loved all the Shreveport Sports, Harry Heslet was her favorite. Harry had a heart as big as a watermelon. He doted over her, often helping her from the car to her wheelchair and rolling her into the ballpark. Harry, all 230 pounds of him, was a sight to see as he wheeled little old Mrs. Curry to her special seat in the park. She loved that big lout, as well as the rest of her Shreveport Sports. She gave me five dollars at the end of the season in appreciation for my efforts that year. I didn't want to take her money, but as I looked into her sincere and grateful face, I couldn't find it in my heart to refuse her. She was a remarkable woman with enthusiasm and kindness for everyone in spite of her condition.

Karl Spooner, in my opinion, had the best-moving fastball in the Texas League that year. In fact, Spooner had one of the liveliest fastballs ever. In 1954, I had started to keep a book on all the pitchers and what they threw to me on each pitch. I would go back to the hotel after the game to write it down, pitch by pitch. It gave me an idea of what to expect in certain situations if I met the pitcher again. Spooner must have figured I was a fastball hitter, because when I saw him early in the season he threw me slow stuff—curves and change-ups. I was very successful hitting off him in those early games. Toward the end of the season he changed his tactics. All I saw was "smoke." Spooner had a slow windup and his ball seemed to explode, rising over a foot on the way to the plate. He must have struck me out at least 10 times the last three or four games I faced him, as I consistently swung under his hopping fastball.

Karl won 21 games in '54 for Ft. Worth, giving up only 165 hits in 233 innings. He led the league in strikeouts with 260, and I contributed greatly to that number. Karl had bad feet and bad knees, though, and could do very little running to keep his legs in shape. He went up to the big leagues at the tail end of the season. Pitching for the Brooklyn Dodgers, Spooner beat the New York Giants in his debut on September 22, 1954. He ended up setting a major-league record with 15 strikeouts in his first game. The second game he pitched, he struck out 12 Pittsburgh Pirates. To boot, his first two games were shutouts. Since the big leagues have been around, no pitcher had ever come on the scene like Karl Spooner, but later he hurt his arm and never was able to fulfill his potential. I don't claim to be an authority, but in my few official times at bat in the majors I did see some outstanding pitchers. Allie Reynolds, Billy Pierce, Warren Spahn, Don Drysdale, Virgil Trucks, Larry Jansen all pitched to me, but none threw as hard as Duren and Spooner. And Spooner was the most overpowering pitcher with the greatest-moving fastball I ever batted against.

During the month of August 1954, there were many eventful occurrences in sports. Bobo Olson and Rocky Marciano were the talk of the boxing world. Roger Bannister broke the four-minute mile. Ken Boyer hit safely in 30 consecutive Texas League games, and the Shreveport Sports were on their way to their first full-season Texas League pennant. Back in 1919, Shreveport had won a split-season championship.

In non-sports events, John Wayne was starring in *Fort Apache*, James Stewart was in *The Glenn Miller Story*, and Dean Martin and Jerry Lewis were in *Living It Up*. On a Thursday evening of television, starting at 7 p.m. you could see Liberace, *This Is Your Life*, *Dragnet*, *Ford Theater*, *Inner Sanctum*, *Place the Face* and the news at 10 in the Central Time Zone. On radio every afternoon was *Road to Life*, *Ma Perkins* and *Young Dr. Malone*. An Oldsmobile 88 two-door sedan sold for $2,595. Sport shirts were on sale for $1.95, straw hats for $3.15, men's slacks for $4.95 and Hart Schaffner and Marx suits were reduced to $32.50.

It was common among ball players to invite each other to dinner while they were on the road, especially if you had played with them before and had established a friendship. When they were in town for a series, my buddies Ryne Duren and Charley Hopkins from the San Antonio club came out to our apartment for dinner. The local butcher was a baseball fan and really gave us choice cuts of meat for nominal prices. Jo Ann had spent extra time and care to prepare an excellent meal. We chatted about the season and the happenings at San Antonio the previous year and the well-being of their wives and sons. As Duren was about to leave, he said, "Thanks a lot, Jo, for a great meal. And Mick, I'll see you in San Antonio in a few weeks."

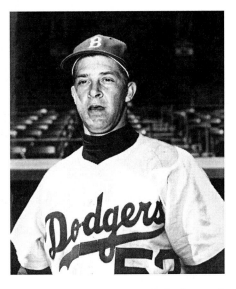

And a few weeks later in San Antonio, Ryne Duren was on the mound with the Missions six games behind us and fading. I came up in the first inning with a man on first base and Duren was throwing his usual, out-of-control smoke. The first pitch was head-high and behind me. A ball thrown at over 90 miles an hour from 60 feet, 6 inches, is upon a batter in a fraction of a second. Fortunately for me, I reacted in that split second by moving downward and forward. If I had fallen backward, the ball would have struck me in the head. The pitch ended up at the

Karl Spooner went on to pitch the last week of the 1954 season with the Brooklyn Dodgers. I thought he was the most overpowering pitcher I ever faced. He threw a phenomenal rising fast ball directly over the top, with tremendous velocity. For his first major league start, he struck out 15 Giants on three singles and shut them out. In his next start against the Pirates, he struck out 12, allowed four hits and had another shutout. That's 27 strikeouts in 18 innings and two shutouts. Those two games removed any doubts I had about my inability to get hits off him. The major league hitters didn't do any better than I did. Unfortunately for him and for baseball, he injured his arm the next spring and was never the same. Just think what an incredible career he might have had. (National Baseball Hall of Fame Library, Cooperstown, New York.)

screen, and the runner advanced. As I lay on my right side in the dirt, gathering my wits, these thoughts quickly went through my mind, and in this order:

That son-of-a-bitch threw at me, he could have killed me, that's the last time I'll feed him.

But Ryne had said, "I'll see you in San Antonio." He saw me all right. Even friends become enemies during ballgames. I won't say I wore Duren out as a hitter. He was tough. He got me out sometimes, but I got my hits too.

I recently saw Charley Hopkin, who was the catcher for the Missions in '54, at a St. Louis Browns dinner in St. Louis. I asked for years if he had called a knockdown pitch from Ryne, and he always said, "No!" This time I asked and he said, "Yes!" I asked what kind of signal he gave Ryne. Generally the catcher would waggle his fingers when a knock was on. Charley said, "Mick, he could hardly see my fingers. I had to waggle my whole mitt back and forth."

We were hot in August of '54 and so was I. We took three straight games from San Antonio late in August at Shreveport, knocking them out of contention. We went into Houston with eight games to play. Oklahoma City was four down and in second place, while Houston was five back. We won that first game in Houston 6–1 before 11,483 Buff fans. Oklahoma City lost that night, too, so we were now five games ahead with just seven to go. It was a good thing, too, because a hot Houston team took us the next three games. Close to 35,000 fans saw that four-game series and Houston had drawn 310,531 fans that season, best in the league. The payoff to the Shreveport organization for the four-game series was $6,514—an all-time record payday for a visiting club in the Texas League.

As I toured the league, I found that the cities of Dallas and Tulsa were clean and cosmopolitan. Houston, with its multitude of freeways, was fast-moving, fast-growing and exciting. San Antonio resembled the Old West with an interesting Mexican flavor. Ft. Worth was called "Cow Town," with a very redeeming quality—the best-looking women in the United States. Oklahoma City was hot—the temperature reached 115 degrees at one point that year—but the humidity was low and the breezes were dry. Dry or not, 115 degrees is hot. Beaumont, Texas, though, was the end of the line in the Texas League. The temperature was high, the humidity oppressive, the mosquitoes were trophy-sized, the ballpark and hotel were the worst, and the whole darn town shut down every night at about 9 p.m.

But on Saturday, September 4, 1954, on the Labor Day weekend, Beaumont became a paradise for the Shreveport Sports. The *Shreveport Times* carried this headline in the Sunday paper: "Sports Win First Regular Season Title!" Jack Fiser wrote it like this: "Let 'em ring out the bells in Caddo, boys. The Sports are in—the mighty men of Mel McGaha— paced by the skipper himself, gave Shreveport its first straight-way Texas League championship tonight by mauling Beaumont 8–1, while second place Houston was absorbing an 8–3 shellacking from the San Antonio Missions."

It had been a long, hard-fought season. We may not have had the best talent in the league, but we had earned the championship. Several cases of beer came into the clubhouse, and in that small, dimly-lit room, we had a hell of a time. We sat there for at least an hour after the game in our sweaty shorts, drinking, laughing, joking and dousing each other with beer. All the pent-up emotions of five long months were released in that jovial locker room. From there it was out on the town for the rest of the night in celebration. I drank my beer, shared in the jubilation, and later returned to the hotel with a deep sense of gratitude for what we accomplished—the team and myself. An intense feeling of self-satisfaction welled up within me.

To me and to the rest of the Shreveport Sports, the rest of the season seemed anti-climactic. All emotions had been spent, and we went flat. This would hold true for the remaining three games of the regular season and, unfortunately, the playoffs as well.

After clinching the pennant, we had returned to Shreveport and were honored with a motorcycle parade and speeches by dignitaries, with the key to the city given to Mel McGaha, our manager. But Mr. Spooner and the Forth Worth Cats took us 3–2 in 12 innings in the first game of the playoffs in Shreveport. We won the second game 7–1. But the Cats swept the next three games 9–5, 9–8 in eleven innings and 2–0, with Spooner getting the last win. Our season had ended.

The minor-league draft took place in Houston on November 30th. The last-place team in the highest minor league was Portland, Oregon, of the open-classification Pacific Coast League. Open classification meant that if a player was purchased by a major-league team, he could choose to stay with his team instead of reporting to the major-league team. Portland chose me from Shreveport for the $10,000 draft price. I received the news with mixed feelings. It was a real honor to know that of 8,500 minor league ball players, I had been picked first in the draft. But I was disappointed that no major-league ball club had deemed my season's credentials good enough to purchase me.

After Portland drafted me I was not aware of what had transpired between Mr. Bonneau Peters, the president of the Shreveport team, and Joe Ziegler, the general manager of the Portland Beavers. According to L. H. Gregory, in his article that appeared in *The Sporting News* in August 1955, Mr. Peters went to Mr. Ziegler and said, "I know you won't take me up on it, but I'm saying it just the same. I'll give you back your $10,000 for Mickelson, and $7,500 besides, if you'll turn him back. That is how I feel about that boy, and how my Shreveport fans feel. He was one of the best kids at putting out and one of the most popular players we've ever had. Even if you did take me up, I know someone else would grab him—but it shows you what I think of him."

The Shreveport story didn't end for me until January 30, 1957. An older gentleman, Mr. Frank Grosjeans, who worked for the *Shreveport Journal* and corresponded with me through the years, sent me a clipping from the paper. It was an article written by Jimmy Bullock about Albert Gaedke, the Shreveport Sports' groundskeeper, who was 65 then. Gaedke had a little cottage in the ballpark adjacent to the dressing room used by the umpires. He was so good at his trade and kept the ball field in such superb condition for so many years that the field was later nicknamed "Gaedke's Gardens."

In this article, Bullock wrote that "Gaedke has a bag full of stories. Most of the tales involve former Shreveport players. Gaedke's All-Star Texas League Team includes Al Mazar at second base, Bob Kennedy at third base, Salty Parker at shortstop and Ed Mickelson at first base. The outfielders were Vernon (George) Washington, Hal Simpson, Pete Fleming, and Paul Easterling. The pitchers he picked were Gordon Maltzberger, Warren Hacker, Doyle Lade, and Ralph "Buzz" Hamner, and the catchers were Bill Sarni, Herb Crompton, and Joe Kracher. Ed Mickelson, Shreveport's first baseman three seasons ago, is tabbed by Gaedke as the best player he has seen in his Gardens."

So thanks, Al Gaedke, for a most cherished compliment about a memorable season. And wherever you are, please forgive me for the times I tore up your bat rack in a fit of anger.

Harry Caray, the Cardinal broadcaster, cornered me in the Cardinal dugout upon my return to St. Louis. The Cardinals were ending the season, and he asked me about Ken Boyer as a possible Cardinal third baseman. I said, "Harry, he is great. He can run, he has a strong arm, he is a splendid fielder and a good power hitter." Boyer did go up with the Cards the next year and became one of their all-time greatest players. What I wanted to scream into Harry's ear and in the ear of baseball executives everywhere was that, in the same league and against the same pitchers, Boyer hit .319 and I hit .335. Boyer drove in 119 runs, I drove in 139. His team came in second, mine won the pennant. It may sound like sour grapes, but I was getting resentful watching other guys get a shot.

10

The Pacific Coast League

The days Jo Ann and I spent with Portland, Oregon, in the Pacific Coast League were the most enjoyable in our baseball travels. Portland and the Coast League had a number of pluses. The weather was a most welcome change. After spending most of my baseball summers in the hot sunbelt states, it was a pleasant change to feel cool summer breezes, see snow-capped Mt. Hood and dangle my feet in the fresh mountain streams of Oregon.

At the time there wasn't a great discrepancy between salaries in the Coast League and in the big leagues. In fact, some ball players were making more money in the Coast League than they did in the majors. The major-league minimum salary at that time was $7,500 and there were more than a few major leaguers around that figure. The travel in the Coast League was by plane, and at that time most major-league teams were still traveling by train. Except for holidays, every Monday was an open date, with double headers played on Sunday. This gave a player time off from Sunday night until late Tuesday afternoon. Each series at home or away was played for one whole week, and when we played the Los Angeles Angels and then the Hollywood Stars, we wouldn't even change hotels. The Coast League wasn't the big time, but it was the next thing to it. In those years it was referred to as the Other Major League.

The Coast League had some of the best scenery and the greatest cities in baseball. Its cities in '55 were exciting and beautiful. Some places had flowers, palm trees and grass growing the year around. Los Angeles and Hollywood were starting to become too crowded. But apart from that, and the smog and the traffic, they were exciting cities. The San Francisco-Oakland and San Diego areas had it all—beauty, weather, entertainment, lush vegetation and the best restaurants in the world. Sacramento was hot during the day, but by 10 p.m. the cool, dry breeze often led one to don a sweater. Portland and Seattle were more "down home" kinds of cities with less hoopla and excitement, but both had a natural beauty that was unsurpassed in most other places in this country.

Robert Clay Hopper, manager of the Portland Beavers, was born October 3, 1902, in Porterville, Mississippi, and was living in Greenville,

YOU HANGIN' IN THERE, SAMMY? SAMMY...

Illustration by Ron Joyner.

Mississippi. He had been a minor league outfielder from 1926 to 1941. In '46, he was named Minor League Manager of the Year as he led Montreal to the pennant, the Governor's Cup and the Junior World Series. In '52 he was named Manager of the Year in the Pacific Coast League by the PCL Baseball Writers. Clay Hopper, who came from the Deep South, was Jackie Robinson's first manager in pro baseball at Montreal in '46. Black players should have been playing in the major leagues long before, and Jackie's entrance into professional baseball, I feel, led the way for the civil rights movement that followed.

Clay had a thick Southern accent and a gravelly voice. He was rough

Last-Place Finish Brought Beavers First-Base Prize

Portland Grabbed Mickelson as Lead-Off Choice in Draft

By L. H. GREGORY
PORTLAND, Ore.

Does it ever actually pay to be a tailender? "Yes," emphatically replies Joe Ziegler, general manager of the Portland Beavers of the Pacific Coast League, and proceeds to give name, date and occasion.

It was at the minor league draft session in Houston last December when their 1954 tail-end Coast league status gave the Beavers first call in the draft. They selected Ed Mickelson, six-foot, three-inch, 205-pound, .335-hitting 28-year-old first baseman from Shreveport of the Texas League.

"That's an instance when it was worth close to a general manager's weight in gold (Ziegler isn't a very heavy man) to have been a lastplacer," continues Ziegler. "Every other club in our Open Classification league, and each of the 16 Class AAA clubs of the American Association and International League, had a greedy eye on Mickelson. In short, 24 clubs would have snapped him up, but being tailenders in Open Classification gave us first choice, and our man, at the bargain price of $10,000.

Ed Leads Club at Bat

"And we haven't regretted it. Mickelson leads our club at bat with a .313 average, he is first in runs batted in with 84, he has made most hits on the club with 165, and on top of all this he's the best fielding first baseman in the league. All this came to us on a platter from having had the luck to be tail-ender at just the right time!"

In fact, as a fielder, Mickelson set a new league record in action through August 21 by handling 504 chances without an error. The previous mark for first basemen was 498, held by Chuck Stevens, now a player-coach with the Seals.

An interesting sidelight on Mickelson is that after Portland had taken

Basement Bargain

Ed Mickelson

him in the draft, Bonneau Peters of the Shreveport club came to Ziegler and said: "I know you won't take me up, but I'm saying it just the same. I'll give you back your $10,000 for Mickelson, and $7,500 besides, if you'll turn him back. That's how I feel about that boy, and how my Shreveport fans feel. He was one of the best kids at putting out and one of the most popular players we've ever had. Even if you did take me up, I know someone else would grab him—but it shows you what I think of him."

After coming to the Pacific Coast League from the Texas loop, Mickelson was slow to start and there were a few early fears that he might not make it. But once he got going, there was no stopping him. Other first basemen may be more spectacular and one or two will hit more homers and drive in more runs. But for a combination of allround, reliable play, he can't be beat. One impressive thing about this

earnest-minded college graduate, who expects to have a master's degree in physical education next spring to go with his present AB degree, is the way he fights his way out of slumps. He has them, like all other players. But when he goes into one it never affects his general play, as with so many. It merely seems to make him more determined and rougher at bat. Gradually he battles his way out of the slump, a quality that has won praise from Manager Clay Hopper.

"Hangs Tough in There," Says Hopper

"He hangs tough in there," says Hopper. "Give me a player like that and you'll never hear a complaint from me. That's the type of player we are always looking for, and so seldom get."

Mickelson attended Oklahoma A & M, and thought so much of his college degree that he was late at some training camps rather than let his college work slip. Since graduating he has been putting in winter work at Washington University of St. Louis, working for a master's degree in physical ed. He is about half through the prescribed course and eventually hopes to become a high school coach. He played high school basketball as well as baseball. He also does child welfare work.

Of course, Ed has major league ambitions. Twice he had brief tries with the St. Louis Cards, and again with the former St. Louis Browns, but each time he was returned to the minors. He has never had what would be called a real trial—and Beaver fans, though with best wishes for the always amiable young man's future, hope he can leave Portland for the majors next season.

Ed's batting specialty is long drives to right center. Though he has 12 home runs for the season, he's more the line drive type of two-base hitter, with 30 for the Coast league season to date.

I felt much honored being the first draft pick of 8,000 minor league players. L.H. Gregory is very generous. (*The Oregonian*, used by permission.)

as a leather boot. In one of our first team meetings, I was ready to request an interpreter as Clay Hopper said, "Boys, ya'll gonna git rail soah these fust few daies—specially yo ahms, yo laeggs and yo ahss." Sam Calderone, who would soon become my roommate and close friend for the next three seasons, just about fell off his stool trying to suppress laughter. Don't get me wrong. We respected Clay immensely. But whenever things got dull during the season, Sam would look at me and exclaim, "Hey Mick, remember you got to take good care of 'yo ahms, yo laeggs, and yo ahss!'"

He must be at park by 9:30 for at least a six-hour workout, batting, catching, running, often a game.

Above, opposite page and page 142: I was featured in "The Beavers ... New Faces of 1955," in *The Oregonian*.

During spring training at Glendale, Ed and Jo Ann Mickelson stay at motel near field. She cooks hearty breakfast.

Sunday Oregonian   Portland, Oregon
                                                     April 17, 1955

Northwest   ROTO MAGAZINE

Ed Mickelson, First Base (See "The Beavers: New Faces of 1955." Page 6)

Jo Ann and I stayed in a motel with a kitchen, bath and bedroom. We got a special rate but the quarters were really cramped. Spring training was slow-paced, with much time being spent getting to know new teammates and their wives. Jo Ann and I established relationships with Angie and Sam Calderone, as well as Muriel and Bob Hall, which lasted well after the baseball days were over. Angie, Muriel and Jo Ann became inseparable that season and in the ones to follow.

We opened in Los Angeles against the Angels in early April. The ballpark was called Wrigley Field after P.K. Wrigley, the chewing gum magnate, who also owned the Chicago Cubs. It was a beautiful ballpark with a white stucco exterior, large grandstands and bleachers in right field. The dimensions were 349 feet to left field, 339 to right and 412 to center. The alleys in left field and right-center were short. During the day, the ball carried well because the air was dry, but at night, with the ocean breeze, the air became denser. The seating capacity was major league at 25,000.

The opening game, whether it is played in the home ballpark or the visitors', is a time of apprehension. We were in our spacious clubhouse on the grandstand level above the playing field. As I remember it, we all gathered around Clay Hopper, listening to his pre-game words of wisdom. After that chat we were anxiously awaiting the start of the game. Time hung heavy and the tension grew. Glen Elliott, a stellar left-handed pitcher for that Portland club, was sitting on the hard concrete floor in the corner of the room. He broke the silence with a deafening fart that bounced off the concrete floor, the walls, the ceiling and back off the floor again. Everyone was laughing and the air of tension had been broken. The Elliot-relaxed Beavers marched out of the locker room only to be annihilated by L.A. in the opener, 9–5.

For our second series of the season, we drove through northern California to get to San Francisco. The weather in Frisco was cold and windy. In the series opener, long underwear was the order of the evening as we beat the Seals 4–2 with Bill Werle pitching a four-hitter. San Francisco's weather is cold and damp in the spring months and even during most of the summer. It is not unusual for the temperature to be in the chilly 50s at midday in July. Nights can be very chilly and extremely windy. A pop fly went up one night in Seals Stadium and I thought it had gone completely out of the ballpark. But the wind caught it and kept pushing it back toward the field. I made a late dash to catch it, but the ball landed in foul territory, just a few feet in front of the first row of box seats. A leather-lung fan got on me for my negligence on that popup. Some fans, like people in general, never forget or forgive. That fan was on my butt for the next three seasons.

The San Francisco fans had one idiosyncrasy that, as far as I know, was exhibited only at their ballpark. Royce Lint, a knuckleballer who had pitched the year before for the St. Louis Cardinals, was removed from the game in San Fran one night in the fourth inning when it happened: Out came the white handkerchiefs of the Frisco fans as they waved goodbye to Lint as he was striding off the mound for the dugout. On Sunday doubleheaders with a large crowd in the stands—Frisco also sat 25,000—thousands of white handkerchiefs would flutter in the breeze as a chagrined visiting pitcher left the mound to a silent, but visible, parting gesture.

A LA CARTE LIST

RELISHES AND SALADS

Anchovies (for 2)	1.00	Shrimp Cocktail	.75
Cracked Crab	1.25	Crab Cocktail	.75
Roman Antipasto (for 2)	1.50	Crab Salad	1.25
Prosciutto	1.00	Avocado Salad	1.00
Stuffed Celery	.50	Salad Bowl	.75
Pigs' Feet	.50	Lettuce, Sliced Tomatoes	.75
Ripe or Green Olives	.50		

(Roquefort Dressing . . . .50c extra)

SOUP

Soup du Jour	.35	Consomme	.35

FISH

Broiled Lobster	2.50	Abalone	2.25
Lobster Thermidor	2.50	Scallops	2.25

ITALIAN PASTE

Homemade Ravioli	1.35	Spaghetti	1.00
Lasagne	1.35	Sauce, to order	.50c extra

STEAKS AND CHOPS

Broiled Porterhouse (for 2)	8.30	Frog Legs Florentine	3.00
Broiled Filet Steak	4.15	Filet Mignon Tips Brochette	3.15
Broiled New York Cut Steak	4.15	Filet Mignon Tips Brochette with	
Broiled Lamb Chops		Wild Rice and Mushrooms	4.15
(extra thick)	3.00	Veal Scallopini	2.75
Broiled Chateaubriand (for 2)	8.50	Sweetbreads and Mushrooms	2.75

(Bordelaise Sauce . . 50c extra)

POULTRY

Chicken, en Casserole	2.75	Chicken Cacciatora	2.75
Boneless Squab with Wild Rice and Mushrooms	3.25	Half Chicken, Broiled or Fried	2.00
Chicken Saute au Sec, with Mushrooms	2.50	Chicken Florentine	2.50

VEGETABLES

Potatoes—Shoe String, Hash Brown or Cottage Fried	.60	Vegetables, du jour	.35
		Vegetables, to order	.50
French Fried Onions	.75	Mushroom Saute	1.25

EGGS AND OMELETTES

Fresh Mushroom Omelette	1.50	Cheese Omelette	1.25

SANDWICHES

Steak	1.75	Cheese	.75

CHEESE

Camembert Cheese	.50		
Monterey	.35	Gorgonzola	.35

DESSERT

Zabaione	.50	Fried Cream	.50
Ice Cream	.25	Sherbet	.25

COCKTAILS

BACARDI	.65	GIMLET	.65
DAIQUIRI (West Indies)	.65	MARTINI, DRY	.55
SCARLET O'HARA	.75	MARTINI, MEDIUM	.55
ALEXANDER	.75	OLD FASHIONED	.55
BRONX	.65	PRESIDENTE	.65
CHAMPAGNE	1.00	PINK GARTER	.75
DUBONNET	.50	PINK LADY	.75
GIN DAISY	.60	SIDE CAR	.75
FRENCH 75	1.25	AMERICANO	.65
ZAZERAC	.75	SQUIRREL	.75
CUCUMBER	.75	TEQUILA	.65
MANHATTAN	.55	STINGER	.75

MIXED DRINKS, PUNCHES and FIZZES

SCREWDRIVER	.60	NEW ORLEANS FIZZ	.75
SHERRY FLIP	.65	GRASSHOPPER	.75
TOM COLLINS	.60	GIN FIZZ	.60
JOHN COLLINS	.60	GOLDEN FIZZ	.75
COFFEE ROYAL	.50	ROYAL FIZZ	.75
COFFEE BRULE AL DIABLO	1.00	GIN SOUR	.60
GIN SLING	.75	WHISKEY SOUR	.60
SINGAPORE SLING	.75	WHISKEY PUNCH	.60
SLOE GIN RICKEY	.60	AMER PICON, IMPORTED	.75
CAMPARI	.65		

We never ate better and we never ate more. What a night we had. That was the occasion when I learned the difference between eating and dining. This menu is from Alfred's, 659 Merchant Street in the financial district. (Courtesy Al Petri, owner of Alfred's.)

    Dick Waibel and his wife Nadine, Sam and Angie Calderone, Jo Ann and I went to Alfred's to eat. Frisco has restaurants one better than the next. We didn't know what a treat was in store for us. Alfred's was located at 886 Broadway and was famous for good food since 1929. We started eating at 5:30 p.m., ordering a New York steak dinner for $4.85, which was a lot of money to us in 1955. The price of the entree included an appetizer choice of cracked crab or avocado shrimp cocktail. I selected the shrimp, followed by prosciutto and salami, stuffed celery, pickles, radishes, pickled pigs feet, peperocini and green and ripe olives. By this time we were getting full, for that relish platter was a large portion. Soup du jour (minestrone) was next, accompanied by Italian bread. The pasta course was a choice of delicious homemade ravioli or spaghetti. Almost two hours of steady eating had gone by and we were bulging. I really didn't know where I could put my steak when it arrived about ten minutes later. It was an inch thick and came with a baked potato and salad. I ate slowly, hoping that my digestive tract might possibly hurry and make room for at least one more course. Slowly, cautiously and with perseverance I finished every morsel. It was now 8:30 p.m. and the waiter asked, after clearing the table, "You have a choice of dessert. You may have fried creme in blue flame, ice cream, sherbet, Camembert, or Monterey cheese and coffee." We sighed,

The Portland Beavers, 1955. These guys were the last team to play on the Vaughn Street Field. Back row, left to right: Don Eggert, Carl Powis, Joe Taylor, Luis Marquiz, Dick Whitman, Tip Bert (trainer); middle row, left to right: Bill Werle, Bob Alexander, Ed Burtschy, Carl Schieb, Royce Lint, Dick Waebel, Red Adams, Glenn Elliott; front row, left to right: Jim Robertson, Frank Austin, Ed Basinski, Clay Hopper (manager), Bill Fleming (pitching coach), Ed Mickelson, Artie Wilson, Don Lunberg. (Used by permission of Portland Beavers.)

ordered and very slowly stuffed ourselves to the bursting point. We didn't leave the restaurant till 9 p.m. That had to be one of the best dinners I have ever eaten. I still have the menu. Alfred's, are you still there? It would almost be worth the trip back to San Francisco just for another meal there.

Jo Ann and I left Frisco on Sunday after the game and headed for Portland to open a series on Tuesday. We encountered snow in the mountains of northern California. In fact, the snowplow was ahead of us on one stretch of the road. Our old blue 1950 Ford slipped and slid, but it got us through to Portland, where it was the season for rain. That season we had 13 games postponed at home due to the rain. They would be played at later dates, and at least 13 others should have been called but were played anyway. It could certainly be said of that season that we'd win some, lose some and some would be rained out.

Because of the rain, our home opener on Tuesday took the form of a double-header on Saturday afternoon and evening instead. We lost both games to San Diego. On Sunday we played another double-header, winning the first game 9–5. The second game went 20 innings but we won that one as well, 3–2. Sam Calderone caught the entire Sunday double-header. As Marlowe Branagan, the sports editor of the *Portland Journal*, wrote, "Statisticians will delve into the records to see if any other two clubs played 29 innings on a Sunday afternoon and night. They will find other records, including Sammy Calderone's catching all 29 innings for the home club. Never, old-timers asserted late on Sunday, has that happened in this league—or any other."

We took Sacramento in a seven-game series at Portland, winning the series 5 games to 2, and moved on to San Diego. Bob Hall won for us on our first night in San Diego. I went 0 for 5 despite hitting three balls well, including one against the fence in left-center that was caught. On Wednesday, Thursday and Friday, I was collared and we lost all three games. On Saturday, Hopper was making out the lineup. Sam came over to me as I was playing pepper down the right field line. "Hey Mick!" Sammy hollered, "The skipper's got Dino Restelli in your place today, you better go in and tell him you want to play." I did want to play, but after going 0 for 19 in the last four games, Shreveport was starting to look good to me. Sam was right. Hopper had Restelli in my spot. So I went to see Hopper feeling angry and frustrated.

I said, "Skipper, I hear I'm not in the lineup." "Thaet's raight, I'm gonna play Restelli," Hopper said. "Clay," I replied, angrier now, "I can play in this caliber of ball, but I'm not the type of guy who can work out of a slump by not playing. I have to battle it through. But I've got to be in the lineup to do it." "Yaw'll mean yaw'll wanna plaigh?" he asked. "You're damned right I do," I replied. "Okay, yaw'll in thayer ta-day," he said. So, in what was, as far as I'm concerned, the most eventful three-minute conversation that season, everything had been worked out. All Hopper wanted was to see me assert myself and let him know my confidence was still there. So I let him know that I hadn't lost my guts.

But I had then talked myself into a bit of a corner. I needed a hit that Saturday in San Diego, and I needed one bad. The one I got was more of a dying quail, but it got me started as I went 1 for 4. Then I went 1 for 4 in each game of Sunday's double-header, but we had lost six in a row and were now at 14 wins and 16 losses.

My roommate on the road in those first few weeks of the season was a bespectacled, wiry, erudite-looking gentleman. Eddie Basinski looked more like a professor than a ball player. He had played with the Brooklyn Dodgers during the war years of the forties while in his teens. He had also spent some time as a violinist with the Buffalo Symphony Orchestra. The "Fiddler," as we called him, had a very interesting background. Besides being a ball player, Basinski was a businessman while on the road. He would get up promptly at 7:30 in the morning, shower, shave, put on his business suit and make calls for Consolidated Freightways. He did this in every town in the league. Eddie had a lot of stamina and a strong desire to get ahead. How he maintained the pace of playing ball at night and soliciting sales during the day, I'll never know. Eddie was a utility man, but there were some stretches during the season when he played regularly, and it began to tell on him. But the last I heard, Eddie had worked his way up to a good job with Consolidated Freightways.

Joe Taylor arrived by plane at 8 a.m. on Sunday, May 15th, from Columbus, Ohio. Joe was known on occasions to take a nip or two, but there was no way that could happen on that day, for Joe went directly to the park from breakfast at the airport. He was inserted in the lineup immediately and hit a 400-foot shot off Karl Drews for a homer in his first time at bat in the PCL. The next time up, with Don Eggert on first base, Drews threw Taylor a curve ball, which he then deposited high into the left field stands. On Taylor's third trip to the plate, he found himself facing relief pitcher Dick Strahs. Taylor hit a ball that the centerfielder caught while leaping high against the fence. In Taylor's fourth and final time at bat, with Bill Black on the mound, he hit his third home run of the game. L.H. Gregory, the sports editor for the *Portland Oregonian*, called Joe's performance "the most sensational debut any player ever made in Vaughn Street Stadium in 52 seasons of PCL baseball."

Luis Marquez joined us a few days after Taylor. Luis had played a lot of minor and major league baseball, and he was a student of the game— the club's "friendly philosopher." Lu talked a mile a minute, and his rich Puerto Rican accent made you work at listening closely to each word. Lu had a big toothy smile with a lot of gold showing and a deep, raucous laugh that was often heard in the Beavers' clubhouse that season. Lu had a worldly wise intelligence about him and was quick to size people up. He played with a fire and intensity far beyond that of most players. He had a great deal of confidence and pride in his work.

Marquez used one of the biggest and heaviest bats in the league. Most players were moving to lighter bats to allow for a quicker stroke that could handle the slider. The slider was now being used widely by pitchers in baseball, and it had become a very successful pitch. But Lu insisted on using a 36-inch, 40-ounce bat when most players had gone to a 33- or 34-inch bat that weighed between 33 and 34 ounces. Lu's bat looked like a wagon tongue. But he got it around and balls seemed to jump off that club of his. Marquez had a lot of theories about baseball, and I listened and learned. Blacks weren't managing at that time, but Luis Marquez, a black man himself, would have done very well as a manager. Lu ended his four-year career in the Negro Leagues with a .371 batting average. He reached the major Leagues as a much-wanted player. His contract was purchased by the New

York Yankees, but in a dispute between New York and Bill Veeck's Cleveland Indians, baseball commissioner Happy Chandler awarded Lu to Cleveland.

Five years had elapsed since I last hit against Larry Jansen in my first at-bat in the major leagues before I saw him again in Seattle in 1955. Larry resided in Verboot, Oregon, and wanted to pitch regularly in the PCL rather than become a pitching coach for the New York Giants. He looked good to me as he beat us for his fourth straight win. I did manage to get a hit and RBI off him. Seattle had another pitcher, though, who seemed to have an easy time getting me out regularly. Elmer Singleton must have pitched to me in 40 at-bats over a three-year period, and I doubt that I got more than two hits off him. He threw a good slider, a fastball that he rarely threw for a strike and the illegal spitter that he loaded up whenever he really needed a good pitch.

The Coast League had some excellent umpires in '55. Several went on to the major leagues and had lengthy careers. The umpires were grouped in threes in the higher minor leagues. One ump was behind first base down the right field line, another opposite him down the third base line and the last behind home plate. In the lower minors, two umpires worked the game, and situations came up on the bases that were very difficult for two men to handle. The performance of the umpires improved with each step up in classification. The poorest umpiring occurred on the lower levels of Class D, C and B. Class A got a good deal better, with good umpiring being done on the Double A, Triple A and major-league level.

The umpire's life is a difficult one, to say the least. When an umpire left home in late winter for spring training games, he would see very little of his family until the following September or October. An umpire and his partners are always on the road, with only an occasional visit from family or friends. The frustration level for an umpire has to be extremely high. The working hours are short—some games then were played in as little as an hour and 45 minutes—but the pressure is intense on each pitch and each play. Once back in Pocatello, a young lad was umpiring at first base. He was feeling the strain of having bungled a few previous calls and taken a lot of abuse. After the game I saw him in front of the ballpark and he began opening up, telling me all the problems that he was encountering as an umpire. Before long, tears were rolling down his cheeks. I really felt sorry for him. And a few weeks later he quit.

The umpires in the PCL were quite competent, though, and with the following umpiring teams, not too many calls were truly blown: Mutart, Orr, and Valenti; Pelekoudas, Smith and Carlucci; Iacovetti, Ashford, and Ford; Somers, Passerella and Steiner; and Anske, Yuhase, and Nenzich. Umpires are moved up, down and around just like ball players. I believed

Illustration by Ron Joyner.

that sometimes politics played a part in an umpire's movement—again, just like ball players.

The umpire I really got to know the best was Chris Pelekoudas. He and I enjoyed talking about basketball. I refereed basketball games in the winter at various high schools in St. Louis, and he also worked basketball games in his off season. Playing first gave me a lot of time between pitches to carry on a good conversation with the first base umpire. I didn't do it to any great extent, though, because I did want to concentrate on what I was doing. Some infielders and catchers talk constantly to the umpires during the whole game. It's a means to break the tension. I also talked a lot to the other players after they got on first. Most players usually felt pretty good just after a hit, and they would talk glibly about anything. Next time you watch a game on television and they zoom in on first base after a player has just gotten a hit, see if the first baseman and the runner aren't carrying on a light-hearted conversation. I would generally say, "Nice hit," and the jubilant player would jabber on and on and on.

Pelekoudas was a good umpire, but he had a gigantic honker. Everyone called him "Nickel Nose," because if a player thought Pelekoudas had missed a call, he would yell remarks from the dugout like, "I wish I had your nose full of nickels," or other such endearing remarks. Umpires took a lot of abuse, and I wondered if I would consider the hassle worth it if I were an umpire. Pelekoudas went up to the big leagues for a lengthy career—he also got his nose bobbed.

Emmett Ashford was the only black umpire in the PCL. He too went on to the big leagues. He was an excellent umpire, but he got the reputation for being a showboat. He dramatized every decision, putting a lot of body English into every call. Not only did I like Emmett as a person, I very much enjoyed his antics on the field, and so did the fans. He livened up a ball game, but he had his detractors who felt he should have toned down his act. The constant travel, months away from home and family, low pay, constant pressure and frustration, abuse from fans, players and owners, having only your fellow umpires to confide in and little or no praise for a job well done, led me to wonder why anyone would put on that monkey suit and become a baseball umpire. It takes real courage and perseverance to remain in that capacity for very long.

Ball players like to play tricks on one another and on umpires, too. We were in the dugout in Oakland when I noticed a brand new ball on the field near the umpire who was standing behind third base. The National Anthem was being played, as it always is before each ball game. The umpire (whom I shall not name) saw the baseball, too. Umpires are fastidious groundskeepers and I could tell that this umpire couldn't wait until the end of the Anthem so he could rush over, bend down, pick up the ball and clear the field. Before the last note had sounded, the umpire began to lean toward the bright, shiny, new baseball a few feet away. As he quickly darted to pick up the ball, it was jerked away from his fingertips. He made one more futile attempt to grab the moving baseball as it was rapidly nearing the dugout steps. By this time, we were all in hysterics as the umpire looked in the dugout and realized it was a hoax. One of our guys had drilled a hole in the ball, inserted a green string which was indistinguishable from the grass and planted the ball on the field. A barrage of profanity was spat our way by Mr. Umpire.

We lost the first game to Hollywood on June 14 as George Vico hit a homer that beat us in the 10th inning, 6–5. From there on we took them four in a row, coming up to Sunday's double-header. Hopper was beaming after Saturday's game. Bill Werle had beaten them, 4–2, as Marquez was the batting star. Early in the week, Carl Powis, Joe Taylor, Dick Whitman, Artie Wilson, Frank Austin and Jim Robertson had all led us at bat. Bob Alexander, Red Adams, Royce Lint and Werle had pitched masterful games.

After Saturday's win, Sam Calderone and I were in the bar of the Hollywood Plaza Hotel having a beer and listening to the Plainsmen, a group patterned after the Sons of the Pioneers. The Morgan brothers, who were the group's members, came over to talk with us. And before long, the subject turned to baseball. They were not baseball fans, but both decided that they wanted to see the next day's double-header. Sam and I promised to leave them two tickets.

The next day, Sunday, June 19, we won the first game, 9–2, getting another good game out of Bob Alexander. From first base I could see the Morgans in their box seat between home and third. They were soaking up both sun and beer, and they were sure doing it at a fast pace. Both were fair-skinned and appeared not to have seen daylight for months.

We won the nightcap, 5–1, as Carl Powis hit his fourth homer of the series and the Beavers beat my old roomie, Red Munger. The Morgan brothers (whose sister is singer Jaye P. Morgan), had risen to their feet earlier in the second game to give one last cheer for the Bevos before passing out.

We had then won six in a row. Calderone and I dressed and headed for a cab and something to eat at the airport. We really hadn't eaten since breakfast at 9 a.m., just two beers in the clubhouse to quench our thirst before heading for the airport for another beer and a sandwich. We were a little light-headed as we dashed to the gate to catch our plane to San Francisco and then on to Portland. Who should fall in beside us then but our manager, Clay Hopper. Like Sam and I, he glowed for more reasons than a six-game winning streak. We went up the steps to board the plane with Hopper keeping up step for step. The stewardess shut the door behind us as we heaved a sigh of relief—but not for long. Before we could get seated, a voice came over the plane's intercom announcing, "Welcome aboard ... Airline's flight ... to Hawaii." I don't remember the name of the airline, but I sure as hell remember our reaction when we heard the word "Hawaii!" The three of us scurried out of the plane, down the boarding steps and across the Los Angeles airport to get the proper flight back to Portland. After running several hundred yards, Sam started to slacken the pace. He turned and started laughing. "Hey, Mick," he said, "Why are we worried about missing the plane—hell, how can the skipper fine us when he's right here with us?" This broke the old man up, but he didn't break stride as we hustled to the right gate and onto the right plane.

We traveled Western Airlines for this, the correct flight. The route was along the beautiful Pacific Coast. During the day you could see the Pacific Ocean to the west and land to the east. It must have been around 9 p.m. when our plane took off. The sun had gone down but it was still light to the west. Sam and I settled back contentedly to relax. The stewardess asked us if she could get us something to drink. "Hey Sam," I said, "I think we need a drink after all that running." Although that was just the thing that had gotten all three of us in this mess to begin with, we told her we would like some champagne. Western served drinks on the plane with no charge, and we kept them coming. By the time we hit Frisco, Sam and I were in great spirits, and we deboarded to change planes for our flight to Portland. We had some bacon and eggs at the airport, and even

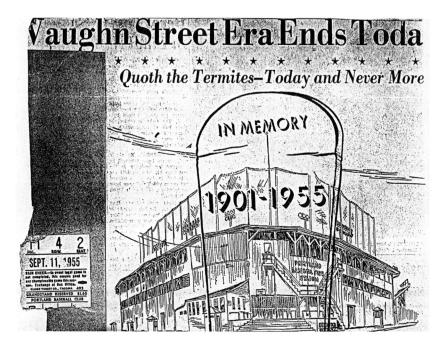

Vaughn Street Era Ends Toda

★ ★ ★ ★ ★ ★ ★ ★ ★ ★ ★ ★ ★ ★

Quoth the Termites–Today and Never More

IN MEMORY

1901-1955

SEC 4 ROW 2 SEAT
SEPT. 11, 1955

RAIN CHECK—In event legal game is
not completed, this coupon good for
any championship game this season. Exchange at Box Office.
GLOBE TICKET CO., TACOMA 695
GRANDSTAND RESERVED $1.65
PORTLAND BASEBALL CLUB

I was glad to see Vaughn Street Park go because the new ballpark would have a green space in center field. Fans, mostly men in those days, usually came to the games in suits with white shirts and straw hats. When they took off their jackets, all that white background made it hard to pick up the ball when they were seated in center field. (*The Oregonian*, used by permission.)

more champagne on our second flight. It was early in the morning when we arrived in Portland.

The wives were generally out at the airport to greet us. Sam and I were the last ones off the plane, and we were a little wobbly, to say the least. I decided to play it up. I had taken my partial plate out (three teeth in the front) and placed it in my shirt pocket. This left me with a tooth-less smile. I had run my hand through my hair to give it a tousled effect. I also pulled my shirttail out. I really didn't have to exaggerate the condi-tion I was in, but I did for a joke. And as I swayed and stumbled off the plane, I sang at the top of my voice. I could see Jo sandwiched between Angie and Muriel along with the other wives. As we entered the termi-nal, the players were greeted by their wives and young ones, but Jo kept her distance from me all the way to the car muttering, "I don't know the guy," over and over.

The Vaughn Street Park was starting to creak in 1955. L.H. Gregory wrote in the August 30, 1955, *Oregonian* that it had been built in 1912 by the McCredies. Gregory's account of the ballpark went, "It may not seem so to modern eyes, but this plant at its time was the absolute last word in baseball modernity, visibility and comfort for spectators. There was nothing like it anywhere in the minor leagues. Indeed, many a major-league park, except in size, could not compare with it. This was the first minor-league park to have individual theater seats in the grandstand. It seated 12,000, and that is how many were there on April 14, 1912, to dedicate it.

"The first professional ball game played in Portland occurred on May 22, 1901, as Portland played Seattle that afternoon at 3:30. Rain had been a problem all day and the rain-abbreviated contest was won by Portland, 8–6, in four and one-half innings. Except for one season, 1918, the Portland baseball team had made Vaughn Street Park, its baseball home. Now, after fifty-four years, comes its farewell. The property has been sold for industrial purposes with the new owners taking possession on December 31, 1955. Multnomah Stadium would be the new home of the Portland Beavers," wrote Gregory.

I mention this to point out the ballpark's tradition and its condition. It was in dire need of renovation, which it would not get since it was being torn down. The centerfield bleachers, a somewhat recent addition, had been painted with a silver-colored metal paint. That backdrop made it difficult to pick up a high fastball during a day game. George Witt, a hard-throwing right-hander with the Hollywood Stars, once hit me in the head with the bases loaded. It was the toughest RBI of the season for me. The plastic insert in my cap had been dented, but it had been my salvation. That night, after a quick trip to the hospital, I was lying in bed wishing we were already in Multnomah and away from the "silver-painted monster." Hollywood was wearing batting helmets similar to those in use today. Joe Ziegler, our general manager, got one for me and I wore it from that day on.

Dwight "Red" Adams had been in the Coast League for years and was trying to stick it out for another season. Adams was soon to be 34 (baseball age) in October and the life had started to go out of his arm. He still had fairly good stuff, but what had always made him an effective pitcher was his savvy—his ability to throw almost every pitch to a specific spot—and a bulldog determination. In '55, though, Red came across a bit of bad luck, going 12–12 despite a low 2.05 ERA. He also led the league in fielding for pitchers with a 1.000 percentage—no errors.

Red was a heck of a swell guy along with being a tough competitor. I used to watch him closely when he came in from the mound while we were at bat. Either he or the trainer would rub "hot stuff"—the penetrating salve which is used to keep the muscles loose—on his arm. I flinched each time he rubbed it in. The stuff was really hot. As Red rubbed the salve in vigorously, an expression on his face seemed to say, "Damn you, arm, I'm going to get another good inning out of you whether you like it or not." I later talked to Red when the L.A. Dodgers came to St. Louis. He was their pitching coach for quite a long while, and he is still enthusiastic about baseball. I had to chuckle when I watched television and saw Red saunter to the mound giving an L.A. pitcher advice. My memory instantly went back to Portland, with Red hanging on to the game he so loved to play.

Frankie Austin, our shortstop, was honored in Portland for playing in his 600th consecutive game. A truckload of gifts came that Sunday afternoon of July 28th. Frank was born in the Panama Canal Zone and he had played for the Philadelphia Stars in the Negro American League. He came to organized baseball with Newark in 1949 in the International League. That same year he moved on to Portland and he had played excellent baseball for them ever since. Frankie was still a good hitter, but he had lost some of his fielding range and his arm had lost some zip, though not its accuracy. Frankie was about the nicest gentleman I have ever known in baseball.

Most of the guys were in the clubhouse dressing and chatting about the kinds of gifts Austin might get later on for his "day." Down the corridor from the clubhouse we could hear the loud voice of Joe Taylor in song. "Old Taylor," someone suggested, "has been out on the town." Joe was a great hitter when sober, but he was useless when inebriated.

Clay Hopper was the first to hear the strains of Taylor's tune. It was as if a father had been waiting patiently for his recalcitrant son and had risen to meet his return. Hopper rose, not to greet Taylor, but to go directly to the bulletin board to insert Marquez's name in at right field, scratching the too-happy Taylor right out.

Joe was definitely tipsy. Hopper sent him down the left field line to sleep it off in the bullpen. But as L.H. Gregory wrote in the *Oregonian*, "The evening also produced a specialty not on the schedule, an old-fashioned, country-fair type bonehead play on the Portland side, and at that, by a player not in the lineup at all. This freak of baseball stupidity certainly cost the Beavers a chance to tie and probably an opportunity to win the first game, for it killed off a rally that had just started. The one who committed the boner, and he'll never make a bonier one if he plays 100 years, was Joe Taylor, outfielder.

"It happened in the fourth inning, just after the Padres in their half scored both their runs on four consecutive singles by Dick Sisler, Ray Jablonski, Earl Rapp, and Ed Bailey. Eddie Basinski, with the bases loaded, slammed a sure-fire double over the third baseman that then hooked toward the bullpen where several players, Taylor among them, were gathered. As the ball sizzled past them, Taylor put out his glove and stopped the ball.

Basinski, who reached second base, was called out for interference and a promising Beaver rally was killed off."

What had really happened, as I viewed the incident, was that Taylor, dozing on the bullpen bench, was startled as the bullpen pitchers jumped out of the way of Basinski's fair ball. The only one remaining on the bench was a groggy Taylor who, awakened by the jostling, opened his eyes, saw the ball coming and instinctively fielded it cleanly, making what would have been a hell of a play.

At the time, it didn't seem funny at all. Basinski was furious, shouting at Taylor after being cheated out of a double. Hopper, trying hard to get the words out that just wouldn't come, slowly paled, reddened and then turned a ghostly white. When the words came to him later, boy, did they come! I never heard the exact words, because Hopper was headed out to the bullpen with a vengeance, head-hunting for Mr. Joe Taylor. After a heated exchange of words (or shouts, really), Joe took the walk of shame toward the clubhouse—for the day. Like the rest of my teammates, I was really ticked at Taylor at the time. As the season wore on, we were able to joke about it plenty—even Taylor. We would be sipping a cold brew after a game and someone would say, "Hey, I really thought Taylor showed a great pair of hands that day in the bullpen." And we would all crack up.

Jo Ann had gotten tickets for us for the Bobo Olsen–Jimmy Martinez fight at Multnomah Stadium. She surprised me with them when we got off the road in early August. We played our game Saturday at 2 p.m., allowing time for the grounds crew to get the ring set up for the fight that night. We had excellent seats at ringside. It turned out to be a beautiful night under the lights with Bobo winning and looking every bit the middleweight champion that he was.

On that Portland team, Bob Hall was different kind of guy. He was frank, outspoken and very independent. He was far ahead of his time when it came to eating natural foods, exercise, and proper body care. Bob read a great deal, especially about subjects pertaining to health and exercise. Most ball players at that time couldn't care less about proper diet, exercise or the latest deep-breathing techniques. The prevailing mentality was: Eat French fries and hamburgers, drink beer and soda, and what the heck's wrong with that? Bob Hall was preaching about food preservatives, refined sugar and white flour, and so he became a "kook" or a "flake." Because of his views, which he expressed and practiced, Bob became known as "Nature Boy." Besides his strong beliefs, he had the best-proportioned body on the team, and by far. Bob's fanaticism toward bodily care even carried over to the showers. He would take ice-cold showers because he felt that they toned up the muscles. "The gamest fish are found in the coldest waters," Bob always said.

One day, Bob and Muriel went with Jo Ann and me on a picnic, to a river the girls had found on one of their sightseeing adventures when we were on the road. The current was so swift that you had to start way upstream to swim across to a sandy beach on the other side. Bob had done this several times, telling me how great the water was. I kept wading up to my knees, but in just a few seconds my legs and feet would be numb from the cold. The water was actually freshly melted snow from nearby Mt. Hood. Not to be outdone by "Nature Boy," and goaded by my wife, I dived head first into the icy water and started swimming for the other side. It was a short distance, but when I got to the sandy beach I lay down on my back, my body aching with pain from the cold. It seemed like knives were sticking in each of my sinus areas . As I lay there dying, Bob yelled, "Great, isn't it, Mick?" All I could think about how was I possibly going to make it back? My skin was a mass of red blotches as I got out of the water on my return trip. The pain in my sinuses was excruciating. No one laughed or said a word as they saw my pain. I thought to myself, "If this is what it takes to keep the body in shape, then count me out!" But Bob Hall reveled in this type of activity.

As the season wore on, I began to understand Bob and appreciate his ways, even if I didn't always agree with him entirely. He did make a lot of sense, though, and I guess I felt a little indignation toward some of the guys for putting him down because he believed in something, spoke out about it and practiced it. There was a crusader-type spirit in Bob. He felt the right thing to do was to stand up for his convictions, even though it meant some ridicule and loss of belonging. I respected him for that. Most ball clubs have their so-called characters. To me it is sad that, because of an inability to communicate feelings, a chasm can develop between the group and an individual.

The middle of August found us fourth in the PCL behind first-place Seattle. Marquez was leading us with a .323 batting average. I was second with .319, followed by Dick Whitman with .312 and Artie Wilson at .310. Bill Werle was our best hurler at 12 wins and 6 losses. For our last series in Seattle, Jo Ann drove the blue Ford up to see us play. Generally wives didn't accompany their husbands on the road, but Joe Ziegler and our general manager gave us permission. We stayed at the Olympic Hotel in Seattle. We were 7½ games behind Freddie Hutchinson's Seattle Rainiers. We lost the opener 5–3 as Ewell Blackwell, the former Cincinnati great, beat us. I had homered off Blackwell in Portland, but he collared me in Seattle. The next night we beat Seattle in front of 12,000 spectators on Ladies' Night. Seattle took the next three games behind three former major-league pitchers: Howie Judson, Elmer Singleton, and Larry Jansen. Before Saturday night's game, Jo Ann and I ventured out to the University of Washington's football stadium to see the San Francisco Forty-Niners take on the New York Giants in an exhibition game. It was the first professional football game we had seen. The San Francisco players stayed at our hotel, and it was sure a sight to see those huge guys walking around the lobby. Today, some of the baseball players could match them for size.

On Sunday, the 21st of August, we took two from Seattle, 9–4 and 4–0. Bill Werle (13–7) and Royce Lint (7–9) were the two stylish lefties who beat the Rainiers and got us back to within eight games of the lead. It was fun having Jo with me on the road, and we both enjoyed the fresh clean city of Seattle.

Around the end of August, we were playing in Hollywood. The telephone rang, and I got to it before Sam did. The party on the other end asked me if Sam and I would care to go out to one of the movie studios to see the filming of a movie called *Giant*. I said sure, and the voice at the other end said that he would pick us up around 1 p.m. He said he was a Hollywood agent and that he would have a young starlet with him. He said he was taking her out to meet an important executive on the lot.

I don't remember the agent's name. But the executive liked baseball, and this agent was using us to get in to introduce his starlet. In Hollywood, it seems like everybody is being used by somebody for one reason or another. The agent picked us up at the appointed time and, sure enough, he had the starlet with him. Being the gentleman that I am, I held the door for Sam to get in the back seat. I got in the front. The agent introduced us to Gloria Marshall. She was a knockout, about 20 years old, and she had big "bazoomas." She was ahead of her time, too, because she was going bra-less. I was sitting straight up in my seat gazing down to check them out. Every now and then I could hear Sam in the back say, "Hey Mick, how's everything look up front?" I straightened up, sitting as tall as I could, peeking over my left shoulder, saying, "Just fine, Sam, just fine."

When we arrived on the lot, I found out that Gloria was blind as a bat. She couldn't see doodle-do without glasses, which she refused to wear. Contact lenses weren't the thing at that time, so every time we would approach somebody coming toward us Gloria would ask me, "Who's that? Who is that?" She kept wondering if the person was a movie star. Finally I got perturbed and said, "Gloria, why don't you just wear your glasses?" She ignored the question altogether.

We finally got to see Mr. Executive, and it was a boring half-hour spent listening to him try to impress us with his baseball knowledge and his command of suggestive language. All the while, the agent was trying to impress Mr. Executive with what he had to offer—Gloria Marshall. I felt some hostility toward both men before we concluded the meeting and headed for the set of *Giant*.

It turned out to be an epic film starring Rock Hudson, Elizabeth Taylor, James Dean, Mercedes McCambridge and Chill Wills. Many years later as I look back on that afternoon that started so uneventfully, it now ranks as one of my highlights from that season. And for one reason. I met James Dean.

Sam and I struck up a conversation with Chill Wills, who turned out to be a big baseball fan from his baseball days with the New York Giants. Mr. Wills was really an affable guy, and he latched onto Sammy right away. Sam and I must have talked with him for a while and he asked us if he could tour us around the set. He introduced us to Mercedes McCambridge and Elizabeth Taylor. We spoke briefly with both ladies. Miss Taylor was more beautiful in real life than on the screen. We were standing by a trailer, which was parked on the set as a home for one of the stars. I asked Chill whose trailer it was. He said, "James Dean is in there. Would you like to meet him?" He continued, "Well, he's kind of funny sometimes, a little moody. Sometimes he'll talk and other times he won't have nothing to do with anybody, but I'll see." With that, Chill went inside the trailer.

Before long a rather short, thin young man came out with his straight, blond hair combed back. He had on black shell-rimmed glasses and was wearing blue denim pants. It was James Dean. In the short span of time he had been in Hollywood, just a few years, his star had ascended as quickly and as brightly as anyone before or since. I had seen him in *East of Eden* and *Rebel Without a Cause*. Watching him in those pictures left me with the feeling that he didn't act those two parts, he lived them.

Sam and I stood there conversing with James Dean for over 45 minutes. The look on Chill Will's face as he left us talking showed surprise that Dean was so amiable and talkative. I asked Dean why the yellow Bull Durham tag was hanging from his shirt pocket. He said, "Well, in the movie, the part calls for me to roll my own cigarettes, so I do it all the time off the set to practice. I want it to look natural." All the time Dean was talking to us, I felt a sense of detachment from him. It was as if you could only get so close to him, but no closer. It wasn't a feeling that he was staying away because he was a big shot. It was more like he was afraid to get too close to people, at least right away. During the time we talked, he had a rope with a large knot tied at the end. He would let the rope dangle almost to the floor, and then he would flick his wrist and wind the rope around the knot in a figure eight. He said that if he got good enough with it, he was going to ask to make it a part of the picture. Later, when I finally got to see the movie, Dean has a scene with Rock Hudson in Hudson's office. Dean is asked to sell his property. He refuses. And before he shuts the door, he does his rope trick. James Dean's portrayal of Jett Rink in *Giant* won him an Oscar.

Sam and I returned to the hotel that day feeling that we had an enjoyable afternoon, meeting the stars and the stars to be. We had to chuckle when we thought of Gloria Marshall. I did see her on TV in *The Bob Cummings Show* a few years later, but I haven't seen or heard of her since.

That fall, back home in St. Louis, I picked up a newspaper to discover that James Dean had died on September 30, 1955, in an automobile accident. The headlines jumped out at me. I remembered those few precious minutes spent with a truly great actor who seemed scared and unsure of himself.

A few days after our visit to the movie set, Sam and I were eating in an upscale restaurant called the Villa Capri. As I glanced around the room I thought I spied Nat "King" Cole. I asked Sam to take a look and he assured me that I had it right. Sam said, "He is a great baseball fan and used to come in the New York Giants clubhouse. Would you like to meet him?" I said, "You bet I would." We finished our meal and Sam led me over to his table and introduced himself as the Giants' catcher. They conversed for a short time and then Sam introduced me. Mr. Cole was sitting at the table with his wife and a very young child. He took the time to introduce us to them. What a thrill for me because he was one of my favorite vocalists. When I hear him sing "Unforgettable" with his daughter Natalie, that table scene always comes to my mind.

On our last trip to Hollywood that season, I picked up the paper in the coffee shop of the Hollywood Plaza Hotel. I had gone 55 games without an error, handling 504 consecutive chances perfectly. I really didn't realize that I had gone that long. My streak ended 22 games later when, on August 11th, I not only made one error but two in the same game. Until then, I had handled 704 consecutive chances in 77 consecutive games without an error. For the season, I handled over 1600 chances and made only six errors. My .996 fielding mark set a PCL record for first basemen. I also ended the season hitting .307 with 85 RBIs.

The last three weeks were a real bummer for me and for Portland. We lost a lot of one-run games, and the flu bug hit me in Hollywood with just a month to go. During the last three weeks, I drove in only three runs. On the last day of the season, September 11, 1955, we won a double-header, and after 55 years the Vaughn Street Park closed for good. I got the eerie feeling that I was either shutting down ball clubs (the Browns) or ballparks (Vaughn Street). As I think of 1955 and my first season in the PCL, I remember the guys in the league—the way they looked, walked, swung a bat, threw a ball and talked. How could you forget George "The Cat" Metkovich, the cut-up and great hitter with Oakland? Or Steve Bilko, my long-time past rival with his size and gigantic home runs with L.A.? Earl Rapp, the clutch-hitter with San Diego, Joe Ginsburg, Seattle's talkative catcher, Bobby Del Greco, Lee Walls, and Bobby Balcena with their great gloves in the outfield, and Ed Bailey's and Ray Jablonski's big bats are also vividly remembered.

Some of the managers who were a big part of that league's success at that time were Lefty O'Doul, Bobby Bragan, Tommy Heath, future Cardinals manager Freddie Hutchinson and, of course, Clay Hopper.

The Coast League then was a Who's Who of former major leaguers with experience and know-how. To name just a few: Walt Judnich, Wally Westlake, Dick Sisler, Spider Jorgenson, Bill Serena, Ed Kazak, Vern Stephens, Jerry Priddy, Hoot Rice, Bob Hall, Sam Calderone, Russ Bauers, Ben Wade, Dick Whitman, Gene Mauch, Red Munger, George Bamberger, Cal McLish, Bill Werle, Elmer Singleton, Royce Lint, Ed Burtschy, Carl Scheib, Earl Harrist, Vic Lombardi, Joe Hatten, Lou Kretlow, Al Brazle, Turk Lown, Gene Beardon, Bud Dailey, Bubba Church, Al Gettel, Howie Judson, Larry Jansen, Ewell Blackwell, Chuck Stevens, George Vico, Nippy Jones, Monte Basgall, Lucky Lohrke, Carlos Bernier, Steve Ridzik, Milo Candini, Bill Kennedy, Hector Brown, Bob Usher, Al Heist, Tom Glaviano, Bob Swift, Jim Brosnan and Clyde King.

Through the years the Coast League has sent some great players to the majors. A few from that season did go up and make it big, like future Hall of Famer Bill Mazeroski, Ed Bailey and Rocky Colavito. But in '55 the Coast League was certainly not the lifeblood of the major leagues. It was more like the place where old elephants went to die. The names of the future coming out of the minor leagues then were from the American Association, where mistakes and inexperience were compensated for by fervor, zeal and a youthful raw talent.

The day after the season ended, L.H. Gregory, the kindly old gentleman who was then nearing 70, got a rag-tag group of people to go over to the ballpark to play the "last game" at Vaughn Street. I could tell that he was losing a friend that he dearly loved as he cavorted under the fall sunshine. He had seen some 30 years of baseball in that old park as a reporter. I looked around the wooden stands, with their green paint peeling, and thought that I would miss that place, too. Until I looked toward center field and the silver-painted bleacher gleaming in the sunlight. I shuddered to think that there was a miserable, even dangerous, hitting background that I sure as heck would not miss!

At the end of the season Jo Ann and I headed to Long Beach, Washington, on a peninsula in the Pacific Ocean just north of Astoria, Oregon. I had won a couple days of free lodging there and wanted to enjoy a few days of rest and relaxation. We met a family from Portland in Long Beach that we knew and they showed us how to have a clam dig and prepare what we found for dinner. It was our first time eating clams and they were thoroughly enjoyable. We couldn't say the same for our accommodations.

So we stayed only one night and headed home, following the Columbia River route. The view was magnificent as we motored through the gorge, with high cliffs on the northern side of the river. We wound our way up the Cascade Mountains, through high fir trees, ferns and other greenery as waterfalls spewed from the side of the bluffs. West of the Cascades, the rainfall is heavy. The air pushing upward and inland from the Pacific Ocean rises over the mountains, dumping the moisture on the west side. But as the air pushes eastward and comes down on the flat plains east of the mountains, all the precipitation has spent itself and the land is semiarid. The Dalles is just on the eastern side of the Cascades, where the land and vegetation look somewhat like Arizona desert. Portland, on the west side, receives 39.91 inches of rain annually compared to the less than 10 inches that The Dalles receives.

At The Dalles we watched the Indians fish for salmon. They had rights which permitted them to use nets attached to long aluminum poles. The Indians had built wooden platforms over the water's edge of the Columbia River. At The Dalles, the river had narrowed. Huge boulders were scattered in the water, which was very swift and treacherous. Some of the fishermen had ropes tied around their waists while they stood on the platforms. The poles they used were 10 to 12 twelve feet long, and it took a lot of strength to pull out a 20-pound salmon swimming upstream to spawn. The salmon sold for around fifty cents a pound. The Indians— seven or eight of them fishing at a time—pulled in salmon in every eight to ten minutes. And every time I saw one pulled out, I thought that 10 bucks per fish could amount to a tidy sum at the end of the day.

We had gone to The Dalles earlier in the season and bought a couple of salmon. The Indians throw them in the trunks of their cars, and at the end of the day journey to Portland to sell their catch to the fish markets or canneries. Lee Anthony, one of our pitchers, and his wife Aileen had told us about buying salmon at The Dalles and taking them back to a cannery in Portland, where the fish would be canned for a nominal fee. Lee was quite a fisherman himself and had done that the previous years with his own catches. We enjoyed our salmon during the winter.

From The Dalles we went to Pendleton and arrived the day after the big cattle roundup had finished. The town was quiet as we rode through the streets early that September morning. The signs and banners stretched overhead across the street and told us that the activities had come to an end. The streets were still littered from the previous days' activities. Indian teepees were still set up in one section of town. Pendleton was asleep as we passed through. Oregon is quite an agrarian state with its cattle, dairy products, wheat, barley, fruits and vegetables, but it is still probably best known for its lumber and fishing products. Oregon's lush vegetation, mountains, valleys, streams and ocean make it a scenic paradise. We said goodbye to Mt. Hood, which is about 75 miles east of Portland and rises 11,245 feet. On clear days, Jo and I appreciated being able to see so easily its beautiful silhouette all the way from Portland.

Another season and a great many new and wonderful friendships, places, and experiences had ended. I was hopeful that something might happen during the winter months. I hoped that a major league club would pick me up after seeing what I had done in the Coast League in '55. My spirit was buoyed by Bob Broeg, sports editor for the *St. Louis Post-Dispatch*, who through the years had written some supportive comments about my play. But Bob Burns, the sports editor for the *St. Louis Globe-Democrat*, really lifted my spirits with a lengthy article that winter. He was very complimentary of my minor-league credentials and questioned why they weren't good enough to interest a major-league team.

I was asking the same questions. The only answer I could come up with was that, at 29 years of age, I was too old. I felt that I was now in a race against the clock. It created a sense of desperation as the glimmer of hope started to fade in my mind.

11

The Neon Twins

The off season is really a part of the year-round baseball program. Some players don't seem to realize that what you do then can greatly influence your performance in the upcoming season. An obvious example is the ball player who sits and eats all winter and then reports to spring training overweight and out of physical condition.

Equally important is the mental aspect of off-season preparation. It was crucial, at least for me, to have parents and friends with whom to relate our experiences. Jo Ann and I enjoyed our respective parents. We were a close-knit family and spent many holidays, birthdays and other social occasions together. We also enjoyed sharing happy times with some special friends in St. Louis, such as Lloyd and Alice Brewen. Lloyd taught and coached basketball at University City High School. I often worked at the high school, teaching and assisting with the athletic teams, so we shared many good times together during the winter months.

Sam and Angie Calderone came through St. Louis on their way to Glendale, California. They stopped at our house about the first of March, and together we drove out to spring training for the 1956 season. Sam was to report on the 5th of March with the pitchers and catchers. The other team members were to report on the 12th. We motored across the country with the Calderones, enjoying their good company. It was fun to go back to the same training base with friends we had made during the previous year and rejoin teammates from the past season. This was the first time we could do this, and it felt good.

The look was new for Portland as the club, now community owned, had sold stock to shareholders. The board of directors was composed of prominent local businessmen. The board president was Clay Brown and the directors were Cal Souther, Ted Gamble, A.B. Graham, Milo McIver, Harold LeDuc, G.A. Kingsley, Graham Griswold and Clyde Perkins.

The Portland Beavers were to move into a refurbished dog track renovated for baseball purposes. The Multnomah Stadium would be the largest in the Coast League, seating 28,870 fans. The left field fence was just 305

LOOK OUT, BIG CITY -- HERE WE COME!

Illustration by Ron Joyner.

feet down the line, but the wall was 20 feet high to compensate for the shorter distance. It was 389 feet to center field and 335 feet to right.

Crafty Joe Ziegler, our general manager, had, in the period of one short year, moved us from Vaughn Street to Multnomah and established a working agreement with one of the best farm systems in baseball at that time—the Brooklyn Dodgers.

Thomas Francis "Tommy" Holmes was our new manager. He was 38 years old and had managed in the minor leagues for several years. Tommy was a great outfielder for the Boston Braves of the National League, batting over .300 for five of his nine seasons. In 1945 he posted a .352 average and hit in 37 consecutive games, a National League record until broken by Pete Rose's 44-game hitting streak. In 1945, Holmes was named the Most Valuable Player in the National League by the *Sporting News* and was picked for the Major League All-Star team.

Bill Fleming, our pitching coach, was coming back for his fifth season. Lloyd Merriman, who had played football at Stanford and baseball in Cincinnati and Chicago for the past six years, would join the outfield crew. Tom Saffell, who had played outfield for Pittsburgh and Hollywood, also joined us.

I was the only holdover in the infield. Jack Littrell came to us from Kansas City in the American League to be our shortstop. Jim Baxes was now at third base and Dick Young, who had played at the Dodger farm club in Mobile, was at second.

Sam Calderone would do our catching. My roomie would have a splendid season in '56, avoiding the broken thumb, split fingers and sundry other injuries that had kept him from respectability the year before. Sam had played with the New York Giants from 1950 to 1953 and spent the '54 season with the Milwaukee Braves. He was a major-league hitter with a .292 batting average but wound up in Portland because of trouble with his throwing arm. His arm had still been a problem in

Sam Calderone was my roomie for three years. Sam's natural friendliness led him to talk to everyone. I had more adventures with him than I ever would have on my own. I always met interesting people when I was with Sammy. There is no more decent individual than Sam Calderone. Sammy's wife Angie and my wife JoAnn were also very close. Photo ca. 1950. (National Baseball Hall of Fame Library, Cooperstown, New York.)

'55, but it improved throughout the season and we had little need for our utility catcher, Ron Bottler. Unlike me, who had to learn to let the high fast ball go by, Sammy loved the high hard ones. And he would kill most every one that a careless pitcher threw his way.

Our pitching crew was solid, led by returnees Bill Werle, Royce Lint, Red Adams, Bob Alexander, Ray "Snacks" Shore, Dick Waibel and Bob Hall. Along with additions Darrel Martin, Dick Feidler, Rene Valdes, Bob Darnell, and Alex Konikowski, the Beavers' staff proved to be tough to beat in '56.

Off the field, we had the "Neon Twins." Every ball club had a few like them. When the sun goes down and the lights come on, these night prowlers came alive. The Portland Beavers of '55 and '56 all agreed that

Rocky Benevento, behind his mower, with an unknown onlooker. Rocky and his Ford pickup arrived at the Vaughn Street ball park in 1927, and Rocky stayed on as head grounds keeper until he and the Portland Beavers said farewell to the old ballpark in 1955. He was typical of most groundskeepers. He had a passion for the quality of his work and the ballpark became his second home. Because of dedicated people like Rocky Benevento, the baseball fields in most higher minor league parks were in excellent condition. I still hold the fielding record for first basemen in the PCL, making 6 errors in 1600 chances for a .996 fielding percentage. Rocky, I share this honor with you for your passion and hard work. (Photograph courtesy David Eskenazi.)

our Neon twins—who shall remain nameless—were the smoothest, most sophisticated, most-intelligent, best-looking operators in the league. Their shrewd nighttime exploits were unsurpassed.

My formula for every ball club is that 25 percent are straight arrows, solid as a rock, never going astray. Another 50 percent infrequently but occasionally go astray. And the other 25 percent are on the prowl constantly. The Neon Twins definitely fell into the last category. Their selective manner enabled them to come up with the most beautiful women each town had to offer.

Tip Berg was our trainer. He was quick with a quip along with the valuable ability to stretch out sore and aching muscles. Rocky Benevento was our groundskeeper, readying Multnomah Stadium for its first season. Rocky had been with Portland at that position since 1926 and was probably better known to most fans than their everyday players. Rocky smiled frequently and had a pleasant word for everyone. He was popular with everyone, but especially kids.

At the microphone for the Beavers were Bob Blackburn and Rollie Truitt. They were sponsored by Blitz Weinhard Beer and could be heard in Portland on KWJJ. They advertised that they were the largest minor-league baseball network in America, with broadcasts funneled through seventeen cities in Oregon.

Televised baseball games had come to most of the PCL cities. Los Angeles, Hollywood, Oakland, San Francisco, and Seattle all had some of their home and away games on TV. The color man on television for the Los Angeles Angels was Chuck Connors, the former Dodgers first baseman who would later go on to acting fame in the *Rifleman* TV series.

Our attendance in Portland for the '55 season was 785 people short of 200,000. In '56 we drew 305,729 to lead the PCL. The new ballpark, excellent front-office leadership, great community interest, not to mention a pretty good ball club, caused our attendance to be one of the highest in the minor leagues. But the minors as a whole had a drastic problem at this time. Teams were dropping out and leagues were folding. The reason for this could be summed up in one word—television. The minor leagues were quickly dwindling from 59 in 1948 to just 27 in 1956, a drop of more than half. It was easier to turn on the tube and watch a major-league ball game than to go out to see the local nine. Why pay money to see the "bushers" play when you could see the major leaguers on the tube ... for free? In the next few years, the ranks would lessen even more as minor-league baseball was in a fight for its life. The major leagues expanded, taking in hot-spot minor-league cities, many of them from the PCL like Los Angeles, San Francisco, San Diego, Oakland and Seattle.

Baseball would be the lesser after losing teams in towns like West Frankfort, Illinois; Pensacola, Florida; Roanoke, Virginia; Meridian, Mississippi; and Moultrie, Georgia. Greater sums of money would be invested in fewer players. Scouting services would be diminished along with the need for executives, managers, coaches, trainers, bus drivers and office workers. By 1956, minor-league baseball was a skeleton of its former self.

Economic factors were keeping good young players from entering professional baseball. The booming postwar economy had provided young men with good employment opportunities at reasonably attractive salaries. A skilled tradesman could make as much as the average Double A player, without uprooting his family and leaving his friends. But the Portland fans, Joe Ziegler and the Beavers appeared oblivious to all of these depressing forces.

Spring training went by quickly at Glendale. Jack Littrel, a spunky

Front Row: Sam Calderone, Alex Konikowski, Darrell Martin, Bob Darnell, Ron Bottler, Luis Marquez, Don Green, Batboy; Jerry Delavan, Batboy.
Center Row: Lloyd Merriman, Bob Borkowski, Leo Thomas, Dick Young, Jack Littrell, Bill Sweeney, Manager; Bill Fleming, Coach; Tom Saffell, Eddie Basinski, Tip Berg, Trainer.
Back Row: Frank Carswell, Ray Shore, Ed Mickelson, Bob Alexander, Bill Werle, Royce Lint, Dick Fiedler, Jim Baxes, Rene Valdes.

1956 PORTLAND BEAVERS

The Portland Beavers, 1956. This team opened the season in brand new Mult-nomah Stadium. The stadium had formerly been a race track and seated 26,000 people. Of the 22 players on the roster, more than half had previous major league experience. Of the rest, most would eventually move up to the majors. We finished third that year in what was a very competitive league. (Used by permission of Portland Beavers.)

shortstop with a strong arm, kept us alive with his constant chatter like, "You've got to have enthusiasm!" Jack repeated that sentiment constantly, and it picked up everybody.

Artie Wilson, our regular second-bagger from the previous season, had the same upbeat personality and chatter. Artie kept us alive with his infectious, positive spirit, saying, "Never fear, Artie's here!" Artie, like so many other good black players, had missed out on a lengthy career in the majors. The color line prevented him from coming into organized baseball until an advanced age in 1949. He had been one of the greats in the Negro Leagues with the Birmingham Barons, never hitting under .300 in that league. And he hit .316, .332, .336, and .307 in his previous seasons in the PCL.

Artie's forte was a line drive over the third baseman's head, just inside the left field line. Even though he was a left-handed hitter, the defense bunched him to the left, but he would still manage to drop the ball the opposite way, safely down the left field line for a base hit. Artie had a right thumb that was severed at the first knuckle. He had played that way for so long that I really don't think that it hampered his throwing at all. The stories on Artie's play in the Negro League were legendary, about as good as Ol' Satch's. He was a speedy shortstop with great range, a super arm as a youth and a bat that constantly made contact. I was playing with a for-

Pacific Coast League Ball Parks 1957

Name of of Club / Park	Seating of Park	Right Capacity	Center Field	Left Field
Hollywood-Gilmore	12,000	335	400	335
Los Angeles-Wrigley Field	25,000	339	412	340
Portland-Multnomah Stadium	28,870	335	389	305
Sacramento-Edmunds Field	10,500	326	452	326
San Diego-Lane Field	9,000	329	444	330
San Francisco-Seal's Stadium	25,000	350	404	365
Seattle-Sick's Stadium	15,000	335	415	335
Vancouver-Capilano Stadium	10,000	335	415	335

mer black All-Star. The great Jackie Robinson, in fact, was Artie's backup in a Negro League All-Star Game. Imagine Jackie Robinson subbing for Artie in his prime. Artie, whom I guessed to be either a shade over or under 40, could still run, display an average arm, hit PCL pitching for over a .300 average and, perhaps most importantly, display a love and zest for the game that was unmatched by most. God! How I would have loved to have seen Artie Wilson play in his youth.

Jo, Angie, and Muriel were busy with their venturous trips to the Farmers' Market and a few other places. The grocery stores in California were a real treat because all their fruits, vegetables and baked goods were so fresh. Shopping for clothes meant looking, wishing and buying some inexpensive items of necessity, not much more. None of us had the money to provide our wives with expensive clothes.

My salary was $1,400 a month—not too bad for 1956—but the season lasted only five months. I was making $7,000 a year. A new Ford, Plymouth, or Chevy cost $2,500. A brand new, three-bedroom home was about $15,000. My salary sure didn't give Jo Ann anything extra. But that was okay, because our ladies knew how to have fun anyway. And no matter what they were up to all morning, they were always at the ballpark in the afternoon for exhibition games. We had a fine spring training, and everyone seemed ready for the opening of the season.

One time, I recall quite vividly leaving the game in about the sixth inning. Holmes was giving me a breather, so I went into the locker room. I had undressed and was in the shower with soap on my head and in my eyes when I heard this loud, exuberant voice singing at the top of his lungs. I thought that I had heard that voice many times before. I wiped the soap from my eyes, blinked and blinked again to make sure I was seeing right. And then I realized that I had heard the voice before. Standing under the showerhead to my right was Dennis Morgan, the film star, fully clothed and happy as a lark in his somewhat "bombed" state. When you get close to Los Angeles, anything can happen!

We opened the season in Sacramento and beat the old Brownie knuck-leballer, Earl Harrist, 3–2. Sacramento was a great town, the capital of the Golden State, California. We stayed at the Hotel Senator across the street from the capitol grounds. It was an old hotel, well-kept and beautiful. I loved the Sacramento weather with its warm days and cool, dry evenings. During the day, the temperature often got into the 100s but had an extremely low humidity. By 10:30 at night, you would usually find your-self in a sweater or a jacket because the temperature in that semi-arid cli-mate might drop into the 50s by early morning. On one Monday off day in Sacramento, we went to start our golf game at 7 a.m. wearing tee-shirts, sweaters and jackets for the cold. By noon, we were down to our tee-shirts. That day at 4 p.m. the temperature registered 105° in the shade.

It's funny how as a kid you have your idols in baseball. Augie Galan, an outfielder for the Cubs, had been mine. I had also admired Ferris Fain, the great-fielding first baseman for the White Sox. In the Sacramento series, Nippy Jones, the ex-Cardinal first baseman, was playing for the Sacramento team while Ferris Fain sat the bench. In the back of my mind, I kept wondering, "What are Nippy Jones and I doing playing first when Fain is sitting the bench?" It was hard to comprehend. Idols just shouldn't grow old. I felt a little embarrassed playing as one of the greatest fielding first basemen of all time sat and watched.

I was a poor spring-training hitter. Once the season started and I could play regularly, I generally got off to a good start. That '56 season was no different. After Sacramento, we went to Frisco (God, I hated that cold-ass park), then L.A. (I would have paid to play there), then to Hol-lywood and on to San Diego.

I really haven't talked about the San Diego airport—it was a beauty! We flew in four-motor Constellations with Western Airlines. Those pilots were the greatest. After all, they had to be in order to land in the San Diego airport. It had the shortest runway in captivity. We had a pool among the players on the plane going into San Diego. We would actually bet on whether or not we'd make it. And for good reason. More often than not, the pilots—uncanny with their judgment—would miss the telephone wires by just a few feet. And as soon as the wheels would touch, the pilots would reverse the props and send all the passengers pitching forward. Essentially, what a pilot had to do to land the plane safely was stop it as soon as rub-ber touched ground. We would all get out and look at the tires and meas-ure the distance from the tires to the end of the runway. There always seemed to be about a few feet to spare each time, but some pessimist would always say, "I know damn well that we'll go off the runway the next time … and I'll bet on it!"

San Diego had great weather. And with the Pacific Ocean, the naval vessels in the bay, the seafood, and the El Cortez Hotel along with many other amazing features, it was a fantastic city. The El Cortez had a glass elevator attached to the outside of the building that went up 14 floors. It presented a breathtaking view of the bay area because of the hotel's placement on a hilltop.

We had played on the road forever, or at least it seemed that way, and my plump Italian roommate was beginning to look good to me. It was time to head home. The team was off to a poor start but Sam and I had done well. I was hitting .317 and Sam, determined to make up for last season, was batting .275 when we opened at home.

Portland, the City of Roses, had been built to a fever pitch in anticipation of the home opener, a double-header, in the new Multnomah Stadium. Joe Ziegler, our general manager, and Bill Mulflur, his assistant, had done a masterful job of putting baseball across during the winter in Portland.

Marlow Branagan told the story this way in his first two paragraphs of the *Portland Journal*: "The cash register played a record-breaking tune Friday afternoon and evening as the Portland Beavers—for a first time in history—went on to display a spanking new Multnomah Stadium, but the Sacramento Solons spoiled it all day ringing up 'no sale' on their account.

"Playing before 34,750 people—an all-time record for a day-night inaugural in the PCL—the pesky troops of round Tommy Heath spoiled the managerial debut of Thomas Francis Holmes as they twice biffed the white-clad home band into submission."

The stadium, by the way, seated 26,000. Ziegler charged a separate admission for each game.

Eddie Basinski had been in the Coast League for years and he always planned ahead. Eddie once hit me in the locker room before the afternoon game with this one: "Hey Mick, what do you say we split whatever we get in today's games?" Not even thinking, I said, "Okay, Ed." The next morning's sports headlines blurted out, "Mickelson Gets Most Bevo Loot." For the first game in the new ballpark, over $1,000 in gifts were donated by local merchants for everything from the first hit to the first runner safe on an error. In the home opener I got the first triple, and in the nightcap I got the first double and the first home run by a Beaver. There must have been 25 different prizes, ranging from smoking pipes to dining-room furniture. Basinski spent most of the following Monday, a day off, picking up his half of the loot—much of it the good stuff since I had no way of taking furniture home. "Shrewd Eddie" had made a hell of a deal for himself, considering that he didn't play a single inning or even pinch-hit in either game.

Tommy Holmes was a nice guy and everyone really wanted to win for him. But sometimes when you want to win so badly for a guy, you start losing. Then you try even harder, and you become too tight to do anything right.

Holmes spent a lot of time with his players, teaching fundamentals. He was an excellent instructor in the art of hitting. Tommy really didn't present much that Harry the Hat hadn't already stressed to me years ago, but he sure reinforced the basics of hitting that I had learned from Walker. It buoyed my confidence to know that my mechanics were correct. The hard part is to keep from unconsciously getting into a detrimental pattern. That's when the good hitting instructors can really help. The major-league instructor—hitting or pitching—is valuable not because he can teach a major leaguer much that is new. He can help by just watching a player and advising him once he starts to do something mechanically wrong. But the player must be receptive to his advice.

Eddie Basinski, who had excellent hands, was having a bad night in front of the home folks in late in May of '56. He made four errors in the game, but he hung in there. In the last of the ninth with the bases loaded, he hit a grand slam homer to win the game. 6–5. The goat of the night had emerged the hero in the end. Baseball fans are fickle, and a saying I latched onto went like this, "You're only as good as your last time at bat." Or in life, it goes, "What have you done for me lately?"

I tried to change my hitting style by opening my stance in order to pull the ball to left field. I was trying to take advantage of the short left-field fence at Multnomah and was also encouraged to do so by the management. I was a line-drive hitter with left-center and right-center being my power alleys. Even though my average was well over .300 at the end of May, I knew that I could do better. And in my opinion, I was meeting with only moderate success. Jim Baxes, the stockily-built Greek from Frisco with cat-like reflexes, and Bob Borkowski with his rifle-like arm were hitting the bleachers with consistency. But the truth of the matter was that the opposition made better use of the short left-field porch than we did. So when we went to Frisco late in May, we were 23–25 and spinning our wheels.

San Francisco was a great city and its special attraction, the "Top of the Mark," held a central attraction for me. First of all, it was on top of Nob Hill, one of the highest points in the city. On the top of the Mark Hopkins Hotel was a circular bar, which revolved as you sat on your bar stool, and it had windows on the perimeter of the circular room. Alcatraz, the Golden Gate Bridge and much of San Francisco could be seen as the bar revolved a full 360 degrees. At night, with a myriad lights twinkling in the dark, the sight became even more enthralling.

Just a few steps from the entrance to the Mark Hopkins was the Fairmont Hotel. The Fairmont had four huge nightclubs, all with top-drawer entertainers. Ella Fitzgerald sang in one of the rooms on that trip, and she was always a pleasure to hear. San Francisco had so many places to go and see that it boggled the mind. Visiting teams generally had trouble winning in Frisco with all the distractions.

During our stay in the Golden Gate City that year, the Neon Twins were at it again—hell, they were always at it. Frisco was a big town for them. The weather was cool at night, and a suit and tie were their uniform in that town—as in most towns. The Twins went first-class. They looked like a couple of bankers that night, lawyers the next, and....

We won the last game in San Francisco and went on to Sacramento. The bank building registered the day's date (June 1), the time (12:30 p.m.) and the temperature (a cool and windy 58 degrees). Women were dressed in furs and men donned wool suits. We were traveling by bus because our hotel in San Francisco was only 90 miles from Sacramento, less than a two-hour drive. The temperature rises as you move inland from the Bay Area, and the sun, which is so often shrouded by misty clouds in Frisco, started to shine a few miles out of the city. By the time we got into Sacramento, the temperature was over 100 degrees. For each mile that we traveled eastward, the temperature rose one-half a degree.

We won the first night in Sacramento, and after a bite to eat, Sam and I came back to the hotel. As we entered the lobby we saw Walter Brennan and Edgar Buchanan, who were in Sacramento at the time making a movie. Calderone, never at a loss for words, started talking to them. They were both interesting men. Especially Buchanan. He warmed up to both Sam and me when he found out that we were playing ball for Portland, where he had spent most of his life. Buchanan asserted in his low-pitched, gravelly voice, "I was the best God-damned left-handed oral surgeon in Portland!" I said, "You've got to be putting us on." He said, "No, damn it, I mean it." Both Buchanan and Brennan were a little wobbly, as I surmised that they had been imbibing a little and were about to retire when we met them. Buchanan continued, "I was an oral surgeon for over 25 years, and it wasn't until I was almost 50 before I started acting professionally. I had done bit parts and amateur plays around Portland before that."

Buchanan didn't say it, but you could tell that he was proud of what he had done before he started acting. I thought how much guts it must take to make a career change so late in life. True to Hollywood, actor-fashion, the wealthy Walter Brennan asked if we would leave some tickets for them for the next night. We did, and they came. We ended our conversation just after midnight, with them getting a cab. I wondered how they would look on the set at 6:00 a.m.

It was later in life that I realized how accomplished these two actors would be. Walter Brennan had already won three supporting actor Academy Awards. He would go on to appear in 232 movies. Edgar Buchanan became a household fixture in *Petticoat Junction* and *Green Acres*, two early TV sitcoms.

On June 7th in San Diego, we won our eighth straight game after sweeping the Sacramento series. From there it was all downhill for the men of Tommy Homes. We went into Hollywood and lost the opener. The Hollywood atmosphere, like San Francisco, could cause the best clubs to go into a slump. We stayed at the Hollywood Plaza Hotel on Hollywood and Vine, which in itself was temptation enough. At Hollywood and Vine, you could see anything. We used to stand on the street in front of the hotel and girl-watch. The winner of the most unique outfit for that season was a shapely young lady walking a poodle on a leash. She was wearing a halter top, short shorts, high heels, sunglasses and a fur piece draped over her shoulders. It was the damnedest sight I saw all year.

Prize fighters Tony Galento, Slapsy Maxie Rosenbloom, Buddy Baer and others hung out in the lobby of the Hollywood Plaza. Jack Bailey's popular television show, *Queen for a Day*, played nationally from one of the ballrooms in the hotel. At noon, which was lunchtime for the stars but breakfast for ball players, it was common to see many famous television personalities eating in a booth in the hotel's coffee shop. Bob "Bork" Borkowski, our right fielder, was reminiscing over coffee with George Gobel, an old Air Force buddy. "Lonesome George" and "Spooky Ol' Alice," his oft-mentioned wife, were stars of *The George Gobel Show*. It was about the hottest show on television at that time. Gobel came down to the hotel often and shared old times with Bork. It was truly amazing to me how many of the Hollywood stars loved baseball and would attend the games.

Clay Hopper got his revenge. Our former Portland skipper, who was now managing Hollywood, beat us soundly and started us on an 11-game losing streak which eventually cost Tommy Holmes his job. We won six in a row late in June and early July, but the front office worried that another losing streak might crop up again.

Clyde Perkins, one of our stockholders, had become a vice president of the club. He was the owner of the Perkins Oil Company, a big operation with a chain of 100 automobile and truck filling stations in Oregon and Washington. According to L.H. Gregory, "Clyde Perkins, the businessman from Vancouver, Washington, brought a sizeable chunk of new money into the ball club." Gregory also said that the money he had pumped into the team had put us in good shape.

Steve Bilko and his Los Angeles Bombers came to Portland, and everyone in their lineup was having a good season. The 1956 Los Angeles Angels would go on to win the Coast League pennant by 16 games with a .637 percentage. Bob Scheffing's crew was an awesome batting group, with a team average of .297 and 202 homers for the season. Big Steve hit .360 with 55 homers and 164 RBIs. Gene Mauch hit .348 with 111 RBIs. Then came Gale Wade at .292, George Freese at .291 and K.C. Wise was .287. Bob Anderson, Dave Hillman, Gene Fodge, John Briggs, and Dick Drott were the big winners on the Los Angeles pitching staff. The Angels defeated us on the 10th, 11th and 12th of July, and on that last day, Tommy Holmes resigned as manager.

I hated to see Tommy leave. He was fair, honest, enthusiastic and a good teacher—everything you wanted in a manager. I think we were all down when Holmes left. Parting in baseball is a matter of fact, or at least it's supposed to be. "Well, you know, it's a part of the game," went the old cliché. But it still tore at your guts when you saw a grown man moved to tears as he shook hands with his players before leaving, for good. Tommy was crushed. I had seen that look before. Sure, it was a part of life and a part of baseball, but I hated it. I felt guilty, asking myself why I couldn't have done more to save the man's job. Holmes returned home to Woodbury, New York on Long Island.

His replacement was Bill Sweeney. He had managed Portland from 1936 to 1939 and had returned again from 1949 to 1951. Sweeney, like Lefty O'Doul, had become a legend in the Coast League, starring there as a first baseman before going to the American League with Boston and Detroit. Besides Portland, Sweeney had bossed Hollywood, Seattle and Los Angeles. Obviously, he had been around the Coast League several times.

So Bill Sweeney took over the Portland Beavers on July 13, 1956, as we finished up that home series with the red-hot Angels. They finished us up by scoring 12 runs in the first inning. Sweeney must have had some misgivings about leaving his Arcadia, California, home as we were beaten into submission that night, 19–4. I hit a home run and would continue to do for Sweeney what I had not done for Holmes—hit homers and drive in runs.

Rene Valdes (our Cuban side-wheeler), Bob Darnell, Bill Werle and Bob Alexander all pitched well from then on, with steady help from big Ray "Snacks" Shore. Snacks had been our strong relief pitcher in '55 and '56, coming out of the bullpen with his great variety of pitches—a fastball. That's all he threw—just smoke. I remembered Snacks from the International League when he played for Toronto. He was 6'3" with a huge upper torso, and he never wore a long-sleeved sweatshirt. Even with the temperature in the 30s in Toronto, Snacks would get up to warm up with bare arms showing. He also had another peculiarity: He never warmed up in the bullpen by throwing from the rubber to home plate. He would stand a good 30 feet behind the mound and throw to home, a distance of about 90 feet. Despite his quirks, Snacks was humorous and could always get a laugh out of me.

Snacks was relieving late in the ballgame and was doing quite well. We had a pretty good lead and could afford to clown a bit. I called for time and ran to the mound. Snacks looked down at me and said, "What do you want, Mick?" I said, "Ray, I've never once seen you throw a curve. How about breaking one off for me?" Snacks said, "Mick, I haven't got a curve, that's why you haven't seen it, but I'll spin one up there for you if it will make you happy." On the next pitch, he threw what looked like an off-speed fastball rather than a curve, and a gawd-awful line drive was hit to left field for a base hit. Snacks glowered at me and yelled, "Hey Mick! From now on you hit and I'll pitch." I thought to myself, hell, Sowins would never swing at the first pitch, and here is a guy who has been in baseball for more than 10 years who had only one pitch. What kind of game is this, anyway?

Just as we started going good, we got into Los Angeles again. I always hit in that park but we just could not beat Los Angeles that year. They took us in five straight. We left Los Angeles at the end of July and started to make a run at it, but we were in fifth place, 19½ games out. And time was short.

Then Marquez and I got hot. On August 1st we both hit two homers each against Sacramento, and my second one came in the bottom of the tenth to win the game. In three weeks I had hit seven homers for Sweeney and driven in 22 runs. Luis was having a great season, hitting .349 with 81 RBIs. He was given a night on August 8th, with 7,092 fans honoring the fiery Puerto Rican. Marquez received a shower of gifts, plus $500 from the Portland club and $100 from his teammates. All Marquez could say that night was, "My lips will not speak the words that are in my heart."

The next night, August 9th, Jerry Casale threw me a changeup with the bases loaded in the last of the eighth, and I homered to lead us to a 6–4 win. I felt a great swell of exhilaration as I rounded the bases. To a hitter, there is no feeling in the world like a game-winning, bases-loaded home run. What Tommy Holmes had taught me earlier was now starting to pay off, and I now had 16 homers. Too bad he couldn't have benefited from the lessons he taught me.

The All-Star Game was to be played in Portland. Marquez, Calderone, Valdez and Littrell had made the Northern All-Stars. Calderone had hung in there all season without getting hurt, but just before the All-Star Game he split a finger.

We spent the day that was supposed to be an off day after the All-

Star Game playing an exhibition game in Victoria, British Columbia. Victoria is on the southernmost tip of Vancouver Island, just south and west of the city of Vancouver. Exhibition games are some of the most disliked encounters in baseball. After several months of steady play, you point to an open date in the future and pin your hopes on a week of rest and relaxation at the All-Star break. You tell yourself to hang in for just a little longer, and then will come that break—a few days away from the game for fun and frolic. But when that time is taken away, players react with anger.

Victoria was a beautiful city with its well-kept homes, lawns and flower gardens. Everywhere there were flowers. Prince Edward Hotel was a huge place, taking up a whole city block, and the grounds around the hotel were magnificent. Not a blade of grass was out of place. Everything was in order and beautiful.

We went to the ballpark in Victoria and it wasn't bad at all. We played the hometown Mounties before 3,000 people in a Conquer Cancer fundraising game. Around that time, we had been on the road so much that the days and places started to blend together. Someone asked after the game, "What day is it—what town are we in?" That's a common question in baseball near the end of the season. You wake up in a hotel room and your mind races as you wonder where the heck you are. We played nine innings that night and lost 8–5, but no one was really too broken up over an exhibition loss. Exhibitions are not taken seriously. We ended the game shortly after 10 p.m. and hadn't even used the lights. It still wasn't dark yet as we stepped out of the locker room to board the bus and head back to the hotel. A faint glimmer of light could still be seen in the west at 10:45 p.m.

That night back at the hotel we had a party. It was like the days of old. We were all together and having fun. Snacks was the ringleader. He had said on the bus, "Let's get some food and beer and have a party!" And party we did. We got off the bus and went to the nearest delicatessen. The whole ball club got in on it. Even the Neon Twins called off their nightly adventure to join us. We came back with four or five large grocery bags laden with food and drink. We spread our food out on the bed in Snacks' room. Pickled pigs' feet, tuna fish, sardines, beer, soda, ham, salami, cheese, olives, pickles—you name it, we had it. We ate and ate, drank and drank, and laughed and laughed.

The next morning we got up to leave this regal hotel. We all piled out the entrance to the bus. As we came down the front steps of the hotel, we looked down to our right and spied our dapper outfielder from Stanford, Lloyd Merriman, stretched out in the flower bed, out cold. This was way out of character for Lloyd. He was intelligent, reserved, well-dressed and always conducted himself in a dignified manner. Nevertheless, there was Lloyd—in the flower bed. We picked him up, brushed him off and got him on the bus and on the plane back to Portland. I guess you could call it "letting go." Merriman was having his problems hitting and he let it all out that night in Victoria. I have never seen him before or after that night take more than a drink or two.

Frank Carswell, an aging veteran of the baseball wars, had joined us. Frank had seen some major-league play. He was an excellent hitter, but he looked older in the outfield and running bases than a man in his late thirties. However, his bat did help us in some crucial spots throughout the remainder of the season. We had moved slowly from fifth to fourth and now were closing in on third place.

But Los Angeles came to town and Dave Hillman beat us on the night of August 29th. The Angels had beaten us in sixteen out of nineteen games. If we could have handled them, we would have finished second in the league. Even though we beat them the next three games, the damage had been done. After L.A., we took Vancouver five straight as Calderone was back in the lineup going strong again. We went to Seattle after our successful series with Vancouver and Rene Valdes became that season's first 20-game winner in the PCL by nine minutes. Dave Hillman won his 20th a few minutes after Valdes. The next night in Seattle, my roomie was at bat. Bud Podbelian, a former Dodger, was working his magical curveball on us. Calderone, the "spaghetti-bender," was moaning and groaning at the plate with the score tied one and one in the seventh. Podbelian had made Sammy look particularly bad on several breaking balls. I prayed, "Dear Lord, let Podbelian throw Sammy a high fastball." He hadn't seen a high fastball in a week. So with two on, Podbelian decided to fool Sammy with a high fastball, eye-high. Sam tomahawked it over the left field fence, and it was last seen headed toward Mt. Rainier some 50 miles southeast of Seattle.

Sammy and I came back to the room after winning that night and babbled like a couple of kids. This had been a good season for both of us, so it was easy to celebrate. Sam had hit his 14th homer. He had made the PCL All-Star team, and was hitting .285. I was nearing 100 RBIs and had 20 home runs. I had 172 hits, Sam had stroked 118. Sam said that night in Seattle at the Olympic Hotel, "Hey Mick, we have sure filled our room with base hits this season, haven't we?" In his voice there was a touch of pride a person feels after redeeming himself. I said, "Sam, if we get any more hits this season the room won't be able to hold them all." We slept a contented sleep that night.

Sam loved people—all people. Drunks, kids, old people, blacks and browns, Sam loved them all. I would see Sam talking to people everywhere we went. In the cab to the driver, in the restaurant to the waitress,

Sam talked to everybody. The remarkable virtue was that even with all his talking, you'd be hard-pressed to find him having a bad word for anybody. That's why I got mad in the clubhouse when some of the guys would get on Sam too hard. I called him spaghetti-bender, but in private. That was okay between him and me because he knew how I really felt about him. Besides, he knew I was Norwegian and Italian. Sam loved people and most everyone responded to him in like manner.

We closed out the Seattle series winning twice more. I celebrated my 30th birthday in Seattle by going 0 for 4 and getting hit in my newly helmeted head by Elmer Singleton. My affable Italian buddy, in his cheerful manner said, "Happy birthday, Mick! You're leading the league in getting knocked down this season." Sam had it right. I too was beginning to wonder if, at 30, I was losing my reflexes. I had been thrown at a lot but had never been beaned before Witt got me in the previous season. This year, Dave Hillman and Elmer Singleton both skulled me and sent me to the hospital. I must have been about 1 for 40 against Singleton through the years, so why he would throw at me was a mystery. He should have sent a cab to the hotel to make sure I got to the ballpark on the day he was pitching. After each beaning, as Dizzy Dean said so many years before, "The doctors X-rayed my head and found nothing."

The Dugout Varieties were a big event staged by the Portland Beavers. Some of us would sing, one would strum a guitar and another would play violin as we put on a display of talent that set entertainment back several years. Over 10,000 fans joined in the fun. Some who were already "in good spirits" sang right along with us, only to cry with us at 12:50 in the morning when the second game of the double-header was called in the sixth. We lost the first game in twelve innings, 5–4, and the second one (which was short but official), 2–0. Seattle, the team that we beat so easily at their ballpark, rose up in ours and knocked us back into 4th place.

The Neon Twins, in their subtle, behind-the-scenes way, were having a good season. On almost every road trip, good things seem to happen for them. We were flying Western Air Lines on our last trip to San Diego with two very good-looking redheaded airline attendants. They looked as if they might be twins. The guys on the plane were making all kinds of moves on them with none working. That night at Lane Field, the home of the Padres, as we were taking infield, I looked up over our dugout and saw the two redheads talking to the Neon Twins. The Neon Twins were the best!

Then Hollywood came into Portland in third place, one game ahead of us. The press was helping us out by building the series up so we could go over 300,000 in attendance. We lost the first game but won the second with Carswell and Marquez leading us. In the third game, Carswell had another good night as we won and moved up to third place. The closing day double-header would decide it. We lost the first game, 5–4, but came back to win the second game, 6–5, finishing the season in third place, one game ahead of Hollywood.

That final game saved me as I had a double and a home run to drive in three runs, ending the season with 101 RBIs, 21 homers and a .309 batting average. I had reached my goals, but I had hoped we could have climbed just two places higher.

So we left Portland after a satisfying season. Goodbye Sam and Angie. Goodbye Luis, Carswell, Baxes, Young, Royce, Saffell, Merriman, Snacks, Darrell Martin, Leo Thomas, Darnell, Alexander, Tip, Rocky, L.H. Gregory, Marlowe, Banagan, George Gill, Ted Hoener, Joe Zeigler, Bill Mulflur, Mr. Griswold, Mt. Hood, the Willamette, Western Airlines, Los Angeles, Hollywood, the Mark Hopkins Hotel, smelly locker rooms, sanitary socks, Multnomah, Bottler, Valdes, the San Diego airport, Mr. Perkins, the *Oregonian*, the *Journal* and the Neon Twins. Twins, you're the greatest.

12

Feliz Navidad y Próspero Año Nuevo

Dr. Stanley Hampton was a stockily built man. He had shell-rimmed glasses and the white medical jacket commonly worn by physicians. He talked in a deep, cheerful Southern drawl, and he had fond memories of his alma mater, Washington and Lee. He had just signed our certificate of smallpox vaccination and dated it 9/25/56. He also helped me with an allergy problem caused by dust, and I was to take a serum in a small bottle with me to Venezuela. He told me, "Now Ed, be sure to keep this refrigerated and give yourself injections every 10 days to two weeks." We thanked him as Jo Ann and I left his office.

We were getting everything in order to play winter ball in Venezuela. I was to report to the Valencia baseball team around the 10th of October. The season was to start a few days later. We needed to get a certificate from our local police chief recommending us as reputable citizens of our community. Brown Hairgrove, chief of police in the St. Louis suburb of Overland, gave us the letter we needed. We completed our medical forms by visiting the US Public Health Service in downtown St. Louis early in October, where we received shots for yellow fever. We had everything in order and would leave for New York via TWA a couple days later. As Jo Ann and I left the building, I glanced into the window of a restaurant that had the World Series playing. I asked Jo if she would like to get a bite to eat and take in some of the game. She said, "Sure." The game was in the seventh inning and Don Larsen was in the midst of a perfect game. A chill went up my spine when Dale Mitchell of the Cleveland Indians came to bat, and when he was called out on a third strike to end the game the room erupted with cheers. My mind raced back to our spring training together in '53, and I wanted to connect somehow with Don on this momentous occasion. I was happy for him, and I was in awe that someone I knew was able to do such a momentous feat.

In New York we had to make connections with the Venezuelan consulate to get more papers cleared before flying to Caracas. After landing at La Guardia Airport, we were told by the Venezuelan consulate to stay at the Piccadilly Hotel in New York. We had several days to sightsee at St. Patrick's Cathedral, Rockefeller Center, Times Square, the Empire State Building and, best of all, to have dinner at Mama Leone's. Mama Leone's and Alfred's in San Francisco ran each other a close race. I couldn't distinguish between the two superb restaurants.

The middle of October saw us en route by Venezuelan Airlines to Caracas. We left New York around 9 p.m., flying over the ocean at night. The morning sun brightened the sky as huge, white, fleecy clouds floated by with the blue-green ocean below. It was a breathtaking sight. We arrived at the Maiquetia Airport at 8 a.m. This airport, the busiest in Venezuela, nestles in a valley surrounded by mountains and near the ocean. It is located 18 miles from the center of Caracas. A driver met us at the airport to pick us up and drive us to Valencia. We had an easy time going through customs. I had learned some Spanish in high school and college, and I put it to good use with our driver as I conversed with him during our 102-mile trip. I would make this trip dozens of times during the next four months.

The readying for departure from St. Louis, the flight to New York, the flight to Caracas and the ride over dangerous mountain highways toward Valencia combined to unnerve me significantly. I had slept in almost every hotel in every major city in the United States and rarely felt apprehensive. Even so, I was beginning to feel uneasy and fearful. It was a subtle anxiety that I was not fully aware of, but I felt increasingly uncomfortable.

Caracas, the capital and largest city in the country, had a population then of about 875,000 people. The city is 3,018 feet above sea level as it sits in a narrow valley encircled by a coastal mountain range. The autopista, a new, four-lane highway, enabled us to travel quickly over the 18 miles from the airport to Caracas. The old road could be seen above us winding like a narrow ribbon as it slithered through the rugged terrain. We had to climb from sea level to an altitude much higher than the city and come over and down the mountain into the city. From there we traveled on a narrow two-lane highway, winding down the mountainside to the plains below and to the west toward Valencia. At that time only one highway connected the booming oil town of Maracaibo with Caracas—over 500 miles separated these northern coastal cities of Venezuela. As we traveled that highway we encountered heavy trucks, cars, ox-carts, buses and various other moving objects. We went through the town of Maracay, the midway point between Caracas and Valencia with its heavily populated army base, and arrived at the Hotel Valencia around 1 p.m.

The Association of Venezuelan Professional Baseball permitted eight imports to be split up between each of the four teams in the league. The

I'VE NEVER APPRECIATED THE OLD TEAM BUS -- UNTIL NOW!

Illustration by Ron Joyner.

rest of the players had to be natives. The eight Americans who started the season were pitchers Dick Hanlon, Kelton Russell and Ed Burtschy, outfielders Art Schult and Bobby Balcena, catcher Earl Battey and infielders Ron Plaza and me. The glamour of playing winter ball wears off quickly for some people, though. The change of climate and food, plus being in a strange land with a different language, caused some to have a change of heart. A few had second thoughts about staying even the first few days.

After a few days at the Valencia Hotel, we moved to the Cuatrocientos Hotel (the 400 Hotel) a few blocks away. Our hosts for the next few months were Señor and Señora Vitale, a delightful Spanish couple, very cordial and kind. The rooms, though not spacious, were clean, airy and sufficient. We were located on the second floor and had one large room, a desk, chair, bed and a bath with a shower off a bedroom. The floors throughout the building were terrazzo and the walls were freshly painted. The stone front blended in well with the palm trees and the flowers. The building was old but well-kept. The grounds were well-groomed as well, and we felt very lucky to have a swimming pool. The pool was a problem at times because it had no filter and periodically needed to be drained and refilled. Before long, that became a task we all assumed, and we maintained it regularly all winter. This would be home for the next four months for the Norte Americanos.

The Branger (Bron-jay) brothers, Raul and Armando, were our bene-

The Valencia Industriales, 1956–57 league champions. We lost to Caracas, Venezuela, in the playoffs eliminating us from playing Havana, Cuba, in the Caribbean Series. Back row, left to right: First is Ed Burtschy. Fourth toward the right is Ron Plaza. Fifth is Hisel Patrick. Seventh is Kelton Russell. Eighth is Earl Battey. Tenth and last is Ed Mickelson. Sitting, left to right: First is Emilio Cueche. Second is Bobby Balcena. Fifth is manager Reggie Otero. Eighth is Elio Chacon. The other team members are Julian Ladera, Francisco Cirimele, Manuel Lopez, Jeasus Mora, Levy Rodrigues, Edwardo Monasterios, Tito Acosta, Carlos Castillo. Bat boys: Saturino Pasez and Hugo Pacheco.

factors. They owned the team and provided monetary backing for baseball in Valencia. I had been told that I would be playing for $1,000 per month plus expenses. That salary was pretty standard in that league, and I believe that is what most of the Americans received. But when we got there, we were told that we would have to pay for our meals and hotel room out of our monthly salary. Expenses were high in Venezuela—a bottle of beer was three bolivares ($1), and a pack of American cigarettes was 60 cents. The going rate at that time was one American dollar for three bolivares. In the States in 1956, cigarettes were about a quarter and a beer was about 30 cents at the local tavern. We figured it would cost us close to $600 a month to live in our present surroundings. A minor mutiny occurred among the eight Americans, but an understanding was reached with the owners after a few hours of discussion. We would be furnished our salary, room and meals at the hotel in addition to travel expenses on the road, as per our original agreement.

We opened the season on October 23rd in Valencia's huge stadium, which seated over 20,000 fans. The *fanáticos* filled the stadiums in that country. The rainy season was in full bloom, and it had rained parts of every day since we had arrived. That night in the home opener, I hit a home run with a couple of men on base, and we were leading the Oriente team when the rains came. A torrential downpour flooded the field, and the game was cancelled along with my home run. I hoped that this was not an omen of things to come. Ball players are extremely superstitious, and I was no exception.

Most of our road games were scheduled at the huge stadium in Caracas. Oriente and Pompero played some of their home games there, as did the Caracas team. John Roseboro, Chico Carresquel and Tom Burgess were with Caracas. Mike Goliat, Lou Limmer, and Russ Rac were with Pompero. And Joe Altobelli, Bob Darnell and Harry Eliott were with Oriente. These three clubs plus ours in Valencia made up the Venezuelan Winter League. The soccer stadium in Caracas had been built in '51 for the third Bolivarian Olympic Games and seated at least 45,000. Adjacent to it was the 25,000-seat baseball stadium. The two stadiums, located near Ciudad Universitaria, had a very modern lighting system for night games.

Felix Garcia, a former Valencia soccer great, had been assigned the job of transporting the Norte Americanos in his station wagon back and forth from Valencia to Caracas. Each trip was an adventure in itself with Felix at the wheel. We experienced one harrowing ride after another. The highway between Valencia and Caracas ran in front of our hotel. It was nothing more than a two-lane street and it carried tons of traffic. All eight of us gringos got into Felix's station wagon, rolled out of the hotel driveway and took a right turn onto the slow-moving highway. The Venezuelans, for some reason, disconnect their auto horns. Instead of honking, they just pound the side of the car door with their left hand while sticking their heads out and yelling.

We settled back as Felix plodded through the narrow streets of Valencia. When we reached the open country outside of town, the traffic started to move faster. A driver on that highway faced a never-ending stream of traffic coming toward him, not to mention a long line behind. We soon found that this would be no obstacle for Garcia. Whenever the urge struck him, he made his move.

As we drove along the highway on our first trip, Felix was about to make his first move of many that season. With his right hand he gave himself the sign of the cross, then placed it back on the wheel. With his left hand he banged on the door; then he placed his hand back on the wheel and swung out into the oncoming traffic, passing the car in front and darting quickly back into the right lane just before the oncoming traffic came swishing past us. We watched this procedure with shouts of alarm that fell on deaf ears. Felix would not be deterred. We reluctantly had to accept his driving habits. As soon as we saw the sign of the cross, eight gringos hit the floor. The only erect head in the car was that of Felix Garcia.

We were rained out in Caracas and returned to Valencia having yet to play an official game. Jo Ann said, "Honey, how was the trip to Caracas?" I said, "Great, baby, just great." It took several weeks before I got up the courage to tell her about the utter terror that I felt with Felix Garcia, our chauffeur, at the wheel.

The rain stopped in early November and coincided with the stopping of my diarrhea. The rain and I both had gone on for several weeks, and it was a relief to me when both halted. "Montezuma's Revenge," or gastroenteritis, is a malady that strikes most visiting non-natives in Venezuela. It starts with sharp intestinal pains, slight nausea and in some cases vomiting and diarrhea. I was pleased to find out that beer was the best antidote for me. The natives warned us that though the water in Valencia was good, we shouldn't drink it in other towns, and we shouldn't eat unwashed fruits or vegetables.

When the rain ceased and we finally started playing some games, the team got off to a slow start. Our second trip took us to a farming area and a town called Barquistimeto (Bar-key-stee-may-toe), which had a population of 130,000 people. Only a few buildings stood over three stories in height. The road we traveled to Barquistimeto was the new Pan American Highway, an excellent asphalt surface with two extra-wide lanes. The highway could permit speeds in excess of 70 miles an hour. In deference to the cattle which crossed at will, the legal speed was much slower.

I saw a sign on the highway that said, "Do not enter this area because it might contain Motolones." I asked Felix what the sign meant. He replied in Spanish, "The Motolones are a lost savage tribe of several thousand— very anti-social. They run naked and with shaved heads. They raid other Indian villages and oil camps, and they fight with heavy arrows that are five feet long. You must stay away from them. Expeditions go into their territory and never return. They have been known to shoot their arrows into low-flying planes. They are very bad!"

I asked Felix how far they were from Barquistimeto. He replied, "They roam around and are hardly ever in one place, but they are mostly south and west of us about 100 miles or more." I said, "Felix, yo no quiero por los Motolones acerca de mi." Felix nodded, so I guess he understood my Spanish.

On November 8th at the Cuatrocientos Hotel, Jo and I celebrated our ninth wedding anniversary with our baseball friends. We had champagne and a cake and it seemed to pick up everyone's spirits, especially Jo Ann's and mine. The Brangers had a little Sunbeam car that they left at the hotel for the players to drive. We took it out in that cool air to see the sights of Valencia. In November and December, the rains stop and the nights become cooler, but the daytime temperatures are like the spring days in

America with much sunshine. That November night was beautiful, and we enjoyed very much our ninth anniversary.

Time passed slowly in Valencia. We played only three games a week—once during the week and twice on the weekend. We took all our meals—breakfast, lunch and dinner—in the hotel dining room. Breakfast was served until 9 a.m. If you missed it you had to wait until noon for the lunch menu. The big meal came in the evening from 7 to 9. The Americans couldn't wait for the dining room to open. We were all used to eating much earlier. So as early as 5 p.m., some of us would work our way toward the dining area, anxiously waiting for the doors to open. We would all sit and talk outside the dining room with long, hungry looks on our faces. Our waiter, Daniel, was from Spain and spoke very little English, so we all had to order in Spanish. Jo Ann quickly learned words like *leche* (milk), *mantequilla* (butter) and *carne* (meat).

We spent countless hours in the bar, more to socialize than to drink. Jesus (Hey-sus), our bartender, was also a native of Spain. He was a young lad in his early twenties with a congenial disposition and an ever-present smile on his face. He knew very little English. By the time we left, he knew some English but we had learned even more Spanish. As we were told, the water was good in Valencia but some of the players were skeptical. More beer was consumed than water—for precautionary purposes only—and *cerveza* (beer) became a word we would never lose from our Spanish vocabulary.

Art Schult was hitting well, but for personal reasons he and his family decided to go back to the States. From that moment on, a new word became dominant in our life—*solvencia*. A solvencia was certification from the Venezuelan government that was presented to the proper authorities before anyone was permitted to leave the country. Schult tried for three frustrating weeks to obtain certification to leave Venezuela, but for one reason or another, he was put off. The answer was always "Mañana" (tomorrow). It seemed like he might never get out. Finally, he obtained his solvencia and returned to the United States.

More and more I had the feeling of being held prisoner. I realized that I could not leave the country without a solvencia. It was irritating to know that you were at the will of the owners who would not let you leave, especially if you were having a good season.

Charles Peete, an outfielder, had just led the American Association in batting. He had hit .350 with 16 homers and 63 RBIs in 116 games and was being counted heavily to break into the St. Louis Cardinals outfield in the near future. Charlie's plane arrived at the Maiquetia airport in a morning fog. According to the newspaper reports, the pilot was told to circle the field and wait for further orders. After 20 minutes, the pilot decided to land on an emergency landing strip on the side of the mountain, even though the plane had ample gas and was in no trouble. It ended up missing the landing strip and crashing into the side of the mountain, killing everyone on board. Charlie, his wife Nettie, and their young child were all killed. We were a downcast group at the Cuatrocientos Hotel for quite some time after the accident. From the dugout in the Caracas ballpark, I could see the charred scar left on the mountainside by the fiery plane. Charlie Peete died at the age of 26.

A shipment of baseball bats from the States for our team was on board that ill-fated plane. The bats were strewn along the mountainside with most of them intact. We were not permitted to acquire the bats, a decision made by the Branger brothers. They felt that this would be disrespectful to those who had died.

Before Christmas we were to take a trip to the "Orient," a region in the upper northeastern part of Venezuela. We had not been told before leaving the United States that this would be a part of our schedule. We were scheduled to play games in the towns of Maturín and Carúpano. After Charlie Peete's death, we all became apprehensive about flying with the Venezuelan Airlines. We made our feelings known to the Branger brothers but were overruled.

The trip to Maturín was made on a Venezuelan TACA airline and it was a beautiful flight. Maturín, the capital of the state of Monagas, had a population of about 36,000. It was located on the plains with an altitude of 245 feet. The airport and the landing field were both small, but our twin-engine plane landed on a flat dirt landing strip in a cloud of dust with no problem.

We left the airport and headed for the hotel. Maturín and its surroundings looked like some movies I had seen depicting Mexican towns. I expected Pancho Villa to walk by any minute. We had a few *jamón y queso* (ham and cheese) sandwiches and washed them down with beer. There was no way I was going to touch the water. So Balcena, Plaza and I sat up most of the night sipping beer. No one really wanted to go to bed because that meant sleeping in a dirty room on a sagging mattress. There were no screens on the windows, and bats were flying in and out at will, but by 3 a.m. the beer had taken effect and we were relaxed enough to sleep anywhere.

The next day at the Maturín ballpark, I could hear church bells ringing in the distance and I could see dust coming up from the dirt road as cars, buses and trucks were en route to the game. The ballpark was a few miles outside of town and the entire playing surface was dirt—infield and outfield—and it was very dusty. The Maturín fans who filled the stands were a hearty group and very demonstrative as they yelled, hooted, and howled. They had fun! The fans had seen a good baseball game and left as they came—choking the remaining ball players by kicking up a long cloud of dust behind their vehicles. We changed at the hotel and bid good-bye to Maturín as we boarded our twin-engine plane for Carúpano, which was located on the Caribbean Sea in the northeastern part of Venezuela.

A treat was in store for us as the view of the city from the air was breathtaking. The Isla de Margarita was 125 miles to the northwest, and the island of Trinidad was several hundred miles due east. Carúpano was founded in 1647 and had a distinct Spanish influence in its architecture. Our accommodations were clean and comfortable, not at all like in Maturín. After the game in Carúpano, the local people gave us a feast in a building on the beach. The food was excellent, the beer was cold and a small group of natives played lively Venezuelan music to add to the festivities. I walked out on the sandy white beach and halted under an open shelter. I watched the waves rolling in to shore, and in the cool breeze the sun shone brilliantly. A few white clouds floated gently against the pale blue sky. The ocean was beautiful. Carúpano seemed so remote, so peaceful. I wondered when the tourists would take over this tranquil spot. I drank my first glass of water in 72 hours after returning to the 400 Hotel. Christmas was almost upon us, and we were all looking forward to the holiday.

Carl Powis, a broad-shouldered, barrel-chested lad, was almost six feet tall, but his stocky build made him look shorter. He was a handsome fellow with sharp, chiseled, Valentino-like features, a straight-pointed nose and hair combed back. Carl was strong, had a good arm, fair speed and swung a bat with authority. He really loved motorcycles and was always imitating their sounds. "Va, Va, Voom! Va, Va, Voom!" he would go. As Christmas approached, I thought of home—my mom and dad, Jo Ann's folks, our friends and familiar surroundings. Even with Jo Ann alongside me in Venezuela, I felt nostalgia for home creeping in. I think we were both a little homesick. This was our first Christmas out of the States. But for "Va Va Voom," as we called Powis, the Christmas holidays seemed to present a time of greater loneliness. I mentioned to Carl how I felt about missing my relatives and friends back home. Carl then told me that he felt lonely too, much of the time in fact, but especially at Christmas. He said, "Mick, I haven't got anybody—no mom, no dad, nobody. Oh, I have a cousin here and there. But, no, really, I mean it—I haven't got a soul otherwise." I told him that must be awful. "You're right, Mick. It sure is," he said. I wondered how it would feel to have absolutely no one, to be totally alone in the world.

We drew names, exchanged gifts and had our Christmas party in a large ballroom of the Hotel Valencia. The Branger brothers entertained us with food and drink. We enjoyed eating special Venezuelan dishes appropriate to the season. We broke a piñata, a large papier-mâché container made in various shapes and sizes filled with candies and small presents. People take turns striking it with a baseball-like club while blindfolded. It is an old Spanish custom practiced in most of the Latin American countries. The piñata is mainly for children, who rush in to pick up the presents as they fall from the smashed ornament. And we, like children, rushed to grab the gifts.

As our Christmas Eve party neared midnight, fireworks started to shoot into the sky throughout the city. We opened the doors of the ballroom which led to the balcony, three floors above the street. Children were shooting firecrackers from the sidewalk below, and the sky was ablaze with skyrockets exploding throughout the night. The Brangers had brought fireworks to the party, and we had fun setting off our own display.

New Year's Eve was spent at the 400 Hotel as well, as musicians came by singing traditional Venezuelan carols. The singers were in large groups— young, old, and mixed—with everyone smiling and in a joyous spirit. Christmas had been ushered in with a bang, and New Year's with a song.

The holidays had come and gone and we had just finished a ball game at the stadium in Caracas. Felix was at the wheel of the station wagon heading us back towards Valencia when he asked Ronnie Plaza to drive. Plaza got behind the wheel as Felix rested. A law in Venezuela prohibited foreigners on visa status from driving a vehicle. We were about 18 kilometers east of Caracas on a large four-lane highway, speeding westward with Plaza at the wheel. We passed a sign that said Los Teques. A green-uniformed soldier approached our car on a motorcycle, told us to pull over and asked to see Plaza's driver's license. Felix had slumped down in his seat as his ruddy, brown complexion had paled. The officer got into the car, leaving his cycle behind, and directed Felix to drive to *la chota* (jail). As we detoured off our course, I envisioned spending the night in a Venezuelan jail.

It was about 11:30 at night when we entered *la chota* at Los Teques. The desk sergeant looked up from his paperwork and smiled. The green-uniformed officer did not return the smile but started talking in Spanish instead, too quickly for me to comprehend. I kept asking Plaza what he was saying, but Ronnie's attention was riveted on the conversation. The sergeant behind the desk took our names and some information as he filled out the papers. Ronnie said, "Felix is in big trouble!" We sat on benches for what seemed like hours as Felix paced up and down, smoking one cigarette after another.

Finally, the sergeant looked up from his paperwork with a broad grin sweeping over his face. "¿Ustedes son jugedores beisbol?" We nodded as he continued, "Plaza, segundo base." Ronnie said, "Sí." The sergeant was beaming. He said, "Mickelson, primero base." I said, "Sí." He knew baseball and he knew us. He went on to relate how he had just listened to the game, giving us a blow-by-blow description of who struck out and who got hits. He remembered the game better than I did. Ronnie and I looked at each other knowingly, as if to say, "It can't be that bad, this guy likes baseball." But the guy in the green uniform sure as heck didn't seem to care about what sport we played. He was ready to depart, but I felt like if he had his way, we would be shot at sunrise.

It was a little after 1 a.m. when we got back on the road, this time with Felix at the wheel. It felt like we had been in that building forever. We still had a long way to go before arriving in Valencia and poor Felix was still very subdued, saying nothing the entire trip. We didn't get the sign of the cross even once as we sat erect in our seats, the only time we didn't that whole season.

I kept abreast of what was happening in the other winter leagues through the weekly issues of the *Sporting News*. There were nine winter leagues in 1956–57: The Cuban, Mexican, Venezuelan, Colombian, Puerto Rican, Vera Cruz, Dominican, Occidental and Panamanian. The January 2nd issue showed Wes Covington and Orlando Cepeda among the top hitters in Puerto Rico, with Roberto Clemente leading the league. In the Cuban League, Minnie Minoso was the top hitter. Earl Battey was leading our league, and I was in the Top 10 with a .309 average. The first half of the split season was won by Caracas, but we were well in front in the second half after getting away to a fast start. Mo Mozzali had joined us around Christmastime. I had played with Mo in Columbus, Ohio. He was a fun-loving guy who always had a smile, a laugh and a joke. Mo kept everyone laughing. He came down as a replacement in the outfield, and he was an excellent hitter. Mozzali, a little guy of just 5'8" and 160 pounds, had great timing and excellent wrists. He hit .300 in Triple A at Columbus for many seasons, but he was never given a shot at the bigs for whatever reason. Now at 35, Mo was hanging on as long as he could. He would say, "Don't drink the water ... it'll kill ya!" He loved baseball and *cerveza*, and Montezuma's Revenge was no problem for Mo. "Una más cerveza, Jesus," Mo would say to our bartender, and one more Heineken bit the dust.

During the month of January we were to play a game in Ciudad Bolívar, which was on Venezuela's far eastern border with Guiana. We went by car, and I was wishing I had kept my mouth shut about not flying because that trip was over 350 miles through the hot plains of Venezuela. Ciudad Bolívar had a population of 36,000 people and is the capital of the state of Bolívar. It was located on the southern bank of the Orinoco River, about 240 miles upstream from its mouth. One of the largest iron ore deposits in the world was just 50 miles south of the city. The city was the commercial center for the entire river system.

Piranhas were prevalent in the Orinoco River. The piranha is a small fish with a silver-gray back and bright orange belly, usually less than a foot in length. The lower jaw of the piranha protrudes and the mouth is filled with saw-edged sharp teeth. It is attracted by the smell of blood and is capable of removing a man's finger with one bite. A little blood might attract hundreds of them in no time at all, and in just a few minutes they can pick a cow clean, leaving only a bony skeleton.

Our trip to Ciudad Bolívar was to start from the ballpark in Valencia. When the drivers returned from getting their final instructions in the baseball office, they found all their tires flat. Professional baseball players wouldn't do that, would they? The drivers scolded us and refilled the tires. When they returned we all hopped in and headed for the states of Carabobo, Aragua, and Guarico, with stops for water and food several times along the way. I rode with Mozzali, who kept reminding me about the water. After the first five miles we had come out of the coastal mountain area and hit the pampas (plains). They were hot, flat and dry, with towns miles and miles apart in the jungle-like terrain. Late in the afternoon, we stopped at El Tigre in the state of Anzoategue. We ate in a saloon-type restaurant as I ordered my usual ham and cheese with, what else? *Cerveza.* The adobe brick building in which we ate was covered with plaster and had some huge chunks missing. The building would have blended in perfectly on the set of *Viva Zapata!* It was 7 p.m. when we got back on the road.

We were hot, dusty and half-looped because we had no bottled water in those days. We headed the remaining 70 miles to Ciudad Bolívar, arriving on the northern bank of the Orinoco just as the silver-colored ferry boat filled with autos had pulled out from shore. The lights of the vessel were still bright and the cars were plainly discernible as the ferry moved relentlessly toward the other shore. We were told that was the last ferry boat of the night. The only things I could see on our side of the river were shacks with pigs and dogs running in and out. Ronnie Plaza began talking with some of the youngsters who had gathered around our stranded party at the riverbank. Ronnie quickly had a kid scurrying to arouse a captain who might get his boat going to take us across the river. The boy and the captain came back, and the grizzled-looking captain said he would be glad to take us across for a price. By that time the lights of the Hotel Bolívar were gleaming a half-mile across the river. Those lights looked good to all of us, and so the captain got his price as we all piled into his boat, leaving the cars on the north side of the river to be brought across the next morning.

Bobby Balcena took one look at the boat and said, "Fellas, you're now entering the *African Queen*." Away we went, chug-chug-chug across the Orinoco in a boat that looked like it might sink at any moment. Earl Battey kept reminding us to keep our hands out of the water. Several of us kept busy bailing water out of the leaky boat. There was a lot of laughter and some humorous quips on the 25-minute journey across. What else can a group of guys do when they are scared to death?

After a restful night's sleep in the hotel, I jumped out of bed and pulled up the shade to look out the window to see where we had ventured. I was startled to see young men with wicker baskets balanced on their heads wading ashore as they unloaded merchandise from the boats. I dressed and hurried downstairs to ask one of the bellboys in my best Spanish, "What the hell are those guys doing in water up to their knees? Aren't they afraid of piranhas?" He slowly and methodically explained to me that every few weeks, large charges of TNT were set off to kill the fish or at least to send them out of the area. He finished by saying, "Because of this we have no problem with the piranha." It would have been a comfort to know that the previous night as we chugged along in our leaky old African Queen.

The ballpark at Ciudad Bolívar was cozy, for the stands came almost to the foul lines. I could nearly reach into the crowd from first base. The people of Venezuela are a mixture of several bloods. There are very few pure whites, blacks, or Indians. Many Venezuelans are a blend of races, and perhaps that is one reason why there was almost no racism in that country. One of the most beautiful faces I have ever seen was in the stands that night. She was a mixture of Spanish, Negroid and Indian, and it was easy to distinguish traces of each bloodline in her features. Clearly she inherited the best genes from each race because she was beautiful. We played our ball game, hopped in the cars and headed back to Valencia, arriving early the next morning. It was a rugged round trip, but as I look back on it now, it was one of the highlights of our stay for me.

The Venezuelan people were fiercely patriotic, and their respect for their country and Simon Bolívar, their liberator, was of a fanatical nature. To discredit Bolívar, even as a joke, could mean your life. I soon learned that one could get shot by saying, "Simon Bolívar es bandido."

The season was winding down to a close and we were leading the league. Pompero was playing in Valencia, and the hometown fans were a happy crowd that night as we were about to win the second half of the split season. The Venezuelans had some unique rituals during a ball game. If the home team was losing toward the end of the game, they would light small bonfires in the stands signifying the death of the game. Fortunately, the stands in Caracas and Valencia were of concrete and steel. Occasionally if the team was losing, an empty bottle of white lightning might come whistling by your head. Several times during the season I felt a bottle narrowly miss me and land on the infield grass. But on this particular night, none of these things happened. The bases were loaded in the seventh inning with Balcena on third, Battey on second and Mozzali on first. On that night, if a Valencia player hit a grand slam in the seventh inning, the radio station, 810 AM, would award that player with 810 bolivares. So when I stepped to the plate realizing that the stage was set for me, I started to do some math in my head: 810 bolivares worked out to be $270, and I thought, boy, it sure wouldn't hurt to have 270 bucks in my pocket. So I proceeded to step into the box and hit a towering fly to right-center. I knew the ball was well hit but didn't know if it would carry out of the park. The fence was made of concrete, and instead of being flat on top it came to a pyramid-like point. The ball hit that point and bounced back into the park! I drove in three runs and wound up on third base. The *fanáticos* were jumping up and down, going wild. My bases-loaded triple had given us a 6–3 lead which we were able to hang on to.

That win closed out the season for us, and we finished with a second-half record of 18–8. Emilio Cueche, our winning pitcher that night, had won his 10th straight game. Radio station 810 had decided that, even though I had not hit a grand slam, I would be awarded half of the 810 bolivares—the other half would go to Cueche. We received our checks for 405 bolivares a few nights later at an awards banquet sponsored by the station.

We then played Caracas in the playoffs. The winner of these playoffs would represent Venezuela in the Serie del Caribe, the Caribbean Series, meeting the winning teams from Cuba, Panama and Puerto Rico. The fans were at a fever pitch all during the series. One game in particular stands out. We were playing in Valencia and Reggie Otero, our manager, took exception to something that was said in the Caracas dugout. He raced over to their dugout behind the first-base line and dove in headfirst. Our players, of course, followed him hard. Over 5,000 fans had come to the game from Caracas and were sitting behind the first-base line. The folks in the front row started to look over the iron railing into the dugout to see the fight. The people sitting behind them were all on their feet, pushing to see what was happening. Before long the iron railing, which was embedded in concrete, gave way. The first wave of people hit the ground with the second, third and fourth piling on top. People who had slipped and fallen to the ground were being trampled. It was a horrifying sight. The soldiers on duty at the game pulled out their machetes and started slapping people across the butt with the flat side of the blades, driving them like cattle back into the stands. After 20 minutes or so, order was restored, but several people were severely injured and one little boy suffered a crushed chest.

Caracas defeated us four games to one and went on to the Serie del Caribe. The Valencia Industriales, as we were called, played well and had a good season. The fans and the owners were disappointed in our playoff showing but seemed appreciative of our season-long play.

The Venezuelan people were kind, humble, and fun-loving. They possessed a wisdom and philosophy toward life that we could take a lesson from. I loved their music and the slow-paced lifestyle. Their country was in a state of rapid development and an optimistic enthusiasm prevailed. My early pangs of resentment toward their authoritarian form of government waned as I adjusted to their politics and way of life.

On February the 6th I received a precious piece of paper from the Venezuelan government—my solvencia. It was number 047524, signed by Francisco Ramón Cisneros. I looked at it with thankful eyes. It wasn't that I disliked Venezuela, but I was ready to get back to the United States. I think the feeling was widespread throughout the North Americans who had been there from the start.

On February 8th we left Maiquetia Airport for our trip home. The four pleasant months of the Venezuelan sun had been good to us. We were returning with good memories and money in our pockets. We would miss those friends that we made in Valencia—Jesus, Daniel, Mr. and Mrs. Vitale, the Brangers, Felix Garcia, the Hotel 400, my teammates and all the friendly people of Venezuela. I would not miss the water, the food, Garcia's driving, Montezuma's Revenge and the Spanish-speaking television and radio programs.

Our plane was soon aloft, and our first stop was in Ciudad Trujillo in the Dominican Republic. We then stopped at Port au Prince in Haiti for about an hour. I got off the plane there and looked in the gift shops with Jo Ann. We reboarded and flew from Haiti to Miami and then on to St. Louis, arriving in a soupy fog. That was the worst scare of the whole trip, wondering if the pilot could see the runway. After we landed, they closed the airport because of the weather. Jo and I both heaved a sigh of relief as the wheels touched down. The pilot got our hearty thanks as we left the plane. We were home. And spring training would start in four weeks.

13

April Fool

I was having a good spring in 1957. We were back at Casey Stengel Field in Glendale, California. I felt that I was one of the leaders of the ball club. It was my third year with Portland, where I had batted well, set fielding records and had a good rapport with the fans. I had resigned myself to finishing my career in Portland at that point. I felt good about that, though, because I liked the league, the team, the city and the people. I was enthusiastic and happy about the upcoming season. Most of all, I was confident. But sometimes I had feelings of dread and anxiety which seemed to come from nowhere and for no apparent reason. I asked no one about these feelings because I didn't understand them myself.

I had been pulling the ball to left field and I had success with the change in my hitting style. Bill Sweeney, whom I had at first resented when he took over for Tommy Holmes, was back as our manager. My feelings for him had warmed, and he showed an appreciation for my talent and desire. It felt good having somebody depend on me as Sweeney did for the last part of the '56 season. He would come in after a game, give me a big hug and say, "Mick, I love ya! I love your bat, too!" We had built up a mutual admiration for each other. I had hit 12 home runs and driven in 49 for the man in the last two months of the season. I felt relaxed with him—he knew what I could and couldn't do.

On Sunday, March 31st, in a spring training game, we lost to Sacramento, 7–6. I had a double and a home run down the left field line. I felt ready for the short porch in left field at Multnomah Stadium back in Portland. After the game Sweeney called me into his office. He had Bob Scheffing, the Chicago Cubs' new manager, on the telephone. Sweeney told me I was going to the Cubs and asked if I cared to talk to Bob. I took the telephone and told Scheffing that I liked Portland and the Coast League and really didn't want to leave unless I was going to play. Scheffing's reply was, "Mick, you'll play. You will start against left-handers and Dee Fondy will start against right-handers."

That was good enough for me, and Jo and I were packing again. It was a happy and sad goodbye to all my old teammates, but especially to

WELCOME BACK TO THE BIG SHOW, ED!

Illustration by Ron Joyner.

Sam and Angie. We headed for Mesa, Arizona, where the Chicago Cubs had their spring training. As a youngster growing up near Chicago, I had always been a Cub fan despite spending the rest of my life in rival Cardinal country.

On April 1, 1957, I met with John Holland, the general manager of the Chicago Cubs, in his hotel room in Mesa and signed my contract. The Cubs were about to break camp and start home, playing the Baltimore Orioles on the way. Jo took our car and followed one of the wives as far as St. Louis, where she would wait for the completion of the exhibition games and the club's return to Chicago.

On April 2nd we played at Douglas, Arizona, and I hit a sacrifice fly with the bases loaded to drive in a run. The next day in El Paso I didn't play, but in Alpine, Texas I had two RBIs on a long double to left-center. On Friday in San Antonio I went 1 for 5. On Saturday and Sunday, Dee Fondy, the Cubs' regular first-sacker, played both games.

In San Antonio, we stayed at the Old Gunter Hotel. It was like home, having played in San Antonio, and I got to see some old friends. I visited with the Bennetts, who had been our landlords there. I picked up the April 10th issue of the *Sporting News* at the cigar counter and read an article about my new team.

It read, "March 31st—Holland called a press conference in the Maricopa Inn (Mesa, Arizona) and announced that the Cubs had acquired first baseman Ed Mickelson from Portland.

"The 31-year-old Mickelson, who had previous major-league tryouts with the Cardinals and old St. Louis Browns, batted .309 and drove in 101 runs with Portland last year.

"Scheffing pointed out that he had recommended Mickelson to the Cubs last year. He said the right-handed hitting Mickelson would play against left-handed pitching, and Fondy would oppose right-handers."

I felt good as I read this because I realized that Scheffing wanted me based on what he had seen last season and that he would, in fact, start me against lefties. I was to start at first in Nashville on April 10th but the field was in terrible condition. We didn't take infield or batting practice. We just sat around waiting to start the game. I always got a little nervous before a start. So I usually took a trip or two to the john, checked my equipment several times, flipped the bat in my hands. I'd lived with that feeling for 10 years and it would have felt different not to be nervous. But that day, before that game, each minute seemed to last an hour. I began to wonder why I felt such a strong sense of apprehension.

We beat Baltimore 7–6 behind the pitching of Bob Rush and Turk Lown. I felt pretty miserable after the game because I looked pitiful at the plate and booted an easy grounder for an error. I felt like I had messed up

National League of Professional Baseball Clubs

Parties

Between __Chicago National League Ball Club (Inc.)__

herein called the Club, and__Edward Allen Mickelson__

of __St. Louis, Mo.__, herein called the Player.

Recital

The Club is a member of the National League of Professional Baseball Clubs, a voluntary association of eight member clubs which has subscribed to the Major League Rules with the American League of Professional Baseball Clubs and to the Major-Minor League Rules with that League and the National Association of Baseball Leagues. The purpose of those rules is to insure the public wholesome and high-class professional baseball by defining the relations between Club and Player, between club and club, between league and league, and by vesting in a designated Commissioner broad powers of control and discipline, and of decision in case of disputes.

Agreement

In consideration of the facts above recited and of the promises of each to the other, the parties agree as follows:

Employment

1. The Club hereby employs the Player to render, and the Player agrees to render, skilled services as a baseball player during the year _____ 195_7_, including the Club's training season, the Club's exhibition games, the Club's playing season, and the World Series (or any other official series in which the Club may participate and in any receipts of which the player may be entitled to share).

Payment

2. For performance of the Player's services and promises hereunder the Club will pay the Player the sum of $__9,000.00__ (NINE THOUSAND DOLLARS)__, as follows:

In semi-monthly installments after the commencement of the playing season covered by this contract, unless the Player is "abroad" with the Club for the purpose of playing games, in which event the amount then due shall be paid on the first week-day after the return "home" of the Club, the terms "home" and "abroad" meaning respectively at and away from the city in which the Club has its baseball field.

If a monthly rate of payment is stipulated above, it shall begin with the commencement of the Club's playing season (or such subsequent date as the Player's services may commence) and end with the termination of the Club's scheduled playing season, and shall be payable in semi-monthly installments as above provided.

If the player is in the service of the Club for part of the playing season only, he shall receive such proportion of the sum above mentioned, as the number of days of his actual employment in the Club's playing season bears to the number of days in said season.

If the rate of payment stipulated above is less than $5,000 per year, the player, nevertheless, shall be paid at the rate of $6,000 per year for each day of his service as a player on a Major League team.

Loyalty

3. (a) The Player agrees to perform his services hereunder diligently and faithfully, to keep himself in first class physical condition and to obey the Club's training rules, and pledges himself to the American public and to the Club to conform to high standards of personal conduct, fair play and good sportsmanship.

Baseball Promotion

(b) In addition to his services in connection with the actual playing of baseball, the Player agrees to cooperate with the Club and participate in any and all promotional activities of the Club and its League, which, in the opinion of the Club, will promote the welfare of the Club or professional baseball, and to observe and comply with all requirements of the Club respecting conduct and service of its teams and its players, at all times whether on or off the field.

Pictures and Public Appearances

(c) The Player agrees that his picture may be taken for still photographs, motion pictures or television at such times as the Club may designate and agrees that all rights in such pictures shall belong to the Club and may be used by the Club for publicity purposes in any manner it desires. The Player further agrees that during the playing season he will not make public appearances, participate in radio or television programs or permit his picture to be taken or write or sponsor newspaper or magazine articles or sponsor commercial products without the written consent of the Club, which shall not be withheld except in the reasonable interests of the Club or professional baseball.

Player Representations

4. (a) The Player represents and agrees that he has exceptional and unique skill and ability as a baseball player; that his services to be rendered hereunder are of a special, unusual and extraordinary character which gives them peculiar value which cannot be reasonably or adequately compensated for in damages at law, and that the Player's breach of this contract will cause the Club great and irreparable injury and damage. The Player agrees that, in addition to other remedies, the Club shall be entitled to injunctive and other equitable relief to prevent a breach of this contract by the Player, including, among others, the right to enjoin the Player from playing baseball for any other person or organization during the term of this contract.

Ability

Condition

(b) The Player represents that he has no physical or mental defects, known to him, which would prevent or impair performance of his services.

Interest in Club

(c) The Player represents that he does not, directly or indirectly, own stock or have any financial interest in the ownership or earnings of any Major League club, except as hereinafter expressly set forth, and covenants that he will not hereafter, while connected with any Major League club, acquire or hold any such stock or interest except in accordance with Major League Rule 20 (e).

Service

5. (a) The Player agrees that, while under contract, and prior to expiration of the Club's right to renew this contract, he will not play baseball otherwise than for the Club, except that the Player may participate in post-season games under the conditions prescribed in the Major League Rules. Major League Rule 18 (b) is set forth on page 4 hereof.

This was the most money I ever made in baseball, but I played with the Cubs for only part of the contract. After cut down day, I went back to Portland to play every day, and Chicago paid a portion of the contract, so I still got the same money. The major league minimum salary at the time was $5,000. I felt I finally had some financial success playing baseball.

what chance I had to make the club. Worse, it felt like the end of the world. I was too hard on myself. Instead of shrugging it off with "everybody has a bad day," I found it gnawed at me.

The next day in Knoxville, Dee Fondy hit two homers and gave us the edge in the series as we won 10–8 over the Orioles. We set out for

Chicago and the White Sox in the Windy City Series. The Cubs won on Saturday and Sunday. I got to pinch-hit once and flew out to left field.

Tuesday, April 16th, was opening day at County Stadium in Milwaukee. The Cubs were playing the Braves and Warren Spahn, a lefty and future Hall of Famer, was their starter. I really thought that I would start with a left-handed pitcher throwing, but I ended up watching the game along with over 23,000 other spectators. Spahn beat us, 4–1. I was disappointed because I actually felt good before that game. My anxiety had subsided and I just wanted to play. There was a big letdown after it was over. I felt like I had been misled. And at heart, I was crushed.

On April 18th we played in St. Louis and won handily, 10–2. Fondy started and had three hits. The next morning I picked up the paper and I was shocked to see that William Joseph Sweeney had died in San Diego, California. I had only known "Old Bill" for a few short months, but my heart ached for him and his family.

On Sunday as a pinch-hitter, I managed a lazy fly ball off Sad Sam Jones, the Cardinal pitcher. After sitting on the bench for three weeks I got a chance to start in Cincinnati but went 0 for 4. On Wednesday, May 1st, in Brooklyn, I went in to pinch-hit against Don Drysdale. I remember vividly Roy Campanella looking at my feet as I walked up to the plate and stepped into the batter's box. Some smart catchers like Roy pitch a batter a certain way depending on the position of the feet in relation to home plate. I hit the ball hard on the ground to the shortstop Pee Wee Reese, the Dodgers' legendary captain, on one hop. I was barely half way to first base when Hodges caught the ball. I kept thinking afterwards, "Just two feet either way, just two feet!"

Then Dale Long came to us in a trade from Pittsburgh and Dee Fondy went to the Pirates. They just swapped uniforms, really. Long homered in Philadelphia on May 2nd and was looking good. As a pinch-hitter on Saturday, May 4th, a cold, cloudy, blustery day, I hit a line shot off the hard-throwing Jack Sanford. The first baseman jumped and speared the ball, robbing me of a hit. I kept thinking, "Just one foot either way, just one foot!"

Jo Ann and I had rented a little efficiency apartment near the ballpark in Chicago. We had been in baseball long enough to know that I might be gone at any time. It was the eve of May 12th, a Sunday doubleheader just three days before the May 15th cut-down day. We didn't send out the laundry, nor had we brought in a large supply of groceries, nor did we pay the rent a month in advance. We casually talked of my going back to the minors and how it might be nice to play in Portland again. I was restless, but mostly angry, as I felt once again that I hadn't really been given a chance to play. I couldn't knock any doors down and complain, though. After all, I was 0 for 7 at the plate. I felt a sense of hopelessness and futility. I slept some, but my dreams were fitful, a product of my anguish and my frustration. I told Jo Ann, "If I hit two or three home runs tomorrow, we might get to stay." I knew they had already made up their mind.

On Sunday, May 12th, I was to start the second game of a double-header. I walked onto the field beforehand thinking that I must at least go 3 for 4 or hit a couple balls out of the park. I went 0 for 4 and was feeling that I had blown my chance to make the team. I liked Scheffing. I had known him since 1953 when I was with the Brownies. He was the man responsible for my being with the Cubs. But despite all that, I still responded angrily to him, saying, "Why the hell did you bring me here if you didn't intend to play me?" There was no reply.

Cut-down day is an emotional time for everyone but the established players. Dave Hillman, a 20-game winner in the PCL, and Ed Winceniak were getting the same message I got after that double-header. They too were going back to Portland. Jack Littrell was moving into the clubhouse as we were moving out. He had come from Portland to play shortstop for the Cubs as Ernie Banks would move to third base.

Jo Ann and I packed, left Chicago for St. Louis, picked up things we would need for the rest of the summer and headed for Portland. We had a 1,500-mile trip ahead of us. We talked cheerfully on the Saturday night before the next day's double-header. We were resigned to the possibility that I might be released outright to Portland, but the trip across the country was a relatively silent one. A realization was setting in at age 31. I had made my third, and perhaps last, trip to the major leagues. I believed that when I got back to the Coast League and started to play regularly, all of these pent-up feelings would leave. But I was wrong. I was good at stuffing my feelings and, of course, they just got worse.

We arrived and checked in with Joe Ziegler. We got an apartment near the Calderones and I flew to Los Angeles where I met my old teammates. I was back with Sammy as my roomie, and among my other buddies Marquez, Borkowski, Carswell, Shore, Alexander and Werle. But it was essentially a different ball club. The infield was new and our pitching staff had changed as well. Zeigler now had a working agreement with the Cubs. Though quite a few things had changed, the name on the sweaters was still "Beavers," and it felt good to be back.

As I lay on my bed in our Los Angeles hotel before the first game, I thought, "I'm back home now, everything will be fine, I will start where I left off last season." But my dream had been crushed in Chicago. I felt like a part of me had died. I went 2 for 4 the first night and 7 for 20 for the series in Los Angeles—a pretty good first series. But it wasn't fun anymore.

Portland had gotten off to a dismal start with the death of Bill Sweeney. The team was 15–24 but had won 10 of the last 14 under new manager Bill Posedel. We had taken the Los Angeles series four games to three and split our eight-game series with Seattle. After two weeks in the Coast League, I was leading the club in hitting with a .330 average. Still, it wasn't the same as in '56. Nothing felt right. Everything I did became a chore.

Early in June, we were rear-ended in Portland as Jo and I were returning home after picking up a television set from the repair shop. We had stopped for a red light. I could see the guy coming toward us from behind in the rear-view mirror, but I could do nothing to get out of the way. Driving ahead meant crossing traffic and getting sideswiped. So we were in broad daylight hit by a drunk, a high-risk insurance driver who had numerous other accidents. Fortunately, neither Jo Ann nor I was hurt. After X-rays and a few days out of the lineup I returned to play, badly shaken. We had a poor series in Vancouver but I hit .500 for the week and was batting .392 for the year. For some reason I wasn't hitting any home runs, but I figured they would come soon. Since I hadn't been playing, I was still feeling my way and just trying to make contact to get my timing back.

The people in Vancouver were beautiful. They were very British in dress, talk and customs. One day Sam and I went out to play golf. The gentlemen were dressed in their British-Scotch attire, and the holes were only 75 to 150 yards apart. A putter and a few short irons were all that were needed to play that course. I began to notice that all Vancouverites had brightly colored tassels tied around their tees, and as I gazed too intently and too long at one gentleman's tee, he said, "Well, we're Scots you know, and we hate to lose anything." No way could he lose his wooden tee with a six-inch, multi-colored tassel attached.

Another time, Sam and I went out to a large gorge. It was several miles out of town and a rope suspension bridge hung between the cliffs. We were up what seemed to be several thousand feet above the stream below, which from our vantage point looked more like a little trickle. We walked out on that swaying bridge, holding the ropes on each side. As we got out to the middle and looked down, I wondered if the scenery was worth the harrowing experience. I remembered the sage words of Neal Berry, a utility infielder with the St. Louis Browns, Detroit Tigers and about every other team in the American League, when he had quoted Shakespeare one day: "Discretion is the better part of valor. Or another way to put it, Mick, he who fights and runs away lives to fight another day." Sam and I did a fast retreat from the middle of the suspension bridge back to our starting point.

Seattle took us six out of seven. It seemed as though we were always

Seals Stadium, 1956 era, San Francisco, CA. Long underwear was used in night games because the weather tended to be cold, damp and windy. The prevailing wind carried the ball toward the left field corner, making it a very tough catch for pop flies and fly balls. Left-handed hitters suffered the most. It was tough conditions playing there, but it did have the feel of a major league ballpark in size and seating capacity. (National Baseball Hall of Fame Library, Cooperstown, N.Y.)

coming up one or two runs short. I hit well in that series, but still had no homers. We started to lose and it seemed like there was no way to turn it around. Toward the middle of June, Bill Posedel called me aside as were taking batting practice. He said in a disgruntled tone, "Ed, we need some home run production out of you. Last year you hit 21, and both Ziegler and I are a little miffed because you haven't hit a home run yet." He had every right to say that, but I replied, "Bill, I sat on the bench with Chicago for six weeks and I feel like I'm starting spring training again. Besides, I'm hitting .350."

I guess it was a case of both of us being right. I wasn't hitting any dingers, and I should have been. But I was doing very well for the long layoff. Hell, I was second in the league in hitting! Nevertheless, what Posedel said bothered me way out of proportion. It shouldn't have, but it did. I found it difficult to sleep and everything about life seemed to have lost its luster.

On June 30th, in the last of the 12th inning with two on and two out, I hit a walk off home run to win the game. It also happened to be my first that season. It was a happy crew that marched up the hill and up the steps to the clubhouse in Multnomah Stadium. My hand was being shaken and my back slapped. We were 29–44 and in second-to-last place, but you would have thought we had just won the pennant. My feelings were turned around. I felt no joy, no elation. A year ago, there would have been a flow of inner satisfaction that would have lifted me to the heights. This time, I felt only dejection. I forced a smile and a handshake or two, no longer feeling a part of the joy or the fun. In retrospect, I believe that I was somewhat aware that I was in big trouble with my emotions. This led me to become apprehensive, but I shared what I was feeling with no one.

All-Star pin, 1957. These one-inch pin backs were made for the All-Star players. For me, it is a symbol of the support and encouragement my wife, Jo Ann, gave me through my career. She was the archivist of all the memorabilia of my playing career. Without her squirreling away all that information, I would not have been able to write this book. All I had to do was play baseball! She did the rest.

On July 3rd we played the All-Star Game in Los Angeles. I should have been chosen in '56, but wasn't. I shouldn't have been chosen in '57, but was. Our North team won, 3–1. Jim "Mud Cat" Grant got a fastball outside and I hit it to right-center for a home run. God, I loved Wrigley Field—the one in L.A., not the one in Chicago! I called Jo Ann, who was back in Portland, from a phone booth inside the ballpark right after the game. I had started to become uncomfortable around people and I needed to hear her voice. I was scared and I didn't know why.

After the All-Star Game, playing became drudgery. I loved baseball. I loved the challenge and the competition, the guys, the fans and the humorous happenings. It was my life. It was who I was. But for me, at that point, playing baseball had become a nearly insurmountable task. Airplane rides, which used to be fun, were now becoming a nightmare. Taxicab rides through crowded streets in San Francisco and Los Angeles saw me shrink-

Wrigley Field, Los Angeles. I found it exciting to play at Wrigley Field. The crowds were always good and the stands usually held movie stars, enjoying a relaxing day at the ballpark. I loved to hit here, too, because of the short alleys in left center and right center. The Pacific Coast League All-Star game was played here in 1957, where I hit a home run into right center off Mud Cat Grant. My North Team won 3 to 1. (National Baseball Hall of Fame Library, Cooperstown N.Y.)

ing into my seat and closing my eyes. I couldn't sleep and I had to force myself to eat. Fortunately, we played most of that time in Portland and I felt a little more secure there. I would go into a little room away from the clubhouse and try to relax, summoning all my strength just to go out and play nine innings. Every little problem became monumental. I was swimming upstream against the current, with the current getting stronger all the time. In previous years after the games, I would drink a beer or two, talk and joke, and then be the last to leave the clubhouse. Now I quickly undressed, showered and plopped in the back seat of our car, speaking as little as possible, as Jo Ann silently drove me home to another sleepless night. I had become almost totally preoccupied with a fear of not sleeping.

On the 21st of July we played San Francisco in Portland. I went 3 for 4 in the first game and 1 for 3 in the second game. I had hit .349 for the week and .338 for the season. At that time, Rudy Regalado of San Diego was leading the league and I was second. To complement the good hitting,

I had made only one error in 537 chances, and would end up leading the league in fielding with a .998 mark. How could I be doing so well and be feeling so awful at the same time? I tried, unsuccessfully, to figure my problem out.

On the next day, Monday, July 22nd, 1957, I was pulled apart. I had to get up, get dressed and catch the plane for San Diego, but I couldn't. Jo Ann had a sense of what was going on, but she had no idea that it was this bad. A sense of guilt swept over me as I thought of what the guys would think—would they understand? How could they understand it when I did not understand it? Neither did Jo Ann. I had kept what I was feeling to myself. I tried to reason things out, but the emotions were overwhelming. I felt for my roomie, Sammy Calderone. I don't believe that anyone knew I had become so depressed, not even Sammy. I envisioned the guys saying, "Hey Sam, where the hell's your roommate? Why isn't he here?" And I could predict Sammy's hurt as he would have to respond, "Honestly, I don't know."

Joe Ziegler didn't understand it when I told him I couldn't crank it up any longer. He said, "Mick, you have always been so straight. You need to go out and get drunk and get whatever is bothering you off of your mind." I said, "Joe, there's nothing wrong with me physically, but I haven't been sleeping and I just can't push myself anymore." He decided to put me in the hospital for tests. The hospital report confirmed my beliefs—nothing physically wrong. I was emotionally drained, though. In medical jargon, I was suffering from acute anxiety and depression.

I hated to leave my teammates, I hated to leave Portland, I hated to leave baseball, I hated to leave the money, and I hated to be thought of as a quitter. I had battled hard to hang on those last few weeks in July with every fiber of strength I had within me.

I did not want to quit. Guilt was added to the emotions I was feeling.

But on July 28, 1957, I gathered my equipment from my locker and said goodbye to Joe Ziegler. Jo Ann and I got into our car to share the long, quiet, painful ride back to St. Louis. At that time, I thought that getting away from baseball would alleviate my pain. The stress of baseball had opened the box of emotions I had locked up for years. With the help of Dr. Kenneth D. Michael I was able to work through these issues and through the depression. What in 1957 would take years of talk therapy could now be shortened considerably with talk therapy plus the vastly improved anti-depressant medication now available to correct the chemical imbalance.

For many years after my departure from baseball, I felt a sense of frustration and failure. I felt I had three chances to play in the major leagues and had failed. I beat myself up for many years. Gradually I became aware of all the fun I had in baseball, so many good times and so many successful seasons. Now, I'm proud of the success I had. But what I cherish the most is the time spent with my teammates—the camaraderie.

I understand now that in baseball, as in life, you win some, lose some and some are rained out.

14

Extra Innings

I have enjoyed writing this book. It was fun to do. It has helped me to understand the depths of my feelings and to realize how much I really enjoyed both the baseball years and the people I was associated with. A real attachment still exists to my old teammates.

It has been over 55 years since Ray Sowins hit the longest home run I have ever seen, but I often think of Ray, the little strong man from Chicago. I have a lot of love for the guy.

I see Barczewski every now and then. He lives in St. Louis. When we get together, we spend the hours in laughter, tears rolling down our cheeks as we reminisce about our season in Pocatello.

From left, Tony Williams, running back, Ed Mickelson, and Isaac Byrd, quarterback, 1992. Parkway Central H.S. was about to play for the Missouri State Championship in 1992. Tony played college football and Isaac played wide receiver for Kansas and for the Tennessee Titans in the 2000 Super Bowl. In that game, he caught three passes and recovered a crucial fumble.

**BILKO, CALDERONE, BARCZEWSKI -- EVERYONE -- I LOVE
YOU ALL AND WILL REMEMBER YOU FOREVER!**

Illustration by Ron Joyner.

It's the guys I remember most—so many, many guys. I will not for-get the laughs, the heartaches, the victories, and the fun.

Sack, LeBlanc, DiPrima, Franck, Riesgo, Mauch, Childs, Huff, Clark, Faszholz, Ripulski, Derry, Jabbo Jablonski, Bucha, Harry the Hat Walker, my long-time rival Bilko, Ciaffone, Balcena, Duren, Fridley, Ippolito, Caffrey, Ackeret, Koppe, Barr, Heslet, McGaha, Jones, Moonie, Lade, Smith, Elliot, Adams, Eggert, Austin, Wilson, Taylor, Basinski, Sammy, Powis, Carswell, Marquez, Shore, Littrell, Holmes, and Sweeney.

Bless you all. Most of these men are in their 70s now, some are older and some are no longer with us. But I can still see them all swinging a bat, throwing a ball and sliding into a base.

Recently I had been thinking more and more about my good buddy,

Above: From left: Mary Mickelson, Ed Mickelson and Stan Musial, taken by Diane Ryberg at the 2003 Brownie Banquet, as she prepared to include the Brownies in the festivities for the St. Louis History Museum's exhibition from the Baseball Hall of Fame. Stan always surrounds himself with laughter and good will. *Opposite page top:* Parkway Central High School Varsity Football Coaches, 1992. Standing left to right: Denny Hugo, Ed Mickelson, Al Buckley and in front, Bob Trowbridge. These guys were my buddies and life long friends. We worked hard, laughed hard and the kids played hard. It must have been a good recipe because we won 78% of our games between 1987 and 1993, and never had a losing year. The best part for me was the fun we had with the kids and amongst ourselves. The camaraderie that I cherished and lost in baseball I regained by coaching high school sports. I coached football, basketball and baseball at University City High School from 1958 until 1970. I coached at Parkway Central from 1978 until 1983 in baseball, and football from 1978 until 1993. *Opposite page bottom:* Some of the 1962 University City baseball team at their 1992 class reunion. I coached all these guys and have become friends with many of them over the years. They still get on me for not pitching Ken Holtzman on one day's rest, during the State Championship Series in 1962, which may have caused us to lose. I feel like I made the right decision. If he had pitched and we had won, but he had hurt his arm, I would have had to live with that. Back row, left to right: Stan Shanker, Sandy Melnick, Jerry Smith, Maury Poscover, and Steven Kleinfeld. Front row, left to right: Richie Baum, Ed Mickelson, Dave Willson, Aaron Lubin. I have coached baseball with Aaron, Sandy and Kenny in recent years. What a joy to be with the kids you coached. Notice I said kids; they're all 60ish now.

50th Anniversary of the Browns' final season. Busch Stadium, 2003. Left to right: Don Larsen, Babe Martin, Don Lenhardt, Ed Mickelson, Roy Sievers, Mike Blyska, Ned Garver, Al LaMacchia, Jim Delsing, Bill Jennings, Bud Thomas, J.W. Porter, Fred Heger, Fan Club President, Art Richmond, #1 Brownie Fan, and Bill DeWitt Jr., Cardinals owner. We were introduced on the field and gathered in Bill DeWitt's suite for a buffet banquet and lots of stories. The next day both the Cardinals and the Orioles wore the old uniforms from 1953. Youngster in the middle is Bill DeWitt's grandson, John Kern. (Used by permission of Jim Herron, photographer.)

Sammy Calderone. We had so many good times together during our three years in the Pacific Coast League. I taped an hour of those fun times and sent them to Sam's wife, Angie. She phoned to tell me that she and Sam had enjoyed hearing the old stories as much as I had had telling them, and that they had laughed and cried as they listened to the tape. I said to Sam, "You never told me that you were a .292 hitter in the majors."

And so the new stories join the old ones. We old baseball players never get tired of our stories, and we never forget our love for each other.

The days have been good to me since baseball. There was a deep valley at the end of my baseball days. It took several years before the emotions leveled off. I got my master's degree in the fall of 1957 and went into the educational field. I loved working with kids, and spent 43 years in teaching, counseling and coaching. One of the highlights of my career was watching Ken Holtzman, one of my high school players, become the winning pitcher in the first game of the 1972 World Series, for the Oakland A's. Recently, we became friends while we coached Little League baseball

Hank Arft (in 1950), Brownie from 1948 to 1952, was a gentleman and a good friend. As time passes, so will all the old Brownies. Grantland Rice's poem, "Game Called," saw him off to the next Big League in Heaven, in 2002. The poem, which was first used at Babe Ruth's funeral, is a fitting sendoff for all of us. (Courtesy of Ruth Arft.)

together. Two football players I coached in high school football, Isaac Byrd and Ryan Young, made it big in the NFL. Issac played in the Super Bowl for the Tennessee Titans in January of 2000. Ryan Young was the offensive captain for a great Kansas State team his senior year. He went on the play for the New York Jets and the Houston Texans, and retired from the Dallas Cowboys after playing 6 years in the league. He is now doing color for ESPN foolball and working for a bank. It is always a thrill to see my former players doing well in their lives.

I am amazed at the nostalgia that surrounds the ball players of the 1940s, '50s, and '60s. I would be remiss if I did not mention the St. Louis Browns Fan Club, started by Bill Borst in 1982. He and Erv Fischer, Fred Heger and Bud Kane have kept the Fan Club going and growing. The #1 Brownie fan and chief financial supporter is Arthur Richman. Artie, now an executive with the New York Yankees, never misses the annual May dinner in St. Louis. The fan club has grown to over 500 members and as many as 200 fans have attended our annual banquet. In 1993, the fan club held a 40th anniversary dinner for the '53 Browns. It was truly an honor to be there with 10 of my former teammates.

Much as I cherish my baseball experiences, I found

Ken Holtzman, winner of 174 major league games, played in five World Series with a 4 and 1 record, and is the last pitcher to hit a home run in a World Series game. It was my privilege to be his high school baseball coach. Pitching for the Oakland A's, he provided my biggest thrill in baseball when he started and won the opening game in the 1972 World Series game against the Cincinnati Reds. Bing Devine was kind enough to give me his ticket for Kenny's game in Cincinnati, so I could experience the moment in person. This photo was taken in 1972. (National Baseball Hall of Fame Library, Cooperstown, New York.)

working with kids as a teacher, administrator, counselor and coach to be even more rewarding. Jo Ann was a blessing in my life. She was my soul mate. She passed away in 1999. I am blessed with both my son Eric and my daughter Julie, her husband Scott and my three grandchildren, Eileen, Michael and Matthew. In marriage, I have become a double winner! I was blessed with another soul mate when I married Mary Steffen, a lovely lady, in 2002. She loves me, and baseball, not necessarily in that order.

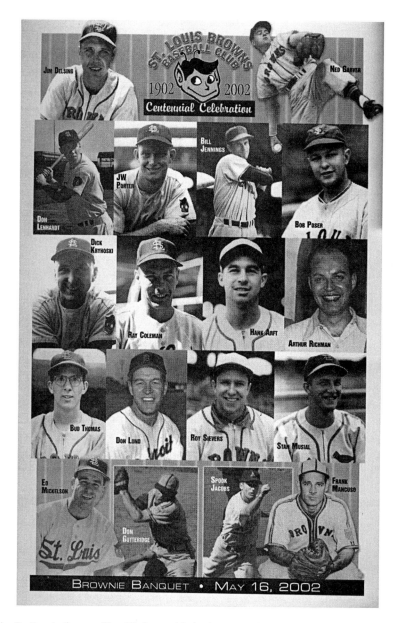

The St. Louis Browns Fan Club, established in 1983, holds a yearly banquet. We all get together in St Louis, tell stories, sign autographs and sometimes get to see what we looked like when we were still playing baseball. Every year the hitters get better as the balls travel further, and the pitchers are more dominating. The stories are longer and funnier. We have had almost 200 people attend our banquets. Artie Richmond, #1 Brownie Fan and chief benefactor, tells us all what is to become of his Brownie baseball cap when he dies. Stan Musial was not a Brownie, but he cannot resist contemporaries and sharing memories and good stories. The old-timers all leave feeling younger. (Used by permission of Ronnie Joyner.)

Bill DeWitt, the president of the St. Louis Cardinals baseball team, and Fred Hanser, the vice president, have been very good to the former Cardinals players by giving them lifetime passes to all Cardinals games. Mary and I go often and root for them and our favorite player and good person, Albert Pujols.

Life is good. Play ball!

Edward Mickelson Lifetime Record

Year	Club & League	G	AB	R	H	Pct.	2B	3B	HR	RBI
1947	Decatur, Ill	55	207	29	52	.251	12	3	1	31
1948	Pocatello, Pionr.	119	516	114	192	.372	32	12	12	143
1949	Columbus, S. Atl	131	440	48	114	.259	22	6	8	81
1950	Lynchburg, Pied.	16	56	10	22	.393	3	0	3	9
	Montgomery, SE	82	300	76	125	.417	33	0	21	102
	St. Louis, NL	5	10	1	1	.100	0	0	0	0
1951	New Orleans, SA	58	166	25	39	.235	4	4	2	25
1952	Columbus, AA	12	26	0	8	.308	0	0	0	5
	Rochester, Int.L.	60	197	19	53	.269	9	3	2	27
1953	St. Louis, AL	7	15	1	2	.133	1	0	0	2
	S. Antonio, Tex.	119	453	60	134	.296	23	8	7	61
1954	Shreveport, Tex.	150	573	96	192	335	43	11	17	139
1955	Portland, PCL.	164	604	67	186	.308	31	2	12	87
1956	Portland, PCL.	159	583	90	180	.309	29	7	21	101
1957	Chicago, NL	6	12	0	0	.000	0	0	0	1
	Portland, PCL	61	219	27	74	.338	12	0	2	28
Totals		1204	4377	663	1374	.314	254	56	108	842

As of this writing, Ed Mickelson still holds the Pacific Coast League record for first baseman playing in 150 games or more for making only 6 errors in 1600 chances, yielding a fielding percentage of .996

Index